Entrepreneurship and Economic Development

Entrepreneurship and Economic Development

The People and Their Environment

Steven G. Koven

LEXINGTON BOOKS
Lanham • Boulder • New York • London

Published by Lexington Books
An imprint of The Rowman & Littlefield Publishing Group, Inc.
4501 Forbes Boulevard, Suite 200, Lanham, Maryland 20706
www.rowman.com

6 Tinworth Street, London SE11 5AL, United Kingdom

British Library Cataloguing in Publication Information Available

Library of Congress Cataloging-in-Publication Data

Names: Koven, Steven G., author.
Title: Entrepreneurship and economic development : the people and their environment / Steven G. Koven.
Description: Lanham : Lexington Books, 2021. | Includes bibliographical references and index.
Identifiers: LCCN 2021018568 (print) | LCCN 2021018569 (ebook) | ISBN 9781793649843 (cloth) | ISBN 9781793649850 (epub)
Subjects: LCSH: Entrepreneurship. | Economic development. | Environmental policy. | Environmental protection.
Classification: LCC HB615 .K728 2021 (print) | LCC HB615 (ebook) | DDC 338.9—dc23
LC record available at https://lccn.loc.gov/2021018568
LC ebook record available at https://lccn.loc.gov/2021018569

This book is dedicated to my wife Andrea

Contents

List of Figures and Tables

FIGURES

TABLES

Preface

Entrepreneurship is of both academic, individual, and geopolitical value. It allows people to survive, prosper, and build private sector empires. It allows individuals to acquire independence, self-respect, and, in some cases, incredible wealth. At the international level, building massive companies within a polity aids in growing aggregate wealth which in turn enables jurisdictions to provide national security and domestic stability. This book serves a few functions. It recognizes that not everyone in the United States becomes a billionaire through their efforts but at the same time the book can encourage people to pursue their dreams, whatever they may be. More than a self-help or "you can do it" proclamation, the book emphasizes the importance of the macro-environment as well as individual initiative in order to create development. It argues that the relatively large number of the wealthiest people in the planet did not create their fortunes in the United States by chance. Specific attributes of the nation such as an excellent system of education, a legal structure that protects property, a process that rewards innovation, and a social environment that tolerates others helped produce favorable outcomes. Personal stories of very successful entrepreneurs indicates that many of them were able to apply breakthrough innovations to amass wealth. Insights of future entrepreneurs were nurtured in some of the most prestigious universities in the world.

Entrepreneurship also is supported by political, social, and economic systems that can encourage or discourage business creation. The book recognizes that social acceptance or rejection of corruption play a role in fostering or reducing effort. It notes that extorting value from private enterprise can clearly have a depressing impact on entrepreneurship and economic growth. The broad economic philosophy of jurisdictions is also relevant. Many associate the United States with relatively strong laissez-faire market philosophies. This philosophy encourages entrepreneurship and freedom for individuals to identify how to maximize their own economic value. The book argues that economic philosophy must be considered in addition to the social and political milieu when assessing environments for entrepreneurship.

In part, the book argues that opportunity is still strong in the United States. Narratives of immensely successful entrepreneurs eviscerate alternative storylines that the "American Dream" is dead, that the U.S. economic system is closed, and that the American economy is in irreversible decline. Entrepreneurship remains a fruitful path for both individuals and nations. Identifying, protecting, and building upon the broad environment or "ecosystem" where the seeds of entrepreneurial development are spread is a logical strategy to follow. Hopefully, this book can both encourage future entrepreneurs and promote conducive environments for wealth creation.

Acknowledgment

Everyone needs help in life, some more than others. It is well recognized that we stand on the shoulders of those that came before us and we benefit enormously from those who have aided us along our paths. First and foremost, I am indebted to the late Professor Bert E. Swanson of the University of Florida. He has mentored countless students through the maze of graduate school, many of whom including me would not be where they are without his concern for the well-being of future teachers and researchers. I am also grateful for the general environment for learning that was accorded to me at Baruch College and the University of Florida. As educational institutions, they expanded my horizons and opened the door to a career in higher education. It is necessary for me to also note the contributions of academic colleagues. It is always good to collaborate with people smarter than oneself. I am indebted to my academic coauthors. Early in my career, my friend, Mack C. Shelley of Iowa State University coauthored publication of a text in American Public Policy. He also helped me navigate the tenure process at Iowa State University. My colleague at the University of Louisville, Frank Götzke, aided me greatly in writing a book on American Immigration Policy. My former colleague at Louisville, Tom Lyons, helped to enlighten me about economic development from the perspective of planners and what role the government can play in the process of development. The University of Louisville and my family generously allowed time for conducting my research. I am appreciative to all.

Part I

THE SETTING, STRATEGIES, AND THEORIES OF DEVELOPMENT

Chapter 1

The Economic and Governmental Setting

No action such as starting a business occurs in a vacuum. Views on the role of government in economic affairs decidedly has an effect on business creation decisions. Governments can play a minimal or dominant part in entrepreneurial affairs; they can ignore, suppress, or encourage entrepreneurship. This chapter describes major perspectives regarding the role of government in business affairs as well as specific government funded ventures in the United States.

LAISSEZ-FAIRE ECONOMICS

Classical Laissez-Faire Perspective

The "father of capitalism" Adam Smith is a logical beginning to explain entrepreneurship, economic success, and failure. In his seminal text *Wealth of Nations*, Smith attacked conventional wisdom arguing that people should be free to pursue the economic interests. According to Smith, individuals are best positioned to maximize their earnings and what types of ventures would yield the greatest returns for their time and efforts. In the view of this perspective, open competition produces the greater general well-being for all. Smith and other Scottish philosophers argued that since the nation consisted of all the people living within it, allowing individual residents the freedom to seek their own fortunes maximizes the wealth of the nation. This view is also attributable to the eighteenth-century French physiocrats who challenged the system of centralized government control in the 1600s and 1700s.

Jacque Turgot, comptroller general of the finances for France (1774–1776) was an early advocate of laissez-faire, free market economics. Turgot eliminated compulsory labor, abolished laws restricting the free flow of agricultural goods from one part of France to another, cut regulations, encouraged competition, and lobbied for the elimination of numbers of layers of French bureaucracy. Not surprisingly, entrenched interests such as manufacturers (who feared entry of competitors), bureaucrats (who feared for their jobs), and members of the royal court (who feared elimination of their sources of wealth through bribes) worked against Turgot (Ebeling 2017).

Adam Smith is the seminal source of what we term today as classical economics or free market economics. According to the Adam Smith Institute, Smith deeply influenced the politicians of his time and provided the intellectual foundation for open trade. In *Wealth of Nations*, Smith argues that it is best for a prospering society to allow businesses to compete in an open marketplace, with free exchange of goods and services. Central to Smith's economic theory are the themes that regulations on commerce are inefficient, productivity rests on a division of labor, future economic well-being is dependent on the accumulation of capital, and that the free market system can regulate itself. According to Smith, in the marketplace, producers identify products of high demand and invest to produce the needed goods. As more producers move into the marketplace, supply increases and prices fall. In contrast, where there is a glut of products, profits are low and producers invest elsewhere; some producers go bankrupt and reduce the supply of goods or services. In this process, producers automatically focus on satisfying consumer demand and the nation's needs without the requirement for central direction. Consumer demand and the profit motive regulates supply in contrast to the "heavy hand" of distant bureaucrats.

Because monopolies, tax preferences, and sheltering products behind tariffs hinders competition and raises prices for consumers, Smith advocated a limited role for government. Smith argued that governments' core functions should be limited to activities such as maintaining defense against foreign enemies, keeping domestic order, and building infrastructure. Smith contended that building up capital is an essential condition for economic progress. By saving instead of consuming societies can invest in new, labor-saving equipment, and enhance productivity. Thanks to growth in capital and productivity increase, the overall "economic pie" expands.

Smith also recognized that capital can be lost, through mistakes, theft, or profligate government spending. To diminish these occurrences, governments should allow people to build up capital in the confidence that they will be able to enjoy the fruits of their labor without fear of confiscation. Jurisdictions should be made aware that excessive taxation and government spending could eat into the community's productivity thereby reducing total wealth as well as future growth. Advocates of free markets such as Smith note that taxes should be predictable; they should be easy to administer, and should have minimal side effects. By showing how the freedom to work, trade, save and invest promotes prosperity, Smith presents an economic roadmap for future prosperity. In theory, free markets meet challenges through adaptability and flexibility (Adam Smith Institute n.d.).

Later Day Advocates of Laissez-Faire

Nobel Prize–winning economist and champion of laissez-faire economics, Milton Friedman, argued that free trade, smaller government and a slow, steady increase of the money supply were the best formula for national prosperity. The best-selling book *Free to Choose* compares free market economies to more heavily controlled economies (Friedman and Friedman 1980) and contends that free markets are superior in many ways. *Free to Choose* cites vivid examples where free market economies outperformed centralized economies, noting in particular that in the post–World War II period the economic growth of West Germany far outpaced that of the socialist-oriented East Germany despite the fact both areas were of similar history and culture. The book concludes that the market economic system that West Germany adopted explained a great deal of the differences in the economic performances of East and West Germany following World War II.

Highlighting the role of free markets in fostering economic growth, *Free to Choose* observes that millions of immigrants from all over the world migrated to the United States to work for themselves or others. This became a catalyst for the remarkable economic growth enjoyed in the United States where people were free to experiment with new techniques and to profit from risk taking. Profit seeking with little assistance from government represents the essence of laissez-faire and the central feature of market economies. The nineteenth-century golden ages of both the United States and Great Britain coincided with the political and economic freedom enjoyed by citizens of those nations. In contrast, socialist nations such as Russia, satellite neighbors, China, Yugoslavia, and India were less productive due to their reliance on central direction. Friedman and Friedman (6) warn against "creeping government" and ask whether private ingenuity can continue to overcome the deadening effects of central control if the government and bureaucrats acquire more power to spend money supposedly on the behalf of the people.

Laissez-faire principles are largely consistent with the notion that the freedom to create through entrepreneurship is a major driver of economic growth. Under this scenario, free and open competition spurs innovation and risk taking necessary for prosperity. Under the right conditions, open competition rewards those who are creators of the future, who take risks, work hard, produce new products and meet undiscovered needs of consumers. Entrepreneurs create their own demand through innovation and ambition;

they satisfy hidden consumer demand with goods and services derived from the minds and talents of those that create the businesses of the future. Entrepreneurial visionaries assure future growth and prosperity.

The principles that support laissez-faire are still applicable today. They are consistent with policies of lower taxes, less regulation, low barriers to entry of new businesses and a generally favorable business climate. Various scholars, such as Michael Porter, argue for replacing government programs with market solutions. Similar to the ideas expressed by the nineteenth-century British economist David Ricardo (in his law of comparative advantage), Porter advocates identifying economic strengths of an area and specializing in that area of strength. He contends that this strategy is logical and reasonable to enhance wealth of communities (Porter 1985, 1995). For Porter, jurisdictions can create a sustainable economic base through private, for-profit initiatives and investments based on economic self-interest. He views this strategy as vastly superior to policies of artificial inducements, charity, or government mandates. Porter contends that localities must rely on the free market in order to release themselves from dependency; governments must stop trying to cure problems by perpetually increasing social investment and hoping economic activity will follow. Local businesses should be able to compete on a regional, national, and even international scale. They should be capable not only of serving local clients but also of exporting goods and services.

An offshoot of the laissez-faire philosophy is that of supply-side economics. Popularized by Ronald Reagan in the 1980s, supply-side economics stresses the idea that polities can advance economic growth by lowering taxes and decreasing regulation. In a famous aphorism, Reagan viewed government as the "problem," and not the "solution." Advocates of supply-side economics maintain that when the government takes more of a "hands-off" approach to business (such as lowering taxes), consumers benefit, unemployment falls, and the size of the overall economic pie increases. Economist Arthur Laffer, in his infamous "Laffer Curve," argues that in some circumstances, lowering taxes will increase government revenue.

The inherent assumption of Laffer is that high taxes depress economic activity. Laffer explains that one must consider the positive effect of lower tax rates on work effort, productive investment rather than investment in tax shelters, overall output, and employment. In contrast, raising tax rates would have the opposite effect and reduce participation in the marketplace. According to Laffer, if existing tax rates were too high (in the "prohibitive range" of his curve) then a tax-rate cut would expand the economic pie. The economic effect of the tax cut would outweigh losses from the lower rates and overall government revenue would increase.

The insight that high taxes can harm economies, however, is not unique to Laffer. In the fourteenth century, Muslim philosopher Ibn Khaldun wrote that at the beginning of a dynasty, taxation yields a large revenue from small assessments. At the end of the dynasty, taxation yields a smaller amount of revenue from large assessments (Laffer 2004). As taxes increase, people are less motivated, pursue leisure over work, do not see the benefit of risk taking and increasingly engage in barter. Another point made by supply-siders is the negative impact of tax rates on entrepreneurship. Discouraging entrepreneurship, in turn, deprives society of the high returns derived from innovative products. In direct contrast to the laissez-faire and supply-side perspectives, controlled economies rely heavily on centralized planning. The early Soviet Union and China represent extreme examples of such controlled economies.

CENTRALIZED PLANNING AND ECONOMIC DEVELOPMENT

Soviet Union

Diametrically opposing the laissez-faire perspective is the view that centralized planning is the most efficient and equitable means to foster growth. Advocates of centralized planning contend that markets are fundamentally unfair in that the most able succeed in accumulating immense wealth while large proportions of citizens struggle to subsist. Aside from this argument is the view that large economic "leaps forward" can best occur through planning by corps of technical experts. In controlled economies, economic development planners and other bureaucrats replace the lone entrepreneur as the driver of economic growth. Societies such as the Soviet Union have a relatively long history of centralized planning. For example, after the Russian Revolution of 1917, the Union of Soviet Socialist Republics adopted a system of state ownership, collective farming industrial manufacturing and central planning in order to boost economic growth (Hansen 2003). Beginning in 1928, officials introduced a series of five-year plans, with a brief attempt at seven-year planning. Economic development planners mandated amounts of labor and material needed to complete projects; set firm schedule for their completion and established prices (Allen 2003).

The aim of the first Soviet five-year plan was to transition from a weak, poorly controlled, agriculture state, into an industrial powerhouse. Success ensued; during the first five-year plan, growth in industrial production was second only to the growth rates of the United States. However, quality suffered. Nonindustrial sectors of the Soviet economy were sacrifice in order to boost industrial production; the government was forced to adapt Draconian rationing in order to address chronic food shortages. Workers who failed to meet government quotas were branded as traitors; propaganda attempted to stabilize morale amid shortages (Riasanovsky 2011).

Some view the Soviet Union's first five-year plan as a success in that it began the long journey to becoming an economic and industrial superpower (Hunter 1973). The transition to industrialization, however, was accompanied with profound costs. The creation of collective farms essentially destroyed small farmers (i.e., kulaks). Peasants resisted by killing their farm animals rather than turning them over to the state. Collectivization policies led to famine in the Ukraine, Russia, Kazakhstan, and areas of the northern Caucasus. Estimates of deaths from the Soviet famine of 1932–1933 are in the millions. Ethnic Ukrainians, Kazakhs, and land-owning peasants particularly felt the burden of food shortages (Marples 2009).

Prior to the dissolution of the Soviet Union in 1991, the Soviet Union adopted fourteen five-year plans. The twelfth five-year plan (1987–1990) ended in economic crisis and is associated with efforts by Soviet leader Mikhail Gorbachev to restructure the Soviet economic and political system. Gorbachev's reforms allowed for less centralized control and introduced market experimentation. The alleged goal of the reforms was to make socialism work more efficiently; these efforts, however, created shortages and led to the rise of nationalism in former Soviet republics (Kolkin 2001).

China

China represents another example of a nation that embraced centralized economic planning through a series of five-year plans. In 1953, Chinese leaders launched the nation's first five-year plan for industrialization and socialization. The goal of this plan was to boost industry through hundreds of large- and medium-size industrial plants. The first plan (ending in 1957) created a foundation for the nation's heavy industries, including iron, steel, coal mining, cement, power supply, and machinery. Between 1952 and 1957, the value of all industrial production grew robustly. A second goal of the first five-year plan was the establishment of cooperatives in the agriculture and handicraft industries. By the end of 1956, almost all Chinese farmers and handicraft workers had joined cooperatives; private businesses were transformed to state-owned enterprises or state-private joint ventures. As with the Soviet Union, China's efforts to spur industrial development came with a cost to agricultural production and farmers. For more than a generation, Chinese farmers fell into poverty and semi-starvation (Kraujalis 2012).

The Soviet Union provided support for China's first five-year plan and delivered loans as well as the services of Soviet engineers, scientists, technicians, and planners. On paper, the achievements of the Chinese economy were impressive. Steel, coal, and petrochemical production grew significantly. The first five-year plan resulted in an increase in life expectancy, better housing, and more income. China's second five-year plan (1958–1962), however, was less successful. This plan is associated with Mao Zedong's "Great Leap Forward" that established communes in the countryside. The Great Leap Forward focused on the development of small backyard steel furnaces in village and urban neighborhoods, however, steel constructed in these backyard furnaces were of poor quality. Farm equipment was inferior and buildings constructed by the substandard steel deteriorated quickly. In addition, steel production took many workers away from their fields and desperately needed food rotted on the land. Millions died of starvation or diseases related to starvation. The second five-year plan is recognized as such a disaster that it required termination after three years. The period between 1958 and 1960 (known as the "Three Bitter Years") had political repercussions as well for Mao Zedong who lost some of his stature and power. The official death toll from the Great Leap Forward is 14 million, but many scholars agree that this figure grossly underestimates the number of deaths. Some estimated of the death toll from the bitter years range from 20 to 48 million (Szczepanski 2019).

The early disasters of Chinese central planning appear to have abated following reforms of the 1970s. Between 1978 and 2013, the Chinese economy grew by an average rate of 10 percent a year, producing a tenfold increase in average adult income. During this period, China reduced its infant mortality rate by 85 percent and raised life expectancy by eleven years. Some contend that the Chinese economy accomplished these successes only after they embraced market and political reforms (Ahlers and Schubert 2011). Further advances were achieved under the reforms of China's leader Deng Xiaoping. These reforms that began in the late 1970s distributed government power in China more equally; allowed for more debate; rewarded performance; and expanded private ownership of land. Adopting reforms at the local level enabled the Chinese government to test policies in a low-stakes manner before scaling up to massive size. China's free market initiatives drew on models adopted from Japan, Taiwan, and the United States (Tepperman 2018).

In 2016, China adopted it thirteenth five-year plan. This plan focused on moving up in the "production value chain" by transitioning from heavy industry to modern information-intensive industries. The 2016 plan emphasized the need to be competitive in the high-tech sector, a sector that has been in the past dominated by foreign companies (Torrey 2018). The 2016 plan followed a strategy adopted in Germany of connecting small- and medium-sized companies in global production and innovation network so that they can more efficiently engage in mass production and customized products. The plan recognized that the efficiency and quality of Chinese producers were highly uneven, and that China had to meet multiple challenges if the nation was to avoid being pressured by low-cost producers on one end of the value chain and advanced industrialized economies at the other end. The Chinese Ministry of Industry and Information Technology (MIIT) drafted the plan with input from 150 experts from the China Academy of Engineering (Kennedy 2015).

The 2016 five-year plan includes a discussion of principles, goals, tools, and sectors to penetrate. Its guiding principles are to advance innovation in manufacturing, emphasizing quality over quantity, achieving green development, and nurturing human talent. A major goal of the plan is to upgrade Chinese industry in order to occupy the most valuable segments of the global production supply chain. The plan allows firms to set their own technology standards. Ten sectors were identified for emphasis: (1) information technology; (2) automated machine tools and robotics; (3) aerospace and aeronautical equipment; (4) high-tech maritime equipment; (5) modern rail transport equipment; (6) new-energy vehicles; (7) power equipment; (8) agricultural equipment; (9) new materials; and (10) advanced medical products (Kennedy 2015). China's record of economic success partially dispels the notion that planned economies are fundamentally flawed and cannot compete with free market economies. Their recent record of economic achievement is a source of anxiety for Western nations with corporations that are used to being at the forefront of the production value chain with little fear of competition from emerging nations.

Economists and political leaders in the United States historically denounced centralized planning. Economists focus upon the superiority of open and competitive markets to set prices and deliver desired goods and services to consumers. It is often asserted that sets of administrators and technical "experts" cannot assess markets and consumer desires as well as private sector investors and entrepreneurs. Noneconomists on the other hand focus on the loss of individual freedom that is associated with controlled economies. They refer to the highly centralized governments of Mussolini's Italy and Hitler's Germany as examples of what kind of government to avoid. It is said that Mussolini allowed the trains to run on time and Hitler produced full employment. Such short-term goals, however, did not compensate for the military overreach and devastation that awaited both nations. In both the Soviet Union and China centralization was accompanied by gulags, secret police forces, deportations, starvation, loss of private property, and death. Recent economic growth of China represents a test case of whether centralized economies that engage in international market competition can be a successful model for long-term development.

Both the Soviet Union and China represent examples of controlled economies. Needless to say, other models of development exist that include but are not limited to the pure laissez-faire or controlled economy models. A "mixed" model that emphasized incentives to business, some planning, regulation and a safety net for citizens represents an alternative. The following section discusses "mixed models" and attempts of the U.S. government to encourage development through "industrial policy" initiatives.

MIXED ECONOMIES AND U.S. INDUSTRIAL POLICY

Experiences of Mixed Economies

Various perceptions of mixed economies exist. One variant defines mixed economies as economic systems where the government owns some but not all companies. A mixed economy is organized under some free market principles and some socialist principles; it lies on a continuum somewhere between pure capitalism and pure socialism. A mixed economy protects private property but also allows for some government involvement in the economy in order to achieve social aims. Mixed economies regulate business and may nationalize industries that provide a public good. The United States is considered a mixed economy since all property is not privately owned; private entities do not provide all goods and services, governments regulate some activities, and private establishments might require government-granted licenses. The public sector can ban some transactions (such as the sale of illegal narcotics or prostitution) altogether.

In mixed economies, governments own public property, provide public services and use tax policy or subsidies to influence the market. Mixed economies such as the United States allows for government control or partial control of goods and services, such as education, courts, roads, hospital care, and postal delivery. Mixed economies also can provide substantial subsidies; in the United States, subsidies have been provided to farmers, oil companies, banks, utilities and others. Some products (such as tobacco and alcohol) are taxed to discourage their use while other activities (such as home ownership) are encouraged through tax incentives. Regulations also play an important role in mixed economies. For example, in United States, the Food and Drug Administration (FDA) regulates consumable foods and medicines and businesses can only advertise their goods and services if they comply with mandates of the Federal Trade Commission (FTC). Hiring, compensating, and firing of employees must comply with the Fair Labor Standards Act (FLSA), the Employee Retirement Income Security Act (ERISA) and other guidelines from agencies such as the Department of Labor (DOL). The Federal Reserve also plays a role in managing the overall economy through control of the money supply (Ross 2019).

Mixed economies can redistribute income, influence trade, and supply essential public goods. These public goods that are government supplied include public utilities, military forces, police forces, and environmental protection. Governments intervene in order to promote exports, foster new businesses, and stimulate economic growth. Some jurisdictions encourage growth of specific sectors of the economy by protecting companies until they achieve competitive scale. With protection, nations have allowed specific industries (such as textiles, machinery, and electronic components) to acquire competitive advantages. Entire regions specialize in specific sectors such as computer technology, finance, or entertainment. The so-called infant industry argument gives justification for governments to protect emerging industries that are not quite ready to compete with foreign competitors.

State intervention in the marketplace is consistent with export-led growth strategies that nations have adopted in the past. Export-led strategies propelled the economies of Germany and Japan in the 1950s and 1960s. In the 1970s and 1980s, the four East Asian Tigers (South Korea, Taiwan, Hong Kong, and Singapore) successfully adopted export strategies to advance their economies. In the 1980s and 1990s, the nations of Thailand, Malaysia, Indonesia, and Mexico adopted state-led export strategies. In the 2000s, China embraced the export-led growth paradigm. Policies of trade protection, government investment in specific sectors, establishment of a stable currency, and others enhanced exports. Economists, in general, recognize the value of government intervention in order to promote exports (Chang 2002).

The export-led state interventionist model evolved over time (Palley 2011). Some view intervention as occurring in stages. In stage I, personified by 1945–1970 Germany and Japan, the public sector used undervalued exchange rates to foster economic growth. Stage II (1970–1985) captured the experience of the four East Asian Tigers (South Korea, Taiwan, Hong Kong, and Singapore). These nations also focused on an undervalued exchange rate as well as the need to acquire more foreign technology. The mobility of technology across the globe aided the Asian Tigers in Stage II as they acquired needed expertise. A distinction between stage II and stage III relates to the fact that stage III countries started turning themselves into export producers for foreign multinational corporations rather than developing their own indigenous industrial capacity. Elements of stage III development include integrating national economies into the global economy, undervaluing exchange rate, and suppressing wages. The goal of stage III is to become attractive to multinational corporations (MNCs) as a site for export-oriented foreign direct investment (FDI).

The third stage of export-led growth (exemplified by Mexico) represents the beginning of the modern era of corporate globalization. In this third stage, a partnership forms between developing countries, multinational corporations, and developed countries. This partnership also promotes relocating existing production from the more developed to less developed nations. In theory, relocating production benefits less advanced economies by creating jobs and transferring technology to those economies. However, the less developed economies do not own the industrialization process, as was the case in stage I and stage II. This makes the less developed areas more vulnerable to the decisions of corporate executives who reside elsewhere. Stage III development also does considerable damage to the more advanced economies via domestic job losses.

Stage IV development represents an extension of the stage III model. This has been referred to as the "China model" focusing on three policies: (1) placing tariffs on imports, (2) undervaluing the national currency, and (3) building up the local technological base. In stage IV, foreign multinationals are forced to share technology and engage in joint ventures (in which multinational corporations may be minority shareholders). Theft of technology represents a clear strategy of stage IV. China's policies toward banking and automobile production embody examples of stage IV strategies. In the case of China, joint ventures and dependence on domestic producers (rather than foreign ownership of facilities) is the price of entry into the Chinese consumer market. Corporations that accept these conditions hope they will reap future profits from the large Chinese consumer market.

Joint ventures with nation-states can benefit multinational corporations by reducing their capital investment (11). Nations can leverage the size of their large consumer markets in order to gain concessions from foreign corporations. Nations such as China with populations of more than a billion people have significant leverage as corporations dream of making immense profits from the nation's large consumer market. In addition, to global strategies such as described above, nations and local governments also engage in targeted "industrial policies." While embracing free market rhetoric, the United States has always been involved in industrial policies of one form or another. These policies represent strategic efforts on the part of governments to encourage economic development.

Industrial Policy Initiatives of the United States

There is a growing consensus that most developed countries, including United Kingdom, United States, Germany, and France, actively intervene in their domestic economy through industrial policies (Chang 2002). Historically, an "American School" of economics embraced what we now call industrial policy. Consistent with this "American School" is the need to create a strong central government able to promote science, invention, industry and commerce and make the United States strong enough to determine its own destiny. Central to this thinking is support of industry through protectionism, creation of physical infrastructure, and formation of a financial structure.

In recent years, federal, state, and local governments have involved themselves in various forms of industrial policy. These governments are engaged in providing subsidies, enacting trade policies, procuring goods, providing venture capital, and assisting failing companies. In the past, the Obama administration directed part of its $787 billion stimulus package toward specific sectors, including agriculture, military construction, and energy. Much of this assistance was in high-tech or knowledge-intensive industries. A strategy of the Obama administration was to capitalize on the nation's engineering and scientific resources in order to produce new high-tech products and services that would strengthen U.S. exports and expand domestic employment.

Maintaining and extending the U.S. international leadership in high-tech and knowledge-intensive industries, such as health, the environment and energy, was a major priority of the Obama administration. While pursuing alternative energy sources, federal subsidies to fossil fuel producers increased significantly. With public sector assistance, the United States became the largest producer of both oil and gas. Top recipients of state and local subsidies included major manufacturers such as Boeing, Alcoa, Intel, General Motors, and Ford Motor Company (Sensrud 2016). The public sector also supported corporations through tax subsidies, direct purchases, and venture capital. Trade policy has gained increased attention under the Trump administration as the administration pursued "better deals" as a means of pressuring foreign nations to make concessions.

The U.S. military spending targeted to the sectors of aircraft, communications, electronics, and computing has been significant for decades. In the past, large spending for the military led to technological breakthroughs. Many large U.S. firms such as IBM, Boeing, Caterpillar, Lockheed, and Motorola have their roots in U.S. government contracting; many of these corporations still largely depend on government contracts. The government has supported a majority of the industries (under to guise of defense) in which the United States has a competitive advantage including: aircraft, the Internet, semiconductors, genetic engineering, and pharmaceuticals (Sensrud 2016). State and local governments have also been active in aiding private businesses.

In addition, the federal government funds numerous small- and medium-sized companies through venture capital. Government agencies make equity investments, often in small- to medium-sized technology firms. Unlike private funds, whose aim is to generate profits, government agencies use their funding to develop, adapt, and shape commercially viable technologies for public sector needs. Government agencies take a "hands-on" role within these firm, usually via membership in a firm's board of directors or through technical collaboration. The first federal-level venture capital fund was created by the Central Intelligence Agency (CIA) in 1999 with the dual goals of investing in the development of commercial technologies and meeting the secretive needs of the CIA. By directly investing in small- and medium-size companies, the CIA gained direct access to innovations while also partly directing the research. States are also utilizing government-backed venture capital model. In 2015, New York State launched the New York State Innovation Venture Capital Fund to support and attract new high-growth businesses to the state (Sensrud 2016).

The concept of "too big to fail" has provided a rationale for government intervention in recent decades. Large steel companies have received aid because of their strategic importance, financial companies have received government assistance because they are crucial to the long-term health of the economy, and automobile producers have been viewed as essential because of the jobs they provide to U.S. workers. The federal government intervened and altered the corporate governance structures of General Motors in 2008 to make it more competitive. The George W. Bush and Barack Obama administrations provided large loans to Chrysler and General Motors in 2008 and 2009; the U.S. government purchased a large portion of General Motor's assets in 2009 (Sensrud 2016).

Taxes represent another aspect of mixed economies. Tax policy is used to spur growth, create jobs, retain jobs, and support high-value industries. Individual companies benefit from special tax arrangements. For example, two big tax breaks in 2014 were given to Tesla Motors and Intel. In 2014, Tesla Motors received a subsidy package worth approximately $1.3 billion from the state of Nevada in return for a promise to build a new factory in the state. In the same year, Intel Corporation received thirty years of property tax breaks that analysts predicted would save the company $2 billion. Tax deals are coordinated with state economic development agencies. These agencies utilize a number of incentives including tax credits, grants, loans, equity investment, and tax exemptions (Sensrud 2016).

The Trump administration promised to use the power of government to reverse the economic misfortunes of "left behind" Americans. According to University of California-Berkeley professor of sociology Peter Evans (2017), Trump capitalized on failures of the global neoliberal system to address growing inequality, stagnant wages, and the enormous gains to the top 0.001 percent. The immense concentration of wealth in the United States coincided with negative outcomes for vast numbers of Americans that suffered from declining life expectancies (especially for less-educated white men), poor job prospects, high incarceration rates, and feelings of insecurity. Trump blamed the problems of ordinary Americans on immigration, "bad trade deals," "endless wars," poor leadership of past presidents and other factors.

A popular conception of industrial policies is that they are anathema to free market economics and that the government is a very poor judge of picking industrial winners and losers. Industrial policy runs against the grain of the perception that in the United States, success is driven by individual initiative, personal creativity, hard work, and a willingness to take risks. This view prioritizes competition in a free market economy and rugged individualism where political favoritism is eschewed. Industrial policies in a broad sense, however, have always played some role in the U.S. mixed market model. Such policies include providing physical infrastructure, strengthening education (particularly in science, technology, engineering, and math subjects), tax credit to support innovation, funding of university research, and support for workforce development (Bennett 2015).

Some form of industrial policy and government intervention is a reality in the United States. A role of government in promoting development is not a subject of great dispute. Sectors of the economy including agriculture, education, health care, housing, and defense traditionally have benefited from public sector aid. Former Reagan administration official Clyde Prestowitz (2012) contended that the real issue is not whether the United States has an industrial policy. The issue is what kind of industrial policy the United States is going to adopt. Prestowitz argues that the perception of pristine free markets is a fantasy.

The mixed market model of the United States recognizes a place for government in the economy and attempts to position itself between the extremes of the pure "laissez-faire" and the controlled economy models. The mixed model attempts to "thread the needle" by outlawing the harsh labor conditions of the early industrial revolution, promoting competition through anti-trust legislation, establishing a safety net for citizens, aiding vital industries, and stabilizing the overall economy through policies of noninflationary growth. At the same time, mixed economies maintain a robust private sector. This private sector helps to maintain incentives for work, sacrifice, risk taking, and other traits that promote economic prosperity. The mixed economy must walk the fine line between charges of intrusive government intervention and claims that the unfettered private sector economy will oppress the masses while enriching the very few.

The endurance of the mixed model has been strengthened by adjustments to the laissez-faire model witnessed in the reforms of the early 1900s Progressive movement and the New Deal of the 1930s. Some credit these movements with saving capitalism and democracy by preventing violent revolution (such as the Russian Revolution of 1917) or a turn to a "strong leader" who would eliminate individual liberty (such as the rise of Hitler in the 1930s). As alluded to above, the question for the United States is not whether the mixed model exists but in this mixed model how to preserve both incentives to generate individual wealth and a decent quality of life for the majority of the people.

CRITICISM OF CENTRALIZED PLANNING, MIXED ECONOMIES AND ENVIRONMENTAL INFLUENCES

Criticism of Centralized Planning and Mixed Economies

By the late 1960s, most of the world's nations conducted their economic affairs within the framework of a national economic plan and embraced some form of Keynesian economics. In the 1980s, however, public confidence in the ability of governments to affect the performance of the economy diminished significantly. In developing countries, economic planning yielded disappointing results. The Soviet Union and its Eastern European satellites were forced to introduce market reforms to counter waste and inefficiency. These reforms, however, were not successful and were hampered by the rigidness of the Soviet system (Krueger et al. n.d.). The fall of the Soviet Union and the loss of its Eastern European allies diminished the credibility of the controlled economy model of development.

Prominent critics of centralized economic planning include "Austrian School" economists such as Ludwig von Mises and Friedrich Hayek. Both Mises and Hayek were highly critical of planning as a substitute for market pricing and resource allocation. Mises believed that signals from consumers were essential for efficient allocations of resources. He argued that economic planning led to inefficiency since (unlike market exchanges) planners did not adequately consider the preferences of consumers. Both Mises and Hayek contended that effective responses to consumer demand is only possible through market pricing. They advance the notion that distant bureaucrats do not possess a good grasp of consumer desires. The understanding of consumer desires is most likely to be achieved at levels of government where leaders are close to the people and have a greater understanding of their desires. In the private sector, entrepreneurs can assess needs and respond to consumer desires. For Hayek and Mises, this entrepreneurial behavior is more efficient than depending on the foresight of government officials. Starting with Mises, Austrian economists advanced the laissez-faire model, arguing that a mixed economy is not sustainable because government interventions will consistently lead to further calls for ever-increased intervention and will tend to drift toward a socialistic-controlled economy.

At least three major criticisms of planned economies exist. First, some analysts believe governments are ill-equipped to respond efficiently to surpluses or shortages. Second, is the view that corruption in controlled economies far exceeds corruption in free market or mixed economies. Finally, there is a sense that centrally economies are politically repressive and consumers have few choices. In essence, consumers are forced to accept any products offered by policy makers. Central planning is often associated with the former Soviet Union, China, Vietnam, and Cuba. The economic performance of these states, however, generally trailed capitalist countries, in terms of growth (Chappelow 2019).

Economists of the Public Choice School describe how mixed markets can guide policy away from the public interest. This produces inefficiencies and distortions in the economy as governments can incorrectly choose winners to support with subsidies and can incorrectly choose to punish perceived economic losers. Weaker economic players can receive subsidies due to their size and political influence. Established status quo players may unduly benefit from public money while the truly innovative small players are deprived of these funds. Powerful political interests attempt to shape government policy. There is a large incentives for wealthy corporations to engage in lobbying and use political influence to gather greater profits and/or limit competition from others. "Rent-seeking" is the term used by the Public Choice School for seeking rewards through political rather than economic criteria.

Government invariably plays a role in planned, mixed, and predominately market economies. Governments help to shape the environment in which economic activity transpires. Governments can encourage or discourage growth by subsidies, tax policy, or regulation. Governments can influence the overall milieu of entrepreneurs. At least three factors are relevant to entrepreneurs and economic development in general: (1) the political environment, (2) the human capital environment, and (3) the quality of life environment. Businesses seek political environments that are supportive of their needs. They are more likely to invest in areas where they are assured that the necessary workforce exists. Finally, the general quality of life or the quality of amenities is also associated with attracting businesses and entrepreneurs. Innovative people and footloose companies choose to locate to in places they view as culturally and aesthetically desirable (Florida 2012).

ENVIRONMENTAL INFLUENCES

Political Environment

The political environment plays a crucial role in the success or failure of business enterprise. Nobel Laureate Douglas C. North (1990, 5) argues that political bodies (such as City Councils, Congress, and State Legislatures) as well as street-level bureaucrats (such as police officers, safety inspectors, police chiefs, and others) affect economic performance. North (9) contends that on balance nineteenth-century U.S. economic history is a story of economic growth because the underlying institutional framework (i.e., rules of the game of society) reinforced productive activity. North argues that in contrast to nations with favorable institutions, in many Third World nations the "rules of the game" and norms of society discourage productive activity. Productive activity is discouraged by government support of monopolies that restricts rather than expands opportunity. North contends that Third World countries seldom encourage investment in education that could increase productivity (9) and corruption is a major impediment to productivity. A few examples illustrate how the political environment, identified in the extent of corruption, affects the ability of businesses to survive and grow. Fukuyama (2014, 218) relates the story of how government officials in Nigeria influenced a foreign businessman's decision to terminate his company. According to Fukuyama's instructive narrative, a German businessman married a Nigerian woman and set up a plant to process soybeans in his wife's home state. Soybeans were grown locally and there was a good local market for the product. With some perseverance, given the difficulty of purchasing machinery, the plant became operational. After the couple sold their first carton of soybean oil, a local government official appeared at the factory gate, declaring that some regulations were broken, and demanded 10 percent of the factory's revenue, paid to a special account. The couple refuse to pay and went to the police. Subsequently, the couple's car was damaged and the police chief demanded a percentage of the profits for himself. When the factory owner refused to pay, he was arrested for breaking employment rules and bribing officials. To negotiate a release from jail, the German businessman was coerced into bribing the governor, the police chief, the council chairman, and the judge who handled the case. The businessman closed the company, sold the machinery, and moved back to Germany. The 200 jobs that the business created disappeared. Fukuyama concluded that the corrupt environment of the nation and its officials "killed the goose that was laying the golden eggs" since once the factory closed there was no one from whom officials could extract a bribe and no one to tax. A potential win–win situation (for farmers, consumers, employees, and public officials) was transformed into a long-term losing situation (218).

Rothstein (2011, 5) provides a second example of how the political environment affects economic development. In his example, a run-down restaurant serves coffee and food across the street from a Caribbean Island airport. The poor appearance of the structure guaranteed that affluent tourists hardly ever ventured into the establishment although they have ample time prior to their flights and significant disposable income. When asked why there was no effort to make the restaurant more profitable, the servers answered that they were not the owners but squatters and if they did invest in an upgrade they probably could never afford to pay off the health inspectors, and did not know if it was even possible to buy the property or get a permanent lease. This story should not be viewed as anomalous. There are probably thousands of similar cases where the lack of predictable legal institutions that can secure property rights and curb corruption hinders "micro-businesspeople" from making investments that would improve their economic situation. Both of these examples illustrate a theme of dysfunctional government institutions playing a central role perpetuating low economic opportunity and poor economic performance.

The political environment ranges along a continuum of "business friendliness." This continuum describes the extent to which governments are willing to grant concessions to businesses in return for private sector investment. Typical concessions offered by jurisdictions include an array of tax, regulatory and other inducements. Financial incentives such as grants, loans, loan guarantees, and equity financing represent commonplace enticements. Tax incentives include abatements, exemptions, credits, deferrals, and agreements to maintain tax rates (tax stabilization). Communities wishing to create more favorable business environments can also provide direct financial assistance. Site development, land banks, industrial parks, and enterprise zones are examples of types of nonfinancial assistance that jurisdictions may provide (Koven and Lyons 2010). In contrast, places can actively discourage investment through heavy regulation, limitations on building, zoning requirements, special tax assessments, and other means of discouragement.

Human Capital Environment

The academic literature describes an unambiguous link between the educational levels of workers and economic growth (Florida 2002; Lucas 1988; Glaeser 1998). It is highly logical that businesses will not locate in jurisdictions where they are unable to find the workforce necessary for production of their products or services. High-tech businesses with a need for a large pool of well-trained workers in skills such as software writing will find it necessary to locate in geographical areas where those workers are densely concentrated. Florida (2012) finds that talent (defined by education) is strongly associated with both high-tech industry location and higher incomes. This is not a unique finding as many others have noted that better educated localities are well positioned to supply goods and services at the high end of the producer value chain (Reich 1991; Malecki 1997). Various studies identify an association between human capital and economic growth (Glaeser et al. 1995; Rauch 1993).

The quality of higher education and individual creativity is particularly salient in regard to technology-related development. Research undertaken at major universities such as Stanford University, University of California-Berkeley, Massachusetts Institute of Technology (MIT), and Harvard University accounted for growth in Silicon Valley and along Route 128 in Massachusetts. Other universities were directly involved in development of technology clusters. For example, the University of Texas at Dallas helped develop high-technology companies in the area's Telecom Corridor. The University of South Florida was instrumental in the development of a high-tech corridor in the Tampa area. Kendall Square in Cambridge, Massachusetts, contains a high cluster of biotechnology employers. Most of these companies are connected in some way to nearby Harvard University and MIT. Biotechnology companies in particular cluster near universities because companies want access to trained employees and because the research phase of production tends to be lengthy (Koven and Lyons 2010, 202).

The product life cycle theory is useful in explaining the link between technology and economic development. This theory contends that high-value production locates in technologically sophisticated areas while technologically backward areas are relegated to producing lower-priced goods that pay its employees lower salaries (Vernon 1966). In the product life cycle, products are viewed through a prism of a life cycle moving through three phases of development (new, mature, and standardized). Each phase is associated with different markets and production processes. Profits, growth, and the ability to pay high wages are greatest in the new phase of development. Technologically advanced places with highly skilled workforces are positioned to produce the kind of innovative products (i.e., cool games, high speed jet engines, and stealth aircraft) that cannot be duplicated in less developed places and will command a high price.

According to the product life cycle theory, people will pay a premium for new things they cannot obtain elsewhere. A captive market develops for the unstandardized new products. For example, it is unlikely that products such as stealth fighter bombers could be developed without high levels of technical knowledge. Those areas with the technology acquire the benefits of the captive market who demand the newest and most trendy things. Under the product life cycle theory, as demand for new products expand, they become more standardized and more easily duplicated. At the standardization phase, cost reduction is obtained through mass production. Automobile product represents an illustration of the product life cycle theory. At one time, automobiles were the new specialty products but over time their ability to be produce became standardized. Before 1910, automobiles were a new innovation (new stage of product cycle) and were more likely to be handcrafted than the mass-produced autos of the 1930s.

When industries (such as steel, tires, and automobiles) become less dependent on specialized skills, they are transferred to locations where owners do not have to pay workers the wages commanded at the new phase of product development. A hierarchy of geographical wages develops with labor intensive products (such as clothing, shoes, and toys) relegated to areas of the world where labor costs are low. This phenomenon on "offshoring" is associated with the deindustrialization that has plagued developed nations as workers in the older industries are forced into lower paying positions or unemployment. Deindustrialization results in a downward spiral of wages, plant closures, declines in real estate values, and outmigration from once thriving jurisdictions (Howes and Markusen 1993). The history of American rust belt cities, such as Detroit, Cleveland, and Pittsburg, is one of ageing industries shifting production to lower cost areas, declining populations, declining tax bases, and the need to find the next economic engine to revitalize their area (Koven and Koven 2018).

Quality of Life Environment

Amenities are defined as qualities of a locality that make it an attractive place to live and work. Examples of amenities are wildlife and flora, recreational areas, cultivated landscapes, unique settlement patterns, historic sites, and cultural traditions. Green (2001, 67) claims that there are three streams of literature that focus on the role of amenities and community economic development. The first stream is principally concerned with the extent to which business location is affected by the quality of life. The second stream focuses on the effects of amenities on population mobility. Finally, other research examines the effects of amenities on economic indicators such as income inequality, fiscal health, and consumer spending.

The importance of amenities for firm location, however, is a matter of debate. Gottlieb (1994) argued that amenities do not have a strong influence on firm locations. Other studies found that climate and water amenities can influence population growth, especially for retirees. Jurisdictions adjacent to metropolitan areas or rich in amenity experienced population growth (Johnson and Beale 1994). The linkage between natural amenities (climate, topography, and surface water) and population change is weaker for some areas such as slow growth regions, Midwest and Northeast, than for the South and West. Lake areas appear to be especially important for attracting migrants seeking recreation or in retirement (Green 2001, 68). Recreation-based growth has the added advantage of being perceived as "environmentally friendly," however, many of the jobs created in recreational areas are seasonal, temporary, and pay low wages. This pattern contributes to income inequality (Smith 1989).

Studies support linkages between amenities (such as art galleries, museums, entertainment, climate, and quality of government) and development (Glaeser et al. 2001; Gottleb 1995). Research contends that for places to remain strong, they must attract workers on the basis of quality of life as well as on the basis of higher wages. Recently a good deal of research considers factors such as the "character" of a place, how comfortable potential residents think they would feel, the level of tolerance for others, and lifestyle "fit." Florida (2002) argues that tolerance of others is a major contributor to development and that at any given time, places compete with one another for talent. Regions that are more open to diversity are able to attract a wider range of talent by nationality, race, ethnicity, and sexual orientation. Florida states, "Simply put, regions that are open and possess low barriers to entry for human capital gain distinct economic advantage in the competition for talent or human capital, and, in turn, in their ability to generate and attract high technology industries and increase incomes" (745).

PLAN OF BOOK

Part I of the book identifies the governmental setting, public sector strategies, and theories of development. The introductory chapter focuses on macro-economic models of managing economies as an essential starting point. It describes and critiques frameworks of governance and perspectives on managing economies. Distinct differences are noted between the perspectives of laissez-faire economics, centralized planning, and mixed economies. The implementation of one framework or another has significant consequences in terms of business and individual wealth creation. The durability and efficiency of planned centralized economies has long been questioned, however, the rise of China as an economic power has generated renewed attention to the desirability of planned economies (Hsueh 2011; Morrison 2014; Pillsbury 2016). The discussion of macro-economic frameworks is supplemented with a recognition that the environment of place in terms of factors such as politics, skill levels, and amenities plays an important role in encouraging business creation and overall development.

Chapter 2 reviews "waves" or "phases" of development. It moves from the broader theoretical focus of chapter 1 to the more applied perspectives of specific strategies and policies that have been adopted in efforts to foster development. The chapter notes that qualitatively different approaches are pursued in efforts to stimulate economic development. Strategies such as trying to lure other firms, support for existing firms, networking, building skill levels of the work force, improving sustainability, enhancing self-sufficiency, and developing competitive advantages have enjoyed popularity at various times. While the approaches differ, they overlap and supplement each other. Attention to a more current approach does not eliminate application of a prior strategy. Chapter 3 explores the extant literature on entrepreneurship theories. The chapter provides an overview from a diversity of disciplines such as economics, sociology, anthropology, and psychology. The chapter integrates perspectives and places the discussion within the context of entrepreneurship as a function of numerous influences. The chapter contends that looking at entrepreneurship from a purely economic point of view is too narrow. In order to gain a fuller understanding of why people become entrepreneurs, it is necessary to consider the contributions of a variety of academic disciples.

Part II emphasizes the roles of both individuals and the broader context or setting. It argues that both individual motivations and the context in which individuals interact with others are essential for understanding entrepreneurial behavior. Individuals can create, but the environments in which they operate can either foster or inhibit individual business creation. Chapter 4 provides case studies of highly successful self-made entrepreneurs. These cases provide support for the view that visionary individuals can drive development. The large proportion of high-tech entrepreneurs among this group highlights the value of people who innovate and create value-producing goods or services at the beginning of the product life cycle. The chapter attempts to engage readers with the personal lives of billionaire entrepreneurs while at the same time illustrating that immense fortunes can still be generated within one's lifetime. The wealth generated by entrepreneurs discussed in this chapter is illustrative of entrepreneurship opportunity in the United States.

Chapter 5 further delineates the context from which entrepreneurship springs by focusing upon the educational and legal context. The historic development of the U.S. system of education, its openness to a variety of economic groups, and the quality of the nation's universities are examined. As discussed in chapter 4, many leading U.S. entrepreneurs benefited from their experiences at world-renowned institutions of higher learning that are located in the United States. Chapter 5 also highlights the importance of a legal environment that facilitates business creation and assures the protection of private property. Chapter 6 describes the social and political environment. Political and social environments that are accepting of others either in terms of immigration or lifestyle issues are seen as contributing to entrepreneurship and economic development. In an age when attracting talent is a high economic development priority, an atmosphere of tolerance and acceptance is valuable. Such an atmosphere can help places become magnets of talent. The final chapter explores institutional challenges to U.S. entrepreneurialism. It examines contextual advantages that contributed to U.S. entrepreneurial success and discusses practical implications of entrepreneurship for various actors.

Chapter 2

Strategies for Economic Development

There are a multitude of strategies to engage in entrepreneurial activity. At the individual level, an array of homilies such as "work hard," "stay in school," "keep your nose to the grindstone," or "marry up," have been posited over time. At the jurisdictional level, strategies such as becoming "pro-business," investing in "good amenities," developing "favorable institutions," "poaching businesses," attracting or developing "human capital," "expanding exports," and other ideas have waxed and waned over time. No single approach prevails as the "one best way" and instead a patchwork of theories complement each other and provide insight. This chapter explores various phases of development as identified in the literature. The chapter describes the phases, links the phases to entrepreneurship and paves the path for the more in-depth descriptions of entrepreneurship theory, entrepreneurial actors, and environments found in subsequent chapters.

PHASES OR WAVES OF ECONOMIC DEVELOPMENT POLICY

Scholars generally agree that strategies for economic development evolved over time that at different periods of time certain strategies were more dominant, and that dominance of one strategy did not eliminate elements of other strategies. Classifications of strategies differ somewhat in terms of number of categories; however, similarities exist in terms of descriptions of specific efforts. Clarke and Gaile (1992) view economic development as historically falling into two waves: (1) a first wave relying heavily on land use controls, public services, and infrastructure, and (2) a subsequent wave involving the use of revolving loan funds and below market loans. The authors speculate that for a later wave, newer strategies would have to incorporate more entrepreneurial approaches. In a later work, Clarke and Gaile (1997) do not place strategies into specific classifications but introduced newer strategies of human capital development, competitive advantage, and third-wave economic development sustainability.

Others viewed second-wave development strategies as including support for business, business incubators, increasing investment capital, and providing technical assistance. A third wave of state economic development strategies shifts emphasis from firm-based programs to broader regional programs. This wave or phase focuses on policies that emphasize strategic planning, public-private partnerships, technology, human resources, and industrial clusters. The third wave is viewed as a policy direction that focuses rather than replaces earlier strategies. This wave mobilizes established programs to build strategic advantages in industry clusters (Bradshaw and Blakely 1999). For many years, people have speculated that a new paradigm for state economic development would emerge. For example, Fosler (1992) proposed that a new paradigm would include three elements: (1) development rooted in the private sector, (2) building on legal, regulatory, and policy frameworks for private sector activity that enhances human, financial, and physical capital, and (3) development of institutions for shaping and implementing government responsibilities.

Scholars disagree about the exact classification of phases or waves. However, there is general consensus that the earliest phase prioritized business attraction or "smokestack chasing." This strategy relied upon general tax incentives, loans and other incentives targeted to individual firms. A later phase prioritized business retention and expansion of existing firms as well as creation of new firms through business incubation, technical assistance, and venture capital forums. Activity associated with more recent phases include networking, cluster formation, human capital development, strategic planning, metropolitan cooperation, sustainability, and human capital development (Koven and Lyons 2010, 117–118). A contemporary and well-accepted perspective of phases of development consists of five phases as summarized in Leigh and Blakely (2016, 59–63).

FIVE PHASE VIEW OF ECONOMIC DEVELOPMENT

First Phase—Smokestack Chasing

Planning literature identifies five "waves" of "phases" of development with "smokestack chasing" representing the first phase (Leigh and Blakely 2016, 59). This first phase focuses on recruitment of specific companies through financial incentives (such as tax abatement and loans) that lowering the costs of businesses operations. The first phase is firmly grounded in what economic development scholars term the "traditional" or "supply-side" school of thought (Bartik 1991; Eisinger 1988; Olberding 2000). Proponents of this school of thought assert that economic development is impacted primarily by the cost of factors of production including land, labor, capital, energy, transportation, and communication. This perspective contends that changing the costs of factors of production can "poach" firms by directing them away from specific geographical areas where costs are relatively high. Smokestack chasing assumes that businesses are profit maximizing and that they will seek out areas where they can attain higher returns on their investments. Businesses attain higher profits by searching for tax and other incentives that reduce their costs.

In the first wave, policies to induce businesses to relocate include lowering the costs of land, lowering the costs of buildings, reducing taxes, having less regulations, and adopting policies that are hostile to labor. Such an environment directly lowers operating costs for businesses. Jurisdictions are viewed as being in competition for jobs; they create business-friendly environments in effort to lure businesses from other areas. Industrial attraction is viewed as a zero-sum game with some places winning and others losing. Policies of phase one specifically target "footloose" manufacturing plants which are not presently located in the area (Olberding 2000, 57).

One of the earliest examples of the first phase strategy is the Mississippi's Balancing Agriculture with Industry (BAWI) initiative. Created in the 1930s, the BAWI initiative represents the nation's first state-sponsored economic development plan that attempted to lure industry through packages of tax incentives, inexpensive land, low wages, and other subsidies. The intent of these inducements was to entice northern industries to relocate to the South (Johnson 2018). BAWI targeted companies that could create high numbers of jobs and that public officials believed possessed a low risk of failure. Prior to legislature terminating BAWI in 1940, the program brought various companies to Mississippi (Johnson 2018). Southern governors supported the Mississippi initiative and introduced similar plans. Some economists claimed that BAWI had a positive impact of industrial wages in the Mississippi economy and posited the general strategy as a model for post–World War II economic development (Lester 2004).

Critics of the BAWI program, however, faulted it and similar programs for institutionalizing low wages, poor working conditions, anti-union tendencies, and poor environmental policies. These critics argued that the BAWI program was an egregious form of "corporate welfare" that gave too much to profitable businesses and attracted uneducated, unskilled workers to the area. Critics also argued that these programs depressed wages in the entire surrounding area. Opponents of BAWI claimed that the program provided incentives to firms that did not need support and only enhanced profits of already well-established firms. Labor leaders claimed that BAWI did not improve the conditions of Mississippi's working poor and that Mississippi engaged in unfair practices to attract new industries (Lester 2004). Despite the criticism, manufacturing jobs increased in Mississippi after BAWI was enacted in 1936. Other southern states followed Mississippi in developing programs that drew industry from the northern Rust Belt.

Contemporary Use of the First Phase Strategy

Despite widespread criticism of "smokestack chasing" as a poor strategy for development, in more recent times numerous state and local governments have attempted to lure jobs from other areas. These attempts did not exactly follow the strategies of Mississippi but similarities exist in terms of luring companies from other areas on the basis of offering a better environment for profit maximization. In a 1993 bidding war to attract a Mercedes vehicle plant, the state of Alabama prevailed in a competition with thirty-four other states by offering Mercedes a generous incentive package. Alabama's package included infrastructure development, job training, tax concessions, and other benefits. In 1982, the state of Tennessee offered substantial incentive packages for Nissan and Saturn/General Motors plants. Both Nissan and Saturn accepted the offers and chose Tennessee as their new homes.

The desire to lure jobs is also played out globally. In recent times, Spain attempted to lure a Lucent Technology semiconductor fabrication facility that was located in Orlando, Florida. In response, the state of Florida and the city of Orlando granted large tax concessions to the company. In addition, in order to retain the facility matching funds for equipment purchases, and money for relevant research were granted to the University of Central Florida and the University of South Florida (O'Neil 2005). This attempt by Spain to lure the large Lucent facility illustrates that the "poaching" game is alive and well internationally as well as within national borders. All jurisdictions appear to be in a cutthroat competition for jobs, businesses, and general development.

Large and small companies are receptive to offers from other geographical areas. Various factors influence business relocation decisions. Some of the diverse factors to be considered in relocations include a better pool of employees, tax and other incentives, lower costs for labor and land, better amenities, and the need to expand or upgrade facilities. By searching for new locales, business owners can improve their chances of finding a place better suited for company needs and revenue generation (Business Vibes 2015). Large cities find themselves not only in competition with other large cities but also with nearby suburbs and smaller towns. Many examples also exist of companies moving away from smaller cities and suburban locations.

In 2016, McDonald's executive announced that they were putting their sprawling suburban property in Oak Brook, Illinois, up for sale and moving to the West Loop of Chicago. In 2013, Archer Daniels Midland Co. said it will move its headquarters to Chicago after more than four decades in the small city of Decatur, Illinois. In 2013, Coca-Cola transferred 2,000 tech workers from its suburban office in Atlanta to a skyscraper in the city's urban core. In 2015, Kraft Heinz Company announced it will move its Chicago-area headquarters to the city's center after decades in the suburbs. In 2017, Aetna announced that it would move its corporate headquarters to Manhattan from Hartford, Connecticut. Caterpillar, in 2017, announced that it was moving its headquarters to the Chicago area from Peoria, Illinois, seeking a bigger talent pool and better transportation options (O'Connell 2017).

There is growing evidence that companies are moving to larger cities in efforts to find a better pool of young professionals who gravitate to certain place because of the area's lifestyle offerings. These places include the growing cities of San Francisco, Minneapolis, Seattle, Boston, Portland, and Denver that have a reputation of catering to millennials' preferences for high-end apartments, diverse food and beverage offerings, and ample entertainment within walking distance of public transportation (Williams 2017).

Contemporary business relocations differ from the old industrial smokestack chasing of the past. They nevertheless indicate that the game of poaching jobs and businesses from other locations has not died. The game, however, appears to have shifted away from lowering business costs in order to lure manufacturing facilities. Today, it is more likely that jurisdictions will market quality of life amenities or the quality of their workforce in order to attract development. The goal of "winning" in a visceral competition for economic gain, however, remains the same. Companies continue to relocate and jurisdictions continue to offer incentives.

The state of Texas is particularly aggressive in marketing their wares to businesses. Texas has benefited from many relocations, particularly from California. The Texas Economic Development Corporation (TxEDC) and the governor's Economic Development & Tourism division (EDT) have offered array of attractions. The Texas Economic Development website openly boasts about its business-friendly environment and why the state consistently wins awards as the top state for doing business. It details why it has attracted businesses such as Toyota, Boeing, Charles Schwab, Merck, and Kubota. The state has actively used property tax abatements, permit fee waivers, and cash grants to lure businesses. Texas is also home to one of the most competitive, deal-closing incentive programs in the nation, the Texas Enterprise Fund (TEF). The Texas Enterprise Fund claims to be the largest "deal-closing" fund of its kind in the nation. It is used as an incentive tool for projects that offer significant job creation and capital investment.

Criticisms of First Phase Strategies

General criticism of first-wave development strategies abounds. Critiques include the assertion that "poaching" is an inequitable use of public resources since it transfers money from lower and middle-income taxpayers to support large businesses and wealthy stockholders. It also violates free market principles by allowing governments to support less efficient enterprises. Analysts tend to view first phase strategies as "zero sum" in that "poaching" does not enhance the value of the total economic pie but merely moves assets from one place to another. In this scenario, one area's gain is offset by another area's loss. Businesses pit place against each other in order to extract the highest subsidy. As a result, all communities are pressured to offer generous incentives in order to minimize their potential losses.

Declining communities are under great pressure to do almost anything to attract development. This in turn can create a "race to the bottom" as communities compete to offer the most direct subsidies, the lowest taxes, the least regulations, and other perks to attract business. In many cases, existing businesses in communities are burdened by the unfair advantage given to the new business that move in to the area to take advantage of subsidies. Because of its negative effects, "races to the bottom" may harm workers, middle-income taxpayers, and communities in general. Businesses reap the rewards of this competition as they shop around for the best offer and choose from among the many communities that seek to attract firms (Deller and Kures n.d.).

Second Phase View—Retention and Expansion of Existing Firms

Criticisms of the first phase led to the second wave of development that focuses on the retention and expansion of existing small businesses. This phase was initiated in the 1970s in response to doubts about the effectiveness of first phase strategies, failures of urban renewal projects, declines in manufacturing employment, and an increase in global competition. Strategies of the second wave include fostering small businesses through public policies such as enterprise zones, tax increment financing, business incubators, revolving loan funds, and other job creation innovations aimed at enhancing competitiveness (Deller and Kures n.d.). The second phase of development emphasizes creating businesses, increasing investment, and providing technical assistance to help local business expansion.

Enterprise Zones

Many cities have embraced the concept of "enterprise zones" of specially carved out areas that offer tax concessions, infrastructure, and diminished regulations to businesses that are willing to locate to the area of the zone (Clarke and Gaile 1992). In theory, these tax and regulatory concessions will help to retain old businesses and create new business activity. This in turn will enhance local tax revenues and employment. Under the enterprise zone strategy, a community can select specific areas for lower taxes, less regulation, and other inducements. This strategy is business-oriented and consistent with supply-side economics with its emphasis on tax and regulatory relief. Many credit the British professor of urban planning Peter Hall with creating the enterprise zone concept and calling for reducing governmental regulation within economically depressed urban communities. Hall asserted that enterprise zones would initially create low-wage jobs but, over time, small businesses would evolve into more sophisticated enterprises that could pay higher wages. Hall did not intend enterprise zones to be a perfect model for overall urban development, but rather to serve as more of a last resort for reinvigorating declining urban areas. The initial intent of the enterprise zone concept was to spur economic activity in abandoned industrial areas (Hyman 1998).

U.S. Congressmen Jack Kemp and Robert Garcia became champions of the enterprise zone concept in the 1980s. Kemp introduced the first enterprise zone bill in 1980 and later continued to advocate for the passage of federal enterprise zones when he became Secretary of Housing and Urban Development (HUD). During the 1980s and 1990s, other legislators also introduced enterprise zone bills. Lower taxes on capital gains, tax credits on investments, and wage credits for investors in enterprise zone businesses were significant features of these bills. Despite the support of Presidents Ronald Reagan and George H.W. Bush as an answer to inner-city disinvestment, Congress failed to pass enterprise zone legislation until 1993. Many states, however, enacted their own legislation at an earlier date.

A variety of studies assessed the impact of enterprise zones. Wilder and Rubin (1998) concluded that according to most studies, enterprise zones were successful in increasing the numbers of jobs and investment in an area. However, they also observed that conditions in certain inner-city neighborhoods were so intractable that even with the creation of enterprise zones, job losses outnumber job gains. Wilder and Rubin surmised that enterprise zones did not have “magical qualities” that can overcome significant barriers such as decaying infrastructure, high crime rates, and inadequate school systems (481).

Critics of enterprise zones claimed that jobs in many zones paid low wages and had little security. The extent to which jobs benefited the zone residents is uncertain. Some studies show that few enterprise zone residents actually produced the new jobs (481). Lambert and Coomes (2001) noted that in Louisville, Kentucky, enterprise zone mostly benefited large corporations and did not benefit local neighborhoods. Peters and Fisher (2002) concluded that most state and local enterprise zone programs came up short in achieving their goals and objectives. Critics of enterprise zones claimed that they were more beneficial to established firms that wished to increase their profits than to low-income residents or declining communities.

Tax Increment Financing

In addition to enterprise zones, tax-increment financing (TIF) is a widely used second phase strategy. Tax increment-financing dates to 1952, when California adopted the strategy as an innovative way to raise funds. The approach became increasingly popular in the 1980s and 1990s, when state and federal funding for local economies declined. In many cases, TIF became the primary strategy for financing local economic development. The rules for tax-increment financing vary across states, however, generally the TIF designation requires designating an underdeveloped area and declaring that economic development would not take place in the area without some type of governmental assistance. In most cases, specialized consultants produced the needed evidence of underdevelopment. State laws varied in detail but all maintained the basic approach of borrowing money from investors, using the money to make improvements in a designated area, generating increases in property values, reaping added tax revenue from the increases in property values, and repaying the initial borrowing with the increases in tax revenue. When TIF-related bonds are fully paid, the city can dissolve the tax increment-finance district and enjoy the benefits of higher land values for General Fund use.

Cities use TIF financing to make improvements to land (such as street lighting, water and sewage lines, and landscaping) or to fund special projects such as a sports arena. Tax increment financing assumes that growth from the TIF improvements benefits the entire municipality. However, some critics assert that growth in TIF districts is offset by less development in other parts of the community. This implies that subsidies to one location reduces demand in other areas and therefore is a zero-sum game (Dye and Merriman 2006).

There are advantages as well as disadvantages of tax increment financing. Advantages include the fact that the TIF strategy does not entail out of pocket expenses, no additions to a jurisdiction's general obligation debt, and no requirement for voter approval. Critics of TIF, however, note that the strategies avoid accountability by voters, increase the need for services, commit other government funds if anticipated property value increases fail to materialize, and may subsidize projects that would have been undertaken even in the absence of public borrowing (Koven and Lyons 2010, 96). A 2018 report of the Lincoln Land Institute concluded that TIF districts can be particularly problematic for overlapping governments that lose tax revenue due to the creation of the districts. Other TIF-related effects suggest that communities should use tax increment financing cautiously to avoid diverting tax revenues from counties, school districts, and other overlapping governments. According to the Lincoln Land Institute, decades of experience and research indicate that tax increment finance schemes and not a panacea but if used properly can be an important tool to nurture economic development (Merriman 2018).

A negative externality of TIF strategies is that they may create the "race to the bottom" effect when jurisdictions compete with each by offering bigger packages of inducements in the TIF districts. In communities desperate to retain their tax bases, businesses recognize that they are in a favorable bargaining position to extract as many concessions as possible. However, the jurisdictional "winners" may become "losers" in the end if the costs of retaining businesses exceed the benefits. Sometimes general revenue funds must be used to make up for shortfalls in TIF-anticipated revenue. With growth, added costs accrue to jurisdictions in terms of the need for police, fire, and education services; these costs may not be offset by growth due to increases in low-wage jobs. Prosperous domestic and multinational corporations recognize their advantageous position with respect to cities that are desperate for development. It is consistent with free market principles for these companies to extract as many benefits from governmental units as possible. Companies link investment decisions to the array of tax credits, tax abatements, tax deferral, infrastructure development, subsidies, training of employees, and regulatory relief that communities offer. "Footloose" companies can carefully weigh the advantages and disadvantages of the numerous sites.

Business Incubators and Revolving Loan Funds

Jurisdictions use business incubators to facilitate new business formation, job creation, and to improve their entrepreneurial climate. The idea of business incubation has its roots in the planned industrial districts of the 1920s and 1930s. Since the 1970s, the use of business incubators as a tool for economic development has spread across the United States and to other countries (Dickes 2011, 25). Some definitional ambiguity, however, surrounds business incubation. Kuratko and LaFollete (1987) see business incubators as seeking to link talent, technology, capital, and know-how to entrepreneurial talent in order to develop new companies. Others such as Hackett and Dilts (2004) focus on incubators as a means of reducing costs and providing assistance in order to prevent business failure.

Since the 1970s, the use of business incubators as a tool for economic development and new firm creation has spread around the world. Research asserts that most incubators take clients whose firms are in the early or start-up phase of a business. Business incubators are primarily used as economic development tools for job creation, often with additional goals of stimulating entrepreneurial and innovative activity. Incubators can be used to bridge the gap between the idea phase of a young firm and the formal start-up phase (Brooks 1986). They provide a platform for new firms to succeed in the difficult start-up phases.

The most common business support services include entrepreneurial training, business development assistance, and services such as accounting, legal advice, marketing, advertising, and financial management (Bollingtoft and Ulhoi 2005; Dickes 2011). In the 1980s, the number of incubators grew substantially (Stenberg 1993). Nations and individual communities around the world enthusiastically supported incubation programs and used them as a policy instrument to promote local and regional economic development as well as entrepreneurship (Dickes 2011, 36).

Incubators generally provide both virtual and on-site tactical support (Riggins 2019). Some incubators have been very successful. For example, the incubator "Y Combinator" funded over 1,800 business start-ups between 2005 and 2019. These companies included highly profitable ventures such as Reddit, Airbnb, and Dropbox. The Y Combinator's model involves investing a small amount of money in a large number of start-ups twice per year; by 2019 funded companies had a combined valuation of over $80 billion (Pilon 2019).

Dickes (2011) emphasizes the difficulty of evaluating the success or failure or business incubators in the short run. She argues that outcomes after one, two, or even five years may not adequately capture the potential long run benefits of incubators. In the long term, incubators may have tremendous impacts as companies that may have been still born at birth, survive and expand, ultimately achieving great heights. Incubators also possess hard-to-measure positive spillover effects such as improving the entrepreneurial climate of an area, enhancing networking, and increasing knowledge spillovers.

Many business incubators also help entrepreneurs acquire capital through revolving loan funds. These funds are primarily used for development and expansion of small businesses. As a self-replenishing pool of money, revolving loan funds utilize interest and principal payments on old loans for the purpose of issuing new loans. While the majority of revolving loans support generic local businesses, some target-specific industries. Money from revolving loan funds also support minority business development and companies engaged in environmental cleanup. Revolving loan funds can provide critical financing to entrepreneurs when their access to credit is limited. The ultimate goal of revolving loan programs is to create new jobs, new businesses, and foster a healthier local economy. Often revolving loans serve as a bridge between the amount of money the borrower can obtain from the private sector and the amount needed to start or sustain a business.

Revolving loans should not be perceived as free or easy sources of financing since loans must be replenished for future activity. Initial funding of a revolving loan fund usually comes from a combination of public (local, state, federal government) and private sources (financial institutions and philanthropic organizations). Most revolving loan funds have at least one local public source combined with other sources. Loans are expected to result in a public good, borrowers are held to performance measures such as the number and quality of jobs created, increases in tax revenue, amount of private funding and benefits to low and moderate-income citizens (Council of Development Finance Agencies n.d.).

Third Phase—Networks, Clusters, and Human Capital

The third phase of economic development emerged in the early 1990s with a focus on public-private partnerships, regional networks, industrial clusters, and human capital. According to Bradshaw and Blakely (1999, 230), third phase programs do not eliminate first- and second-phase strategies, but they give specific purpose to techniques such as networks, clusters, private-public partnerships, and human capital. Third phase strategies leverage capital and human resources in an attempt to increase the global competitiveness of a group of strategically linked firms. Cluster development is a key aspect of this phase. Third phase strategies aim to develop an overall positive context for general economic growth. This strategy avoids individual incentives and focuses on collaboration to enhance an area's competitiveness in the global marketplace. The strategy of phase three assumes that government activism through industrial policies can facilitate growth, new business formation, business retention, and expansion. It incorporates both the first and second phases with an emphasis on building regional attractiveness, improving productivity, and enhancing competitiveness (Held 1996).

Networks and Clusters

Geographical clusters represent a focal point of third-wave economic development (Bradshaw and Blakely 1999, 239). Industry clusters possess interlocking businesses that benefit from their proximity to each other. Understanding the role of clusters in driving growth informs entrepreneurs about desirable locations that will provide greater exposure, greater access to complementary companies, and added prestige to emerging firms. While the development of clusters is associated with "third phase" development, the concept is not novel. Alfred Marshall (1920) discussed in detail the advantages of business concentrations or "industrial districts" after observing the high density of enterprises specializing in the same product in specific regions of the United Kingdom.

Porter (1998c, 2000) viewed clusters as a product of the interplay of environmental factors. He (1998b) viewed close links with buyers, suppliers, and other institutions as essential, not only for efficiency but also for enhancing overall progress. According to Porter (1998c), the quality of the business environment strongly influenced how well companies would be able to compete. Clusters would allow firms to take advantage of human capital and complementary businesses that operated in close proximity. Porter believed that there is an important role for government to play in networking and identifying impediments to growth. Productivity can build on historic strengths of given areas.

Porter identified a wide array of clusters throughout the United States where specialized sectors formed. He noted that large places such as New York (financial services, advertising, publishing, multimedia), Boston (mutual funds, biotechnology, software, venture equity), Los Angeles (defense aerospace, entertainment), Silicon Valley/San Francisco Bay area (microelectronic, biotechnology, venture capital), Detroit (auto equipment and parts), Phoenix (helicopter, semiconductors, electronic testing labs) and Dallas (real estate development) each have their own clusters of specialization. Specialization, however, is not limited to the largest cities and metropolitan areas of the country. Smaller places such as Dalton, Georgia (carpets); Rochester, New York (imaging equipment); Warsaw, Indiana (orthopedic devices); Boise, Idaho (sawmills, farm machinery); and Carlsbad, California (golf equipment) also developed clusters around concentrated strengths.

Clusters can relate to both growth and decline. Growing clusters benefit their communities, states and nation. In contrast, declining clusters portend a multitude of negative externalities such as declining tax bases, budget deficits, failing public services, and dismal employment prospects. Moretti (2013, 187) stated that ever since Michael Porter popularized the concept of cluster building, cities and states have been trying to engineer clusters through public policies. He concluded, however, that the record of public sector success is mixed and that clusters are more likely to develop from the abilities of individuals and their successful enterprises than to develop through concerted efforts of the government. For example, Zucker and Darby (2001) argue that what really explains the success of biotech companies is the presence of academic stars.

Human Capital

Human capital is vital for third phase development. According to this perspective, development derives from the skills, education, and ability of individuals. Leigh and Blakely (2016, 61) highlight this aspect of economic development and observe that third phase programs emphasize building local capacity through the education and training of local workforces. Third phase programs attempt to link technology, human resources, and capital in order to give firms global competitive advantages. Enhancing human capital involves implementing programs aimed at creating cutting-edge comparative advantages. Comparative advantage can be enhanced by developing human capital at all levels. Certificate programs at two-year colleges can improve the skills of people who do not attend more prestigious four-year institutions. Industry-college partnerships have been useful in enhancing the stock of human capital.

Community colleges have been integral to improving skills of workers. Cooperative efforts between businesses and colleges or "new vocationalism" seeks to satisfy both the market demand for skilled employees as well as the value to society of having knowledgeable citizens. In theory, community college-industry partnerships (CCIPs) have the potential to meet the immediate skill-level needs of area business, improve regional/national competitiveness, and earn a family-sustaining wage. Lower-wage workers learn skills that increase their earning power. Businesses receive workers that are tailored to their needs. Higher education is also available through new vocationalism programs that allow students to obtain occupational licenses, technical certification, associate degrees, and bachelor degrees (Soares n.d.).

Individual companies and government entities work in partnership with community colleges to upgrade skills. An innovative program (Metropolitan College Program) was created in Louisville, Kentucky, with cooperation between United Parcel Service (UPS), the state of Kentucky, the city of Louisville, the Louisville Chamber of Commerce (Greater Louisville, Inc.), the University of Louisville and Jefferson Community and Technical College (JCTC). This program helped to prevent the giant package shipping company UPS from moving its hub away from Louisville. The program was acclaimed as a "win-win" since Metropolitan College assisted students in furthering their education, it provided UPS with a reliable stream of workers, helped the colleges increase enrollment, and improved retention rates of workers at the large package handling company. The perceived success of the Metropolitan College Program led Chicago to adopt its own version of the Metropolitan College model (Soares n.d.)

A second example of community college-business partnerships is that of the partnership between Northrop Grumman, Thomas Nelson Community College, and Tidewater Community College in the Hampton Roads area of Virginia. The Northrop Grumman Newport News (NGNN) facility developed two programs to provide workers for its naval building, designing, and ship repairing facilities. Apprentices in the program received paid, on-the-job training in one of nineteen registered programs. Recruits to the program who showed aptitude during the training were allowed to pursue an associate degree in fields such as business administration, engineering, marine engineering, or electrical engineering, all paid for by Grumman.

Community colleges also partnered with Grumman to provide co-ops in computer-assisted design. Qualified students received full tuition, and were able to seek permission to pursue an associate degree in computer-aided drafting or mechanical engineering. After graduating with an associate's degree, Grumman can choose to employ former students and can provide tuition reimbursement to those who continue to work toward a bachelor's degree. Many of the graduates of the Apprentice School were employed by Northrop Grumman, and about a third of the graduates of the apprentice program earned an associate degree (Soares n.d.). Both the Metropolitan College Program and the Grumman Program are illustrative of cooperate private-public ventures that improved the stock of human capital in their areas. Such partnerships work to the mutual benefit of large companies that seek to secure a stable workforce, workers who seek higher pay, and jurisdictions that want to shore up their tax base.

Higher education, particularly the presence of "world-class" research universities, plays a major role in economic development. A study conducted by the Economics Department of BankBoston identifies the significance of the Massachusetts Institute of Technology (MIT) to local, state, national, and international economies. Among the many findings of the BostonBank report are that companies founded by MIT graduates and faculty produced revenues roughly equal in size to that of the twenty-fourth largest national economy in the world. The MIT companies differed from the norm in that they were more likely to be knowledge-based, focused on software, manufacturing (electronics, biotech, instruments, and machinery) or consulting (architects, business consultants, and engineers). These companies tended to have a disproportionate importance to their local economies because they were export-oriented and because they represent advanced technologies (BankBoston 1997).

The five largest employers started by MIT students (Hewlett-Packard, Rockwell International, Raytheon Corporation, McDonnell Douglas, and Digital Equipment Corporation) were founded between 1922 (by Vannevar Bush) and 1957 (by Kenneth Olsen). Major companies clustered around computers, semiconductors, instruments, telecommunications equipment, electrical machinery and appliances. According to telephone interviews of MIT alumni, MIT faculty had encouraged students to become risk-takers. A respondent noted that MIT instills the entrepreneurial spirit in its graduates and many students start businesses while in school. Advantages of MIT include exposing students to cutting-edge technologies, great mentors (professors), ties with other students, and "hands-on" projects (BankBoston 1997).

Fourth Phase—Sustainable Development and Self-Sufficiency

Sustainable Development

A modern concept of sustainable development is derived from the United Nations Brundtland Report (also referred to as *Our Common Future*) that was issued by former prime minister of Norway Gro Harlem Brundtland, in 1987. The report popularized the term "Sustainable Development," defined the term, and laid out strategies for the world to become more sustainable (Report of the World Commission on Environment and Development: Our Common Future, Chapter 2 1987). Sustainable development was defined as "development that meets the needs of the present without compromising the ability of future generations to meet their own needs." The definition recognizes two key concepts of sustainable development: (1) prioritizing the needs of the poor, and (2) understanding limitations on abilities to meet present and future needs.

The report raised many issues, among them is the assertion that sustainable development must meet the basic needs of all and extend to everyone the opportunity to satisfy their aspirations for a better life. The report also emphasized that sustainable development requires containing consumption of resources to fit within the bounds of what is ecologically possible. The report warns that a society may in many ways compromise its ability to meet the future needs of its people by overexploiting common resources such as water and air quality. The report prioritizes values such as equity and common interest. It states that many problems of resource depletion and environmental degradation arise from disparities in economic and political power. Industries may pollute because the people who bear the greatest burden of industrial pollution are often poor and unable to mobilize effectively. The poor are more likely to suffer when air quality deteriorates, mineral resources decline, and climate change accelerates.

Implicit in the concept of sustainable development is the requirement to reorient thinking away from pure growth toward quality-of-life concerns. The Brundtland Report observes that sustainable development requires a change to make growth less material intensive, less energy-intensive, and more equitable. More equitable income distribution represents an essential aspect of sustainable development. Implications of growth must be considered since rapid growth may be detrimental to overall sustainability and political stability. For instance, the introduction of large-scale commercial agriculture may produce additional revenue, but may also dispossess a large number of small farmers. In the long run, such a strategy may be unsustainable since it impoverishes the many and benefits the few while exploiting the long-term productivity of the land.

Sustainability also calls for supplying education and health needs. Sustainable development calls for more equitable public policies, community support of policies, and widespread public participation in the political process. The Brundtland Report emphasized citizen empowerment and decentralized decision making, stating:

> The law alone cannot enforce the common interest. It principally needs community knowledge and support, which entails greater public participation in the decisions that affect the environment. This is best secured by decentralizing the management of resources upon which local communities depend, and giving these communities an effective say over the use of these resources. It will also require promoting citizens' initiatives, empowering people's organizations, and strengthening local democracy. (Report of the World Commission on Environment and Development: Our Common Future Chapter 2 1987)

Sustainable local economic development (SLED) represents another aspect of fourth phase development. Most definitions of sustainable local economic development share the following principles: (1) quality of life, (2) fairness and equity, (3) participation and partnership, (4) environmental stewardship, and (5) concerns for the future. Sustainable development rejects the view that growth is a cure for all society's problems or that a single-minded focus on global trade and outside investment is always beneficial. Advocate of sustainable development argue that emphasis on attracting foreign investment and competing in global markets suffer from the following deficiencies: (1) vulnerability to changes in global markets, (2) a tendency to bypass marginalized communities, (3) environmental damage, (4) erosion of local character, and (5) a failure to develop local skills, entrepreneurship, and businesses. Newby (1999) claims that local economies can avoid many of these problems by developing strong local economies. Sustainable development questions whether resources devoted to securing investment from the outside could be better spent fostering local enterprises. Sustainable local development focuses on ensuring that economic development is not an end in itself, but a means to the end of sustainable improvements in quality of life. Newby states:

> Too often it is assumed that what is "good for the economy" is automatically good for society. However, in reality, the way in which economic development is undertaken can have profound positive or negative impacts on society and the environment. SLED is thus about identifying the whole range of economic development and regeneration options available. (68)

Sustainable Local Economic Development assumes that communities can create jobs while also promoting inclusion, health, and environmental improvement. Policy prescriptions embrace innovative solutions along with more conventional approaches. At least eight core themes depict the concept of sustainable local economic development: (1) capacity building, (2) access to credit, (3) community enterprise, (4) local business development, (5) sustainable approaches to investment, (6) responsible business practices, (7) access to work, and (8) trading locally (69–70).

Community development includes training as a means to address social exclusion. It aspires to regenerate communities and ensure that marginalized people are able to make the most of available job opportunities. "Micro-finance" schemes assist local business creation by providing greater access to credit for those who have trouble securing conventional loans. Credit unions can assist in providing low-cost funding for higher-risk applicants. Community enterprise encourages people to establish local businesses that meet social and environmental objectives. Local business development refers to building a framework to help emerging entrepreneurs set-up new businesses, and to enable local firms to grow. Sustainable local economic development also considers growth's impacts on the environment and access to work by those who live in marginalized areas. Public policies to increase access to work include provision of good childcare facilities and access to decent public transportation. Another aspect of sustainable local economic development relates to trading locally and developing linkages between local firms. This can reduce "leakage" of wealth from disadvantaged areas. Lifelong education that instils creative thinking and a sense of purpose contributes to sustainability (72).

Self-Sufficiency

Self-sufficiency refers to the ability to provide one's needs without the help of others and the ancient adage that teaching someone how to fish is vastly superior to giving the person a fish to eat every day. Examples of attempts at self-sufficiency include homesteading, living off the grid, and the back-to-the-land movement. Growing one's own food or becoming economically independent of state subsidies are aspects of the self-sufficiency model. Jepson and Haines (2003) proposed embracing a "sustainability paradigm" as an alternative to mainstream perspectives. In this paradigm, the concept of sustainability is used interchangeably with self-sufficiency. The model differs from the traditional perspectives of development with special emphasis on quality of life and local consumption, as opposed to production for export. Whereas traditional strategies hope to attract outside investment, the self-sufficiency model relies on local capacity, and "green" or environmental-friendly investments. In the self-sufficiency model, attempts are made to maximize energy efficiency, recruit "green" businesses to eco-industrial parks, reduce environmental damage, hire the unemployed, and develop blighted areas. In contrast, the traditional model of development measures success by indicators such as numbers of jobs created and additional taxes collected.

Fifth Phase—Market Solutions and Regional Strategies

Market Solutions—Clusters and Gentrification

Porter's discussion of comparative advantage is relevant to the fifth phase element of development. According to Porter (1998a), competitive advantages in a global economy lie increasingly in local knowledge, local relationships, innovations and motivations that distant rivals cannot match. He discounts the contemporary role of traditional inputs or natural endowments (such as good harbors) and states that today competitive advantage rests on continual innovation (78). Clusters or geographical concentrations play a significant role in increasing productivity of individual companies and specific regions. Clusters link businesses and human capital within an area. Factors interrelate to form a sum that is greater than the sum of individual parts. High-tech companies seek out areas with many well-educated tech workers. Companies, in general, seem to be attracted to areas that are "business-friendly" with lower levels of regulation and an effective court system. Clusters enhance competition by: (1) increasing the productivity of companies based in the cluster; (2) driving the pace of innovation; and (3) stimulating the formation of new businesses. Being part of a cluster allows companies to operate more productively because companies in a cluster have better access to employees and suppliers and they can more easily acquire specialized information. As an example of cluster synergy in a tourism cluster such as Orlando, Florida, the quality of the Disney experience depends not only on the primary attraction but also on the quality of complementary businesses such as nearby hotels, restaurants, shopping outlets, and transportation.

Ongoing relationships with other organizations in the cluster help companies to learn about new technologies, machinery, marketing concepts, or methods of production. Clusters encourage entrepreneurship and attract entrepreneurs. Businesses locate in specific geographical areas because those areas already have workers with the needed skills and the area has access to local financial institutions or investors. Porter concludes that once a cluster begins to form, a self-reinforcing cycle promotes its growth. This is especially true when local institutions are supportive and local competition is vigorous. As the cluster expands, it increases its influence with government and with public and private institutions (84).

Clusters form as a result of private-sector market competition. Porter is critical of government-led industrial policy where public officials pick companies to subsidize. He advocates only limited involvement in the marketplace declaring that government should not be involved in industrial policies that chooses winners and losers. Such intervention is likely to reward companies with stronger political connections and discourage aggressive competition over innovation, price, and quality. Porter advises others that the role of government should be to assure the quality of inputs (such as education and infrastructure) and to set the rules of competition by protecting intellectual property and enforcing antitrust laws. Setting neutral rules for all promise that productivity, innovation, and the free play of market forces rather than political connections will govern success.

Another aspect of the fifth phase of development is gentrification. Gentrification is an outcome of growing demand for real estate. As wealth is generated from the successes of new or existing businesses, wages rise, profits rise and those who benefit from those increases are well positioned to build upscale housing or renovate existing housing. Downscale neighborhoods can be transformed by the infusion of fresh money and as a consequence of the higher demand for residence, existing dwellers in the areas are priced out of their homes. The impact of gentrification is dual edged, highly negative for those that can no longer afford to live in what might be their childhood homes, positive for jurisdictions seeking tax revenue and wealthier in-migrants happy with their new environment. Displaced persons are forced to relocate to lower rent neighborhoods that may have higher crime and poorer schools. In these places, the displaced may have few friends or family. Relocations as a consequence of gentrification may also force people into declining suburbs that lack adequate public transportation. Poor transportation is a deterrent to finding employment in the extended area. The social costs of gentrification therefore can be high to individuals.

At the aggregate level, gentrification can be highly beneficial to jurisdictions. Higher property values translate into more tax revenues without increasing tax rates and enhances the ability of places to fund essential police, fire, sanitation, health, education, and other services. Gentrification also changes the nature of entire communities as the movement of higher-income people to new locations leads to the formation of upscale restaurants, bars, and other outlets that serve the new residents. This creates a "multiplier effect" for the entire community.

Gentrification remains a controversial subject with proponents praising its ability to economically revitalize and improve the character and wealth of neighborhoods. Proponents view gentrification as a sign that communities are succeeding in attracting higher-income residents, expanding opportunity and "winning" in the competition for development. Opponents of gentrification point to the hardship on working-class and middle-class individuals who can no longer afford to remain in their homes. As a consequence, these residents are forced to abandon friends and forge a new existence in a fresh location.

Metropolitan and Regional Strategies

New regionalism and smart growth are relatively recent strategies that polities have adopted. These approaches to development are prominent in places such as Minneapolis-St. Paul, Portland (OR), Seattle, the San Francisco Bay Area, New York, Salt Lake City, Atlanta, Toronto, Vancouver, and the state of California (Wheeler 2002). Regional strategies are essential for dealing with problems of sprawl, environmental protection, equity, and quality of life. Regional strategies or "new regionalism" emphasizes coordinating urban and suburban development to ameliorate the effect of uneven development and enhance the ability of metropolitan regions to compete globally (Markusen 1995; Pastor et al. 2000; Savitch and Vogel 2000; Swanstrom 1995). New regionalism represents a holistic approach to development based on the interconnectedness of economic, environmental, and social systems. New regionalism views places from the perspective of global economic competition. It proposes that only the region (not components of the region) has the necessary scale and diversity to compete globally. Proponents of new regional argue that good governance is achieved through cooperation in efforts to achieve common ends (LeSage and Stefanick 2004).

Interest in regionalism evolved from the 1960s and 1970s when metropolitan Councils of Government were established to provide at least a minimum of regional coordination. In the 1990s, concerns with sprawl, traffic congestion, central city/suburban inequities, environmental degradation, and the sterility of the built landscape fostered greater interest in the strategy. Wheeler (2002, 267) observed that the new regionalist agenda advanced efforts to create livable communities, fostered smart growth, and encourage sustainable development. Regional planners began to focus on the issue of managing metropolitan growth, strengthening urban cores, and improving transportation.

An essential component of new regionalism is equalizing wealth disparities between center cities and suburbs through arrangements such as regional tax sharing. The Minneapolis-St. Paul region implemented such a strategy in 1975. Another strategy of new regionalism is to extend municipal boundaries to include suburbs which would give cities access to more resources. While regionalists decry the resource disparity between different geographical areas, many see efforts toward equalization as utopian and unable to defeat resistance that will arise. An array of factors works against such a restructuring and redistribution of wealth, among them are opposition from local and state governments unwilling to give up power to a new regional entity, the hostility of suburban voters unable to see how their interests are tied to the well-being of lower-income residents in central cities, and the reluctance of central-city constituencies to see their voting blocs diluted (275).

CONTEMPORARY RELEVANCE OF PHASES

Each of the five phases provide insight into how the public sector can work to assist local, state, and national development. Rather than a time-related sequence, the phases are better understood as strategies that can be used in concert with each other or selectively depending upon the specific conditions of time and place. The general idea of phase one did not end as new ideas came to the fore. Jurisdictions still seek to generate growth by luring companies from other areas. The focus of luring companies has changed somewhat since the 1930s (a time when the lower labor costs and less regulation induced low-wage manufacturing plants to relocate) to a newer focus on luring professional workers and tech-related firms. The state of Texas has been particularly aggressive in attracting higher wage, high-tech companies away from high tax, high-cost states such as California. This approach is consistent with early strategy of industrial "poaching." Texas has been highly successful in recruiting based on aggressively advertising their advantages of low taxes, good amenities, relatively few regulations, high quality of life, and a skilled workforce.

Second phase schemes such as tax increment financing, revolving loan funds, and business incubators remain popular even as the innovations of other phases were introduced. Briffault (2010, 65) notes that tax increment financing (TIF) is the most widely used local government program for financing economic development in the United States. As the TIF programs grew in popularity, they shifted from what was initially an urban renewal program targeted at depressed central city areas to a more general public investment and infrastructure financing scheme (71). The redirection, or expansion, of TIF is illustrated through the change in the language used to describe its activity. Language evolved from redevelopment (revitalization of a once vibrant but now economically depressed area) to simply development, or increase in economic activity in lightly developed areas.

Various factors account for the appeal of TIF as a strategy for development, among them the fact that TIF does not involve a tax rate increase or require a vote for approval. TIF uses existing taxes at current rates and avoids the political controversy that a tax increase often generates. TIF also avoids legal restrictions on tax limitations (73). The second phase strategy of creating business incubators remains alive and well. Studies indicate that since the Great Recession of 2007–2009 the numbers of new incubators increased significantly in the United States, especially in areas which foster innovation such as Austin, Texas; Atlanta, Georgia; Boston, Massachusetts; Boulder, Colorado; Los Angeles; Silicon Valley; Seattle; and smaller cities. Much of the recent growth in U.S. incubators is attributed to interest in nurturing a new venture as a means of enhancing societal well-being (Zehner et al. 2014).

The third phase of development with its emphasis on networks, clusters, private-public partnerships, and human capital is particularly relevant today as globalization increases pressure on jurisdictions to effectively compete for development. Clusters, in particular, are linked to competitive advantages of geographic areas. Moretti (2013, 187) claims that ever since Michael Porter popularized the concept of cluster building in the 1990s, jurisdictions have been trying to engineer clusters through public policies. Moretti concludes, however, that it is difficult to create vibrant cluster through government initiatives. He notes that looking at the map of America's major innovation clusters, it is hard to find an example of a cluster that was spawned by a big government initiative. Even prominent urbanist Jane Jacobs concluded that major government efforts such as the Tennessee Valley Authority work miserably in practice (quoted in Moretti 2013, 200).

On the international level, some governments claim credit for creating successful clusters. The nation of Ireland used tax incentives and other enticements to form clusters in high tech and finance; Israel leveraged its military spending to develop a high-tech cluster; Taiwan established a cluster of publicly supported research and development that eventually became robust enough to sustain private companies. The human capital element of the third phase also remains vital. Moretti (2013, 215) claims that in the past, good jobs were tied to large-scale production of manufactured goods but today good jobs and salaries increasingly come from leveraging knowledge. He states,

> In coming decades, global competition will be about attracting innovative human capital and innovative companies. . . . The number and strength of a country's brain hubs will determine whether it will prosper or decline. Physical factories will keep losing importance, but cities with a large percentage of interconnected, highly educated workers will become the new factories where ideas and knowledge are forged. (215)

The fourth and fifth phases of development reflect the most recent trends in economic development thinking. Concerns over environmental protection, income inequality, gentrification, sprawl, and the need for regional cooperation are prevalent in these phases. These concerns remind us that benefits (such as wealth and prosperity) are also tied to costs such as crowding, class conflict, and environmental degradation. Concern for quality of life as opposed to mere accumulation of assets has gained attention. While economic prosperity is typically seen as beneficial, it may be accompanied by negative externalities such as gentrification, inequality, and disruptive change in the nature of communities. Recent economic prosperity in places such as Austin, Texas, has worked to the benefit of some yet many "old-time" residents decry the city's loss of character, environmental beauty, "soul" and laid-back lifestyle (Koven and Koven 2018).

LINKS BETWEEN PHASES OF ECONOMIC DEVELOPMENT AND ENTREPRENEURSHIP

Lichtenstein and Lyons (1996) assert that the goal of entrepreneurs is to create and capitalize on new opportunities through innovation by finding new solutions to existing problems or by connecting existing solutions to new opportunities. Entrepreneurs such as Henry Ford applied the existing technology of the assembly line to automobiles and reaped enormous profit, while Bill Gates created new software that improved productivity in knowledge-based industries. Entrepreneurship relates to each of the five phases of economic development described in this chapter. To succeed, entrepreneurs should not only be innovative but also must be effective businessmen or businesswomen. As businesspeople, entrepreneurs have an obligation to maximize returns to investors. They must devise and implement strategies that enhance their competitiveness that in turn grows jobs, and improves the overall economy of an area. As places offer incentives, entrepreneurs carefully weigh offers, and they have a fiduciary responsibility to make decisions that benefit their companies. They view incentives and subsidies as part of their rational profit-maximizing calculations. At the same time, entrepreneurs are part of a broader community and must consider the implications of their actions to the larger unit. The accumulation of individual wealth alone may not be the best long-term recipe for society as a whole if it leads to political instability, class conflict, massive inequality, and a poorer quality of life for the vast majority of citizens.

Phase one development is often criticized for not generating aggregate growth and for offering generous incentives to profitable businesses (i.e., corporate welfare). This characterization assumes a "zero-sum game" where there is a corollary loss for every gain. It denies the possibility that "poaching" enhances overall productivity. However, if we assume that entrepreneurs look for economic advantage, they should be able to freely choose from an array of geographical options. In this sense, the first phase of development should be viewed as an extension of free-market principles where businesses "shop around" for communities and communities compete for development by luring companies. In this market analogy, communities offer options for businesses and businesses choose to maximize their mix of costs and opportunities just as a patron in the supermarket choose from one brand of cereal or another. Charles Tiebout (1956) in his famous model utilizes a similar application in exploring how mobile residents seek to optimize their mix of taxes and services when assessing whether to relocate to other areas.

When assessing locations businesses compare financial incentives, amenities, workforce skills, availability of knowledge workers, linkages with similar businesses in the area, or other factors. It is expected that not all places will offer the same attractions and businesses will select those that best meet their needs. As the Tiebout model (1956) suggests, a "quasi-market" can be created where residents or businesses shop around to meet their needs. Such movement can produce efficiencies in productivity by reducing costs and constructing more modern facilities. Communities feel pressure to enhance their appeal to business interests as they realize they are in a competitive battle with other jurisdictions to secure jobs, enhance their economic base, and secure a better quality of life for their citizens.

The second phase of development offers aid to small and emerging businesses. Loans, subsidies, business incubators, and other forms of assistance help new businesses and entrepreneurs survive their critical start-up period. Many massive enterprises began as minuscule ventures. For example, in 1938, William Hewlett and David Packard launched a two-person company in a rented garage. From their first device that improved measurement of audio frequencies, the company expanded to produce cameras, calculators, computers, printers, and other devices. In 2020, Hewlett-Packard (HP) had a net worth of around $20 billion and employed many thousands of workers. According to popular legend, the massive Apple computer company (Apple, Inc.) started in the family garage of company cofounder Steve Jobs. Original funding was acquired when Jobs sold his Volkswagen bus and cofounder Steve Wozniak sold his scientific calculator. The two cofounders began creating devises that allowed users to place free telephone calls around the world; they sold their devices at University of California-Berkeley dorms to college students. In 2018, Apple became the world's first publicly traded company to acquire a market capitalization of $1 trillion. Not all the business stories are as colorful as those of HP and Apple; however, these narratives demonstrate that visionary leaders can produce massively successful companies. Governments often feel justified in risking public funds on fledgling enterprises with the hope that they evolve into the next wealth-generating machine.

The idea of clusters formation identified in phase three of economic development comports well with the romantic notion of the individualistic entrepreneur who starts with nothing but a vision and through herculean efforts develops an entire region as like-minded individuals seek to follow the "Pied Piper" pioneer. History indicates that single individuals have played a significant role in fostering growth of entire regions. In 1940, the peninsula south of San Francisco was a quiet agricultural region with a comparative advantage in fruit production. William Shockley, the legendary high-tech pioneer, who invented the transistor fundamentally changed the region by becoming "the seed that sparked growth of the local innovation industry" (Moretti 2013, 186). Some of Shockley's disciples created the first integrated circuit at Fairchild Semiconductor. Moretti stated, "it became clear that the seed had germinated: the process of clustering had begun. The serendipitous seedling was the starting point of an economic miracle that eventually brought millions of jobs to the region" (186). Other individuals were also successful in molding the development of an entire region. At the turn of the twentieth century, Henry Ford was instrumental in creating the automobile cluster in Detroit. Andrew Carnegie helped to make Pittsburg a steel-producing center. Bill Gates and Microsoft had an important role in spawning the software development and information technology cluster in Seattle. Michael Dell and his company Dell, Inc. was instrumental in the growth of the Austin, Texas, computer industry cluster.

Phases four and five emphasize concepts such as environmental protection, air quality, renewal resources, gentrification, smart growth, and sprawl. Issues raised in these phases of development represent problems to solve as well as opportunities to exploit. Since the mark of an entrepreneur is to identify opportunities and capitalize on them, in theory, entrepreneurs should be able to leverage new demands for goods such as clean air, clean water, better transportation, and livable cities. Wind and solar energy companies as well as electric automobile companies have sprung up in recent years in efforts to reduce pollution and shift away from the nonrenewable energy sources of coal and petroleum. New means of energy production presents opportunities for entrepreneurs to generate wealth as old energy sources are replaced with the new.

Other problems call for innovative solutions. Gentrification may create market niches to upgrade, modernize, and renovate homes in declining cities. Demand for in-fill construction may create market niches for new development and may aid companies with expertise in smaller home construction. Demand for new modes of transportation may create opportunities for innovations that increase the speed of travel within metropolitan areas and enhance energy efficiency. Change is inevitable and entrepreneurs as innovators are especially suited to respond to new conditions, create new demand or better serve existing markets.

PERSPECTIVES TO VIEW GROWTH AND DECLINE

Many analysts over time have endeavored to explain why some economies grow exponentially, why some seemingly implode, why some become "stuck" at a certain point, and why others continuously move forward at a relaxed but steady rate (Koven and Koven 2018). The five phases or waves of economic development that this chapter describe in detail represents only one lens for viewing economic development strategies. Other perspectives, however, also exist. For example, Professor Jeffrey Sachs (n.d.), director of the Earth Institute at Columbia University identifies four stages of development: (1) pre-commercial, (2) commercial, (3) industrial, and (4) knowledge. These economic stages are driven by innovation, science and technology. Pre-commercial economies are characterized by isolated agricultural sectors, commercial economies by integration between rural and urban areas where the urban sector produces manufactured goods and services and the rural sector produces agricultural products. The industrialization stage moves from commodity production to industrial goods. The knowledge phase offers the highest return. According to Sachs (n.d., 6), Korea and Taiwan represent cases of a successful transition to the knowledge phase of development and grew more robustly than comparable countries such as Mexico and Brazil because of their investments in science and technology and their active industrial policies. The governments of Korea and Taiwan promoted spending on national research laboratories, science institutions, engineering and science, and attempted to attract leading scientists from the United States (6).

Harvard University Professor Michael Porter (1990) proposes three distinct stages of national development: (1) the factor-driven stage, (2) the investment-driven stage, and (3) the innovation-driven stage. The factor-driven stage is dependent on issues such as the cost of inputs (land, labor, political stability, and lowering regulatory cost of doing business) while the investment stage focuses on productivity and attracting foreign investment by integrating local economies with the global supply chain. The final stage involves the transition from a technology importing economy to a technology-generating economy. In this stage, global competitiveness is linked to science-based learning and the ability to shift to new technologies. The innovation-driven economy is dependent upon advanced skills, scientific institutions, incentives that encourage innovation and cluster upgrading.

Michael Porter much as his predecessor Joseph Schumpeter places great emphasis on the ability to innovate. Companies that will be the true leaders will be those that don't just optimize within an industry, but the ones that reshape and redefine industries. In *The Competitive Advantage of Nations* (1990), Porter contrasts the old paradigm of sustaining advantage from cheap labor or economies of scale with the new paradigm of innovation and strategic direction. This new paradigm is based on specialization and countries prospering in areas where they can achieve unique specializations as well as critical mass. The government also plays a role in enhancing innovation. Governments can encourage companies to move toward the next generation of technology and can boost local competitiveness. In the new innovation paradigm, scale is not as important as competitive pressure that drives progress. Porter stresses the need for enterprises to learn quickly, assimilate the learning, and develop new insights (Porter 1998c).

A common thread running through the various concepts of growth and development is the need to innovate, experiment, compete, and take risks. The third phase that Leigh and Blakely (2016) discussed places a special emphasis on human capital development and the ability of clusters to facilitate innovation. The fourth phase encourages entrepreneurship and small business development. Research and development play a continuous role in fostering improvements in productivity. Each of the phases allows entrepreneurs to take risks in their efforts to create and grow businesses. Incubators and revolving loan schemes understand the value of encouraging small ventures that can yield high payoffs in the future. Development of human capital provides the seeds for the flowering of future enterprises. The search for a "greener" and more environmental-friendly environment is tied to the discovery of new technologies such as wind and solar energy.

In the past, entrepreneurs have not only created tremendous wealth for themselves but in the process created demand for labor, fostered a vibrant middle class, and increased the quality of life for average citizens. Wages and working conditions improved over time. Entrepreneurship, innovation, and creativity became a comparative advantage for the United States as millions of people from other parts of the world sought to seek their fortune and attain a higher quality of life for themselves and their families.

Chapter 3

Entrepreneurship Theories

Entrepreneurship is a concept that is both difficult and easy to grasp. On the one hand, theorists identify it with the simplistic view of taking risks in order to achieve profit. On the other hand, theorists conceptualize entrepreneurship as an intellectually complex subject that draws insight from fields such as economics, management, psychology, public policy, political science, sociology, anthropology, and geography. Scholars also see entrepreneurship as a spontaneous and natural reaction of people or something to nurture by insightful and future-oriented leaders. As a subject matter, it holds both academic and pragmatic value. Economists focus on the value of entrepreneurship for wealth creation at the individual and state level. Business schools study it from the perspective of how one can polish skills that should be beneficial to aspiring entrepreneurs; the discipline of psychology prioritizes the issue of what personality traits align with entrepreneurship; sociology and anthropology focus on cultural predispositions of populations. In addition, public policy programs look at developing a proper environment for entrepreneurship through legislation and organizational theorists look to the structure of enterprises. Each disciplinary approach contributes value to our aggregate understanding. Seminal authors (Drucker 1985; Knight 1921; Kirzner 1976; McClelland 1961; Schumpeter 1934, 1976; Weber 1992 [1904–1905]) have established a foundation from which future scholars have built upon. This chapter introduces six distinct lenses (economics, psychology, sociology, anthropology, opportunity, and resources) from which one can better understand entrepreneurship. Other means of regarding entrepreneurship exist, however, elucidating these six perspectives allows readers to gain a reasonable grasp of how entrepreneurship theorists view the complex concept.

ECONOMIC ENTREPRENEURSHIP THEORIES

Economic theories of entrepreneurship comprise of classical, neoclassical, and the Austrian Market Process views. These views overlap while containing their individual distinctions (Walia and Chettt 2020).

Classical Entrepreneurship Theory

Although the introduction of the term "entrepreneur" was originally attributed to Jean-Baptiste Say, Richard Cantillon is credited with being the first significant writer to make frequent use of the term in its contemporary form (Brown and Thornton 2013). In the early 1700s, Cantillon, an Irish banker with French roots, distinguished between entrepreneurs (people with variable incomes) and employees who enjoyed fixed incomes. His conception of entrepreneurship comprises a large portion of society including mine owners, factory owners, owners of buildings, traders, speculators, innkeepers, artisans, seamstresses, chimney sweeps, and others who depend on customers to obtain their variable income. For Cantillon, entrepreneurs play a vital role in establishing an equilibrium of supply and demand in free markets. According to this classical view, the role of the entrepreneur is that of directing the production and distribution of goods. Entrepreneurs assume responsibility for obtaining materials, employing workers, and competing. Risk taking is a critical element of the process. In Cantillon's view, competition assures efficiencies by rewarding the fittest.

Cantillon's work provides a springboard for later-day economists such as Adam Smith and the French physiocrats. One of Cantillon's key insights is his view of the entrepreneur as fundamental to the circulation of goods. According to Cantillon, entrepreneurs are intermediaries between economic leaders who establish patterns of consumption in line with their tastes and others. Entrepreneurs meet consumption demands; they also bear the burden of risk associated with production and distribution. In addition to meeting emerging demands, entrepreneurs can also engage in arbitrage by moving goods from low-cost areas to areas where they are sold at a higher price (Hébert and Link 2006). According to classical economic theory, a central feature of entrepreneurship is uncertainty. Entrepreneurs buy goods at known (fixed) prices in the present to sell at unknown prices in the future.

One of Cantillon's major contributions to economic theory is the "circular-flow model" that explains the distribution of goods, incomes, and expenditures between property owners, farmers, farm labor, and entrepreneurs. In this model, nearly everyone but the property owner and wage laborer act as entrepreneurs including deliverers of services, transporters, manufacturers, and merchants of all kinds. As entrepreneurs, these individuals do not derive a fixed income, they assume risk, some prosper others do not. Brown and Thornton (2013, 414) observe that Cantillon was able to show that entrepreneurship allowed society to escape the heavy constrictions imposed by feudal societies.

Neoclassical Entrepreneurship Theory

The theory of neoclassical entrepreneurship emerged in economics toward the end of the nineteenth century. This theory embraces the concept of marginal utility and forges a path for considering sociopolitical and cultural circumstances in setting prices. Under this perspective, entrepreneurialism serves as a mechanism for change in the production and delivery of products and services. The concept of marginal utility allowed economist to think of equilibrium creation and price formation with supply by entrepreneurs rising to meet demand. In this framework, the entrepreneur assesses and responds to market conditions. The neoclassical perspective focuses on how individuals use novel combinations of existing resources to supply goods and services. From novel combinations of resources, entrepreneurs introduce new goods, new modes of production, expand markets, increase sources of raw materials, and create different organizational forms, or engage in other activities that differ from the past. In neoclassical theory, people assess the situation and make subjective decisions; entrepreneurs both create change and respond to change (Murphy et al. 2006).

Schumpeter (1976) provides significant insights into neoclassical thought. For Schumpeter, anyone seeking profits must innovate; innovation is an essential driver of change that produces gales of "creative destruction." Schumpeter views innovation as a revolutionary process of mutation incessantly destroying the old and creating something new. This perspective is fundamental to our present understanding of capitalism, innovation, and entrepreneurship. Innovation allows for dynamism, improvement, and growth. While Schumpeter is generally associated with innovation, his focus changed slightly over time. In his earlier writings, Schumpeter emphasizes the role of individuals who carry out new activities. Entrepreneurs help to break the stationary economy out of its equilibrium toward a new path. Later, Schumpeter came to accept the view that capitalism would produce monopolistic structures and thereby reduce the importance of individual entrepreneurs.

Schumpeter argues that anyone seeking profits must innovate; he sees innovation as an essential driver of competitiveness and economic dynamism. Schumpeter conceptualizes development as a historical process of change, driven by innovation. The innovation process consists of the following: (1) invention, (2) innovation, (3) diffusion, and (4) imitation. For Schumpeter, entrepreneurs draw upon prior discoveries of scientists and inventors, and create new opportunities for investment, growth, and employment. He views the invention phase as less impactful than the diffusion and imitation stages. He contends that what matters in terms of economic growth is not the discovery of a basic innovation, but the diffusion of innovation, which is the period when imitators begin to realize the profitable potential of innovation and invest in search of profit. Entrepreneurs leverage inventions into goods or services that have a market demand. Innovation is part of the "creative destruction" that advances economies while the entrepreneur performs the function of the change agent (Sledzik 2003).

Schumpeter's early writings stress the role of entrepreneurs as revolutionaries who use their talents to exploit inventions, utilize new technologies, produce new commodities, or open up new markets. The entrepreneur is a pioneer who is able to do something new, innovation is the key function of Schumpeter's entrepreneur. The innovators do not necessarily reap the monetary rewards of their discoveries but rewards go to the owners of companies that commercialize innovations. Schumpeter's later writings embraces a role for monopolies and large business entities.

Schumpeter identifies three possible motivations for entrepreneurs. First, the desire to create ones "own kingdom" drives individuals to strive for a sense of power and independence similar to the situation of the European medieval lord. This frees individuals from close supervision and permits experimentation. Experimentation in turn allows creative individuals to pursue their personal visions. Second, the desire to compete, a wish to fight, to showing superiority over others, and winning for the sake of winning motivates some aspiring entrepreneurs. Competition is natural for many individuals and economists view it as a hallmark of free-market capitalism. Finally, the joy of creation, to achieve something of value, motivates entrepreneurs. Entrepreneurship serves as an outlet for seeking acclaim. Schumpeter proposes that rather than the rugged individualist, a country itself, or its agenda, can act as an entrepreneur. As an immigrant from Austria, Schumpeter's conception of entrepreneurship was influenced by his personal observation of American economic life (Sledzik 2003).

Austrian Market Process Theory

The Austrian Market Process model was also influenced by Schumpeter's (1934) conceptions of the value of knowledge. For Schumpeter, knowledge is used to create value in terms of improved processes or new products. Entrepreneurs enhance the existing base of knowledge. Austrian Market Process theorists formulated a dynamic model; they denied that present circumstances would always be repeated leading to the same outcomes. The model posits that entrepreneurs use new knowledge to generate value and addresses the question of how to harness knowledge to discover opportunities. As knowledge is communicated throughout a market system (via prices), people innovate, entrepreneurs use innovations to satisfy market needs, and system-level change occurs. Knowledge creates benefits to both consumers and producers. The Austrian model borrows from earlier thinkers about entrepreneurship and focuses on entrepreneurial alertness to profit-making opportunities.

An assumption of the Austrian school is that market actors compete to generate changes in prices, outputs, methods of production, and resource allocation. Entrepreneurial choices may or may not yield value. These uncertainties underscored the importance of "alertness" since market actors have imperfect knowledge about opportunities. As market actors compete, they acquire new information and continually revise their plans. A rudimentary principle holds that some individuals have more choices than other individuals do. There is openness in the system since knowledge cannot be solely possession. Primary conjectures of the Austrian school include the ideas that errors create opportunities for entrepreneurs; entrepreneurs always face considerable uncertainty; entrepreneurial alertness leads to recognition of opportunities; knowledge is essential for entrepreneurship; and entrepreneurship is beneficial to economic systems (Murphy et al. 2006).

Israel Kirzner (1979) refined the concept of "alertness" as it pertains to entrepreneurs. He contended that alertness provides the mechanism for market participants to discover information and subsequently to revise their plans. IIn regard to the discovery of new information, Kirzner argued that the value of searches for information cannot be precisely calculated. This would assume prior understanding of the value of the knowledge sought. Kirzner proposed that the discovery of new information must be a spontaneous movement with ignorance of the plans of other market participants. Action is future-oriented; alertness is consistent with a motivation to formulate an image of the future. The motivation to shape this future is profit. Kirzner claimed that individuals are at all times on the lookout for features of the environment that might benefit them. The supply of entrepreneurs is thought to be potentially inexhaustible and is dependent on seeing through uncertainty (Bostath 2013; Kirzner 1997, 51).

PSYCHOLOGICAL ENTREPRENEURSHIP THEORIES

Psychological entrepreneurship theories focus on traits, motivations, and general characteristic of individuals. Three of the main strains of thought for these theories include: (1) personality trait theory, (2) locus of control, and (3) need for achievement. These perspectives are not all inclusive of psychological explanations but serve to provide readers with an overview of mainstream perspectives.

Personality Trait Theory

Personality trait theorists focus on inborn qualities of individuals as they explore how one's inborn qualities relate to characteristics of entrepreneurs. Trait theorists identify general characteristics (such as curiosity, optimism, emotional resilience, opportunism, hard work, competitiveness, and creativity) of individuals. These characteristics provide clues of inborn potential. Other characteristics include a desire to excel, dissatisfaction with the status quo, integrity, foresight, belief in individual ability to make a difference, and a desire for improvement (Kwabena and Simpeh 2011).

The publication of the book *Risk, Uncertainty and Profit* (Knight 1921) marked a key launching point into rigorous and careful research on the personalities of entrepreneurs that set them apart from general business managers (Kerr et al. 2017). In the decades that followed, others have continued to investigate individual traits that prompt people to become entrepreneurs. Baron (2000, 16) suggests that individuals' overall capacity to interact effectively with others (social competence) is an important factor in other outcomes such as romance, personal adjustment, job interviews, yearly performance reviews, negotiations, and even court proceedings. Baron concludes that people possessing well-developed social skills experience more favorable outcomes than people lacking in such skills. Social competence plays a role in entrepreneurs' success for at least two reasons. First, most new ventures consist of more than one person. The ability to get along effectively with partners is critical to enhancing success. Second, entrepreneurs must deal with many persons outside their ventures such as bankers, potential customers, and prospective employees. Being able to interact effectively with such people increases the chances of gaining favorable outcomes in face-to-face interactions. Empirical studies support the value of social competence in predicting entrepreneurial success. Social perception (accuracy in perceiving others) and social adaptability (the ability to adapt to, or feel comfortable in, a wide range of social situations) were significant predictors of financial success among a sample of respondents in the various industries (Baron 2000, 17). Perception and adaptability were stronger predictors of success than other aspects of social competence such as the ability to change views (persuasiveness) and the likelihood of inducing positive reactions in others (impression management).

In many cases, entrepreneurs fail even though their technical skills, experience, and motivation is high, and their ideas are sound. Why some entrepreneurs fail while others succeed is a subject of intense speculation. Research suggests that failures may stem, at least in part, from deficiencies in cognitive and social skills. Psychology and trait theory help to explain why social skills are lacking. Psychologists can devise techniques for helping people cope with personality deficiencies. Providing entrepreneurs with such training can assist them in their efforts to start new ventures. Baron (2000, 17) disparages the deficiency of entrepreneurship research in personality and concludes that researchers run from trait theory because more than two decades ago, efforts failed to identify "key traits" of entrepreneurs. This failure left a strong anti-personality bias in the field.

In the 1980s, researchers concluded that there was little or no correlation between personality and entrepreneurship. However, in the twenty-first century, the entrepreneurial personality literature has enjoyed a resurgence (Kerr et al. 2017, 7). The preponderance of the recent literature seeks to answer two main questions: (1) Do certain traits predict an individual's likelihood of becoming an entrepreneur, and (2) Do certain traits predict an entrepreneur's likelihood of achieving successful outcomes? Since the 1980s, the "Big-5 model" (an approach toward defining personality) has become the dominant model for identifying personality traits. This model focuses on five personality traits: (1) openness (O), (2) conscientiousness (C), (3) extraversion (E), (4) agreeableness (A), and (5) neuroticism (N). This enumeration of personality traits refers to what some characterize as the five-factor model (FFM) or the OCEAN model. The model describes each of the five traits.

People who are high in the openness trait tend to be more adventurous and creative. Standard features of conscientiousness include high levels of thoughtfulness, good impulse control, attention to detail, and goal-directed behavior. Extraversion is characterized by excitability, sociability, talkativeness, assertiveness, and high amounts of emotional expressiveness. The agreeableness dimension includes attributes such as trust, altruism, kindness, and affection. The final trait of neuroticism refers to sadness, moodiness, and emotional instability (Cherry 2019).

Kerr et al. (2017, 10) compared Big-5 traits of entrepreneurs versus managers. They concluded that entrepreneurs are consistently more open to experience than managers, more likely to be attracted to constantly changing environments, and more likely to be attracted to new challenges. Entrepreneurs also differ from managers with regard to conscientiousness with entrepreneurs being more achievement-oriented than managers are. Kerr, Kerr, and Xu found consensus lacking on whether entrepreneurs score higher than managers score on extraversion. However, they found entrepreneurs possessing modestly smaller amounts of agreeableness and neuroticism. Some researchers hypothesize that, because entrepreneurs lead their own ventures, they do not need to worry about pleasing others; others find entrepreneurs to be less neurotic than managers because entrepreneurs require exceptional self-confidence (12).

Locus of Control Theory

Locus of control theory was introduced in the 1950s in an attempt to explain the diverse aspects of personality. In its essence, locus of control refers to an individual's perception about the causes of events in his or her life. This orientation explores people's beliefs about whether they control their outcomes (internal orientation) or whether outcomes are more a result of distant hands of fate (external orientation). According to the locus of control perspective, an entrepreneur's successful or unsuccessful outcome relates to both individual abilities and external support (i.e., internal locus of control and external locus of control). Individuals with an internal locus of control are more likely to believe that they are in control of their lives while those with an external locus of control are more likely to believe that their life's outcomes are the result of external factors.

Rotter (1966) is a pioneer in the development of locus of control theory. He focuses on people's expectations as to whether they can influence the feedback/reinforcements they receive from their environment. At one extreme, people believe that these reinforcements are entirely due to fate or luck. At the other extreme, some people believe that outcomes flow from their own actions; they believe they have significant control over their own destinies. Rotter argued that locus of control relates to expectation of success in a task. Rotter's "Internal-External Locus of Control Scale" measures internal or external orientations. The scale was widely used in the 1970s. Various empirical studies link internal locus of control with characteristics of entrepreneurship such as a strong work ethic, business ownership, entrepreneurial success, or the desire to become an entrepreneur (Bonnett and Furnham 1991; Kerr et al. 2017; Rauch and Frese 2000). Literature supports the association between internal orientation and entrepreneurial behavior such as innovation, risk taking, and proactive predispositions (Miller 1983, 777). These associations also appear to have strong face validity (Knopf 2016).

Not all researchers, however, agree that locus of control provides a good explanation of entrepreneurship. Critics contend that personality studied in isolation from social and economic context is not a useful predictor of entrepreneurship (Shaver and Scott 1991). Gartner (1988) also challenged the legitimacy of personality as a predictor of entrepreneurship. According to Gartner, entrepreneurship researchers should focus on the process by which organizations come into existence. Gartner terms this focus on process a "behavioral approach" that views organizational formation as a contextual event that is the outcome off many influences (57). Gartner views personality characteristics as ancillary to an entrepreneur's behavior, not the main cause of outcomes. For Gartner, what is of the utmost importance is what the entrepreneur ultimately does, not who he or she is. He argues that entrepreneurship is contextual (look at what entrepreneurs do in specific situations) and do not focus on internal traits.

Need for Achievement Theory

Need for achievement has the oldest history of all the psychological explanations for entrepreneurship (Shaver and Scott 1991, 30). McClelland's (1961) seminal work asserts that personality characteristics of successful entrepreneurs relate to a need for achievement (nAch). This achievement orientation research grounds itself in earlier work by Murray (1938) who proposed that features of the brain determine personality. Murray's theory assumes that unconscious processes guide behavior. His Thematic Apperception Test (TAT) quickly became second only to the Rorschach in breadth of application (Shaver and Scott 1991, 31). McClelland's contribution is in identifying the importance of need for achievement (nAch) in individuals. He defines the need for achievement as the need to accomplish something difficult, to master manipulate or organize, overcome obstacles, attain a high standard, excel, and surpass others (164).

McClelland's book *The Achieving Society* (1961) builds on the work of the psychologist Henry Murray and Abraham Maslow. His writings identify three motivators that he believed all people possess: a need for achievement, a need for affiliation, and a need for power. People will have different characteristics depending on their dominant motivator; the dominant motivator is largely dependent on one's culture and life experiences. According to McClelland, individuals motivated by achievement have a strong need to set and accomplish challenging goals, take calculated risks, and often like to work alone. In contrast, those motivated by affiliation needs want to belong to a group, want to be liked, and favors collaboration over competition. Finally, people motivated by a power need want to influence others, enjoys status, and like competition.

McClelland proposed that economic development is largely determined by the level of achievement motivation (nAch) in a society. He asserts that Western capitalists are primarily motivated by the need to achieve; money and profit are not pursued for their own sake, but as a surrogate measure of success and achievement. McClelland's work on the need for achievement initiated other studies on individual characteristics of entrepreneurs. His high need for achievement (nAch) is associated with a preference for challenging tasks of moderate difficulty rather than routine or very difficult tasks, taking personnel responsibility for one's performance, seeking feedback on performance, and looking for better ways to improve one's performance. Various studies indicate that entrepreneurs were significantly higher in need for achievement than managers or non-founders of businesses.

Some research supports the view that people with need for achievement can stimulate economic development at the national level (Frey 1984), while others have uncovered a positive relationship between need for achievement and success of small-scale enterprises (Rauch and Frese 2000). It is important to note that McClelland's need theory does not claim that it is necessary to place people exclusively into one of the three types; it asserts that all of these needs in varying degrees and proportions act to motivate.

McClelland's need for achievement theory is not void of criticism. Critics claim that his theory has less practical effect than other theories because his three needs are subconscious and people may be high on certain needs without knowing. In addition, critics claim that measuring needs is difficult and measurements may not be consistent. A controversial implication of McClelland's theory is that lower-performing economies can boost their overall performance by enacting policies that encourage people to change their personality profiles. Critics claim that advancing achievement needs may be antithetical to the values of some cultures that emphasize well-being, simplicity, and tradition. A specific problem with McClelland's theory as applied to entrepreneurship is that while many entrepreneurs may display a need for achievement, many non-entrepreneurs may also have a strong need for achievement that is satisfied with success in other professional careers. Therefore, the theory offers only a partial picture of the drivers of entrepreneurship.

SOCIOLOGICAL ENTREPRENEURSHIP THEORIES

Until recently, research focusing on the individual traits of entrepreneurs has been dominant. This outlook is associated with the "supply-side perspective" of entrepreneurship since it focuses on the "who" is likely to become an entrepreneur and looks at personality traits of individuals. An alternative approach focus on demand and the context in which entrepreneurship is encouraged or discouraged. The demand-side perspective prioritizes factors in society that influence decisions to engage in entrepreneurism. Context remains essential to the sociological perspective of entrepreneurialism. Thornton (1999, 21) defines entrepreneurship as the creation of new organizations which occurs as a context-dependent, social, and economic process. She claims that despite the large and eclectic literature on entrepreneurship, we know relatively little about the specific contexts of organizational founding. Thornton classifies entrepreneurship literature into two schools, one taking the supply side, the other the demand perspective. Sociologist such as Thornton note the influence of environment on both creating a supply of and a demand for entrepreneurs.

Supply-Side Perspective of Entrepreneurship

The supply-side perspective of entrepreneurship assumes that differences in an individual's characteristics explain why some people and not others become entrepreneurs. From this perspective, to create material wealth, societies need an adequate supply of individuals who possess specific characteristics. Various studies explore how psychological, social, cultural/ethnic, and other characteristics influence predispositions toward entrepreneurial behavior. While psychological studies have looked at motivations of people (such as their need for achievement) and whether they believe they have control over their lives (locus of control), sociological studies tend to explore the role of cultural and ethnic differences on behavior. The idea that psychological traits alone account for entrepreneurship has been largely abandoned (Thornton 1999, 22). In its place, context-related approaches have gained prominence. Various authors consider factors such as religion (Weber 1992 [1904–1905]), social class and ethnicity in assessing conditions that promote individual, group and societal predispositions toward entrepreneurship (Aldrich and Waldinger 1990; Light and Rosenstein 1995; Shane 1993; Thornton 1991, 23). Such research holds that the larger culture and group values of a society as well as individual traits of people influence entrepreneurship.

Scholars such as Max Weber (1992 [1904–1905]) highlight the role of macro-culture on economic development. In what some scholars describe as probably the most important sociological work of the twentieth century, Weber proposes that while the impulse to profit is present in all societies, only in the West did capitalism, as a rational organization of production, take hold. Weber observes that in modern times, the economic prosperity of Protestant nations of Northern Europe began to supersede the prosperity of Catholic nations in Southern Europe. In *The Protestant Ethic and the Spirit of Capitalism* (1992 [1904–1905]), Weber proposes that fundamental religious differences created different value orientations in individuals and that these differences accounted for divergences in wealth. The values emphasized in the Protestant religion (particularly that of Calvinism) such as thrift, piety, prudence, sobriety, the idea of a "calling," devotion to work, and delayed gratification, according to Weber, is consistent with the growth of capitalism as an economic system. Weber recognized that personality alone would not break established traditions of the past. A religious ethic that provided justification for business formation and wealth creation was required. According to Weber, "ascetic Protestantism" and its restraint on consumption support capital accumulation as a way of life. Moneymaking became an end in itself that could be justified as fulfilling a religious calling. This calling diverged dramatically from religious perspectives of the past that prioritized piety and poverty as strategy to ascend to heaven. The devotion to the calling of making money evolved into a pillar of support for the capitalist economic system (Bell 1996, 36).

Protestantism's dogma encouraged an "individualistic" attitude toward religion by seeking their own interpretations of Christianity. According to Weber, the more individualistic ethos of Protestantism laid the foundations for a greater sense of individual freedom, and challenged the "top-down" hierarchy of the Roman Catholic Church. Calvinist preaching of the doctrine of predestination induced people to work hard and live ethical lives in order to prove their value. Calvinist doctrine encouraged people to work for the glory of God and according to Weber, over the decades, this "work ethic" enhanced wealth creation and economic growth. Sociologist Patricia Thornton (1991, 23) emphasizes that macro-cultural paradigms and other external structural influences cannot be ignored when examining phenomenon such as entrepreneurism.

Demand-Side Perspective of Entrepreneurship

The demand-side outlook of entrepreneurism views business creation from the perspective of context-related opportunities. From this perspective, individuals act within social and political contexts that expands or contracts opportunities for wealth creation. Individuals, in turn, perceive and act upon the opportunities that become available. The demand-side perspective emphasizes milieu, environment or context that they propose can foster or discourage entrepreneurial behavior. Factors such as availability of resources, freedom of action, size of markets, barriers to entry, and legal restrictions among others affect the environment for entrepreneurship. Organizational culture can also play a role in shaping the context for business formation. For example, some organizational cultures revere those who leave to found new ventures while others value loyalty to the organization.

The availability of venture capital to provide financing and overcome barriers to new business formation is an important factor in business creation. New businesses are often perceived as too risky for traditional lenders and these enterprises must rely on others that are willing to assume high risk for high rewards. Venture capitalists can also enhance entrepreneurships by providing contacts and can act as a catalyst for action. Venture capitalists have a propulsive effect on entrepreneurship because they sit at the center of networks that can link financiers, entrepreneurs, corporate executives, recruiters, and consultants (Thornton 1999, 29).

An environment that fosters a market for initial public offerings (IPOs) is also conducive to entrepreneurship. Public offerings allow entrepreneurs to profit enormously from their companies and represent a strategy for individuals to acquire wealth by "cashing out" of their ventures. IPOs allow a company to access capital; they provide instant liquidity to expand their operations, experiment and become more attractive to lenders. IPOs provide a publicly traded price, which informs managers about the company's value. Environments for acquisitions that opens up for them a lucrative exit strategy may motivate founding entrepreneurs. Often symbiotic relationships develop between large firms that seek to shift the risk of research and nascent enterprises that seek acquisition. Acquisitions of the new firm by the large enterprise allows the nascent enterprise to gain access to the distribution and financial strength of larger organizations. These relationships are prevalent in research-oriented industries such as biotechnology and pharmaceuticals.

The environment of business creation also relates to geography and social structures (Granovetter 1985). For example, the social environment of Silicon Valley encourages the seeding of future companies that can generate large profits. "Angels" and "serial entrepreneurs" who provide the financial, human, and social capital to start new companies can supply valuable insights that in turn can stimulate profit. The environment for both IPOs and acquisitions builds on its reputation. Geography plays a role as entrepreneurs seek certain areas to benefit from concentrations of vibrant clusters. Clustering helps to explain different birth rates of new organizations between geographic regions. Research on clusters or incubator regions indicates that geographic areas that have large number of venture capital firms and relevant specialized service companies have higher birth rates of business formation (Thornton 1999, 31).

Socioeconomic systems provide the context in which entrepreneurs perish or thrive (Reynolds 1991). Context can be formed by public policy or historical changes. Reynolds maintains that societal modernization and freedom are necessary for entrepreneurship since only when individuals feel there are no impediments to pursuing economic activities on their own can entrepreneurial activity be expected. Slave or serf-type relationships of feudal economies preclude entrepreneurialism. For societies to spawn entrepreneurs, a number of conditions must be present. First, it is imperative that aspiring entrepreneurs believe they will reap some benefit from their efforts. Second, entrepreneurs must believe that they can avoid annihilation by the actions of special interests. Third, they must believe the future of their organization will be effective enough to warrant their capital and human investments.

Political environments either foster or retard development. Social stability aids some organizations since disruption can lead to the disappearance of some firms and the creation of others. War can create opportunities for entrepreneurs as economies shift away from domestic production to military manufacture. Political philosophies that countries adopt can also influence entrepreneurial development. Countries can adopt policies that aid small business through subsidies, special tax treatment, technical assistance, marketing aid, and low-cost access to capital. In contrast, countries can adopt policies that discourage investment and risk taking. Government, therefore, has a larger function than mere mediator of political disputes and implementer of compromises. Governments help create the environment that can lead to economic vibrancy or stagnation. Public policies that protect private property can foster business creation that leads to generating wealth.

ANTHROPOLOGICAL ENTREPRENEURSHIP THEORY

Anthropological theories of entrepreneurship focus on the culture, customs, and beliefs of people in a community. Understanding this context is useful in predicting why some ethnic groups may be more inclined toward entrepreneurship (Baskerville 2003). In addition to ethnicity, social, economic, and political institutions of places affect behavior (North 1990; Shane 1993). The importance of societal rules and norms (i.e., institutions) has gained currency in recent years (North 1990).

Social/Cultural Environments and Entrepreneurship

Research indicates that culture, religion, values, traditions, and other factors influences national rates of innovation and economic growth (North 1990; Weber (1992 [1904–1905]). This perspective suggests that a fundamental reorientation of values may be necessary for some nations and regions of the world to prosper. Cultures that inculcate values of individualism, thrift, hard work, a future orientation have been found to align with greater degrees of economic prosperity (Hayek 1945; Huntington 2004; North 1990; Weber (1992 [1904–1905]). Acceptance of uncertainty is also relevant because innovation requires a tolerance for risk and change (Shane 1993). The link between culture and development has been described in detail in previous studies (Huntington 2004; Koven and Götzke 2010; Weber (1992 [1904–1905]). Ideals of moralism, hard work, justice, and fear of expansive government influence represent core values of the United States. Qualitative differences between cultural values of the United States and those developing nations have been noted in the literature (Huntington 2004, 26). Differences are said to exist in terms of attitudes toward control over one's life, interpretations of history, and willingness to take initiative. Huntington (2004) views cultural values in Latino societies (such as acceptance of poverty as a virtue necessary for entrance into heaven) as fundamentally different as values in the United States and as an impediment to economic development.

Culture also helps to establish the "rules of the game" for societies that in turn shape behavior. North (1990, 3) argues that institutions (defined as societal rules) structure political, social, and economic incentives. These incentives influence entrepreneurialism, initiative, competition, work effort, and willingness to take risks. Rules can also have major consequences for national development. For example, North (114–116) attributed the economic decline of Spain and the rise of England in the seventeenth century to their institutional differences. According to North, England's protection of property rights, impersonal exchanges, and patents encouraged innovation and development while personal relationships remained dominant in Spain. Personal relationships in Spain discouraged productive activity by non-elites. Elites in Spain who enjoyed exclusive franchises had little incentive to become more productive, to start new enterprises, and to compete in terms of cost or quality. This institutional framework is quite different from the perspective of modern capitalism that Adam Smith advanced in his 1776 work *Wealth of Nations*.

Nobel laureate C. Douglas North's writings provides a broad perspective on how a nation's environment can facilitate both individual-level entrepreneurship and national-level growth. According to North (1991, 97) institutions (norms and rules of behavior) provide the incentive structure of an economy. Institutions comprise both informal constraints (taboos or customs) and formal rules (laws and property rights). North states, "together with the standard constraints of economics they [institutions] define the choice set and therefore determine transaction and production costs and hence the profitability and feasibility of engaging in economic activity" (97). North proposes that institutions shape the direction of economic change toward growth, stagnation, or decline. He proposes that macroeconomic growth or decline is not haphazard but dependent upon its setting, stating, "economic history is overwhelmingly a story of economies that failed to produce a set of economic rules of the game (with enforcement) that induce sustained economic growth. The central issue of economic history and of economic development is to account for the evolution of political and economic institutions that create an economic environment that induces increasing productivity" (98).

Institutions also help to explain business creation. "Open-access" societies facilitate business creation, foster open entry, encourages competition, and free movement of goods as well as individuals over space and time. In contrast, "limited access" societies possess a hierarchy of personal relationships among powerful individuals. These personal relationships among elites facilitates individual interaction of a dominant coalition. People outside the coalition have only limited access to organizations, privileges, and valuable resources and activities (North et al. 2009, 56). In the limited access state, elites create special privileges for themselves and exclude others. These "rents" enable elites to become wealthy and limit competition from others who may be more productive and more innovative. The privilege of forming organizations that the state will support is among the most valuable sources of elite wealth. In open-access societies, all citizens have the right to form organizations without government consent. Established interests often resist impersonal economic and political competition since competition can rapidly erode rents (62).

Ethnic subcultures exist within dominant institutional frameworks. Some groups (e.g. Amish, Hasidic Jews) have survived relatively intact within larger cultures for generations while others have assimilated or "Americanized" to a large degree. A substantial body of literature has examined the role of ethnicity on entrepreneurship and the possibility that specific ethnic groups are more likely to take risks and create businesses than others.

Ethnicity and Entrepreneurship

Empirical research supports the view that different ethnic groups in North America participate in entrepreneurship at different rates (Light and Rosenstein 1995, 17). Immigrants in the United States have a higher likelihood of self-employment than for those who were born in the United States. Studies indicate that foreign-born Koreans were self-employed at a much higher rate than others in the Los Angeles area. Cuban immigrants in Miami were self-employed at higher rates than other groups in Miami and Iranian men in Los Angeles were also self-employed at a higher than average rate for the area. Jews, Chinese, Japanese, Greeks, Italians, and Armenians also had relatively high rates of self-employment. Rates of business formation between immigrants and native born differed outside the United States. In the United Kingdom, Pakistanis and East Indians had higher rates of self-employment than the native white population. However, on the European continent, rates of immigrant self-employment lagged rates in the United Kingdom, Canada, and the United States. Institutional factors, specifically laws on the continent that commonly forbade foreign workers from becoming self-employed at least partially, explain this phenomenon (18).

Borjas (1986, 486) noted that probabilities for self-employment of immigrants differed by race, ethnicity, and nationality. The probability of immigrant self-employment was significantly higher for whites and Cubans than for Black and Mexican immigrants. Incomes from self-employment also differed. Asian immigrants enjoy the highest mean annual incomes and Mexican immigrants the lowest. Research also indicates significant variation in self-employment within Hispanic and Asian classifications. Korean immigrants were much more likely to be self-employed than immigrants from the Philippines. Immigrants from Cuba and Columbia had much higher rates of self-employment than immigrants from Jamaica, Mexico, and Haiti (Koven and Götzke 2010, 102).

The sociology literature discusses in detail the presence of ethnic differences. In their widely acclaimed book *Beyond the Melting Pot: The Negroes, Puerto Ricans, Jews, Italians, and Irish of New York City*, Glazer and Moynihan (1963) propose that the "melting pot" (the widely accepted metaphor for assimilation) never really happen. They acknowledged that some assimilation occurred but distinctiveness prevailed. Distinctions were partly attributable to the different skill set of immigrants. Eastern European Jews brought skills useful in the garment trade, while Southern Italians came mainly from agricultural areas. Ethnic distinctiveness was also attributed to family cultures, and places of settlement. Each group acquired economic and social traits that amounted to a distinctive profile. Political and economic differences also emerged between groups (Alba 2019).

Regarding entrepreneurship, a central question is why some immigrant groups are more predisposed to business creation. Group characteristics account for some of the divergence (Zhou 2004, 1046). One model that attempts to explain variation in immigrant entrepreneurship refers to whether immigrant groups can insert themselves into U.S. society as professionals or laborers. Immigrant roles in U.S. society is determined by the following factors: (1) immigrant assets in terms of motivation, human capital, and financial resources; (2) how immigrants come (legal or undocumented) and under what conditions they emigrated; and (3) the contexts of reception that considers the presence of preexisting ethnic communities, government policies, and societal acceptance.

At the societal level, discrimination may inhibit entrepreneurship. This prevents immigrants from competing with the native born on an equal basis. Because of the presence of barriers, immigrants either take jobs that natives do not desire or carve out market niches that native-born Americans ignore. Immigrant niches meet demand for goods and services that are unmet by natives in the mainstream economy. Structural constraints can steer ethnics into specific avenues of economic opportunities. For example, legal exclusion of Jews from landownership and skilled-worker guilds in Europe forced Jews into trading as peddlers, shopkeepers, and moneylenders. The Chinese Exclusion Act of 1882 and general anti-Chinese sentiment pushed Chinese residents into economic enclaves. Chinese entrepreneurs were mainly relegated to businesses such as restaurants and laundries.

Ethnic organizations such as credit associations can also aid in business creation. In Chinese enclaves, an "uncle" could testify for the reputation of a person and facilitate lending. Korean credit associations can supply financing for aspiring entrepreneurs. Korean immigrant churches also serve as centers for support. Trust between individuals in common groups serves as an enforcement mechanism against malfeasance. Other ethnics sanctioned violations of commonly accepted norms and standards (Zhou 2004, 1049). Characteristics such as education, age, marital status, work skills, and language proficiency influence the likelihood of entrepreneurship. Individual characteristics differ by ethnic group. Language differences may also affect rates of immigrant entrepreneurship. Min (1986/87) found that Filipino immigrants were less inclined to become entrepreneurs than Korean immigrants because their proficiency in English allowed for access to well-paying white-collar jobs. This is but one example of ethnic differences in business formation. Research indicates that as a whole, there is little dispute that entrepreneurship varies from group to group (Light and Rosenstein 1995, 25). While ethnicity appears relevant, other explanations such as opportunity-based theory provide insight into entrepreneurship.

OPPORTUNITY-BASED ENTREPRENEURSHIP THEORY

Opportunity-based entrepreneurship theory focuses on exploiting opportunities. The contributions of Peter Drucker (1985), Scott Shane (2003), Howard Stevenson, and Carlos Jarilo (1990) are especially relevant in assessing the opportunity-based perspective.

Exploiting Opportunities for Change

Entrepreneurship is often perceived as an outcome of individuals taking advantage of opportunities that arise from a given environment (Shane and Venkataraman 2000). Individuals interact with their communities and both are instrumental in fostering development (Lyons et al. 2012). Communities create an overall environment; the role of the individual is to assess that environment and, if possible, capitalize on the opportunities it presents. Difficulties arise since opportunities are often opaque. Therefore, risk taking is an inescapable component of entrepreneurial action (Shane 2003).

Shane and Venkataraman (2000, 218) state that research into entrepreneurship involves the study of opportunities that includes the processes of discovery as well as the evaluation and exploitation of those opportunities. Entrepreneurship research involve exploring the actions of individuals. Shane and Venkataraman argue that to have entrepreneurship, you must first have entrepreneurial opportunities and situations where new goods or services can be introduced and sold at greater prices than their cost of production. Drucker (1985) describes three different categories of opportunities:

(1) the creation of new information or the invention of new technologies; (2) the exploitation of market inefficiencies; and (3) the reaction to shifts in the relative costs and benefits of alternative uses for resources. For Drucker, innovation is the key attribute of entrepreneurship. Organizations that survive are those that can adapt through innovation. In turn, innovation consists of a search for changes, and analysis of the opportunities the changes offer. Areas from which opportunities arise include unexpected events, differences between assumptions and reality, discovering a better way to do something, identifying unforeseen changes in markets, capitalizing on population changes, exploiting changes in perception or mood, and exploiting new knowledge.

Drucker proposed that entrepreneurs could exploit opportunities through various strategies. Entrepreneurs can wait until others have established something new, and then develop a product that more closely meets the needs of the customer. Entrepreneurs can also enter an industry, which existing organizations do not well defend. Drucker observed that some organizations are complacent and take customers for granted. This leaves openings for firms that can develop innovative products. Opportunities also exist in finding niches and changing the characteristics of products or markets.

Opportunities are identified (because of a hunch, superior intuition or private information) when individuals make conjectures about prices or about what possible new markets could be created in the future. According to Shane and Venkataraman (2000), better access to information and market errors can lead to opportunities. Investment decisions are not always correct, incorrect decisions or "errors" create shortages, surpluses, and misallocated resources. An individual alert to the presence of an error may buy resources where prices are low, recombine them, and sell the outputs at higher prices. In addition to opportunities that arise from market errors, new information about different ways to use resources produce opportunity. New information arises from technological, political, social, regulatory, and other types of change. Some people are able to obtain information about markets or technologies before others. This advantage opens up opportunities that are unavailable to others. Those with access to the information can purchase resources at below their value and reap the rewards of their knowledge (221). Two factors that help to explain why particular individuals will discover particular opportunities are (1) the possession of the prior information necessary to identify an opportunity and (2) the cognitive ability to value the information.

Information necessary to recognize opportunity is not widely distributed across the population because people specialize in discrete sets of information. Because of differences in their life experiences, different occupations, or different knowledge bases, not all people had the same insight about how to exploit technological change. Even with the same available information and the same educational levels, some people may simply be better at identifying changes that can produce entrepreneurial opportunities. Many examples exist where inventors failed to see the commercial opportunities in their creations. In general, people vary in their abilities to combine existing information into entrepreneurial opportunities. Successful entrepreneurs see opportunities in situations in which other people tend to identify risk.

Shane and Venkataraman (2000, 222) state that although the discovery of an opportunity is a necessary condition for entrepreneurship, it is not sufficient. Potential entrepreneurs must decide to exploit their perceived opportunities. Both the nature of the opportunity and the characteristics of individuals help to explain decisions to act. For exploitation of an opportunity, it is necessary for the expected value of the entrepreneurial profit to be large enough to compensate for lost opportunities and the risk of the investment (Kirzner 1973; Schumpeter 1934). Numerous factors affect willingness to exploit opportunities; these include expected demand for a good or service, the expected profit, the ability of others to duplicate the technology, the competition, and the amount of capital necessary to compete.

Personal differences between individuals matter. Not all people have the same value on their time and effort. Those who do not have many economic opportunities risk less by pursuing entrepreneurial options. In addition, people do not have equal access to capital. Research indicates that exploitation of opportunities is more common when people have greater financial capital (Evans and Leighton 1991). Social ties to people with capital, information from prior entrepreneurship, and information gathered from previous employment enhances the probability of people exploiting their opportunities. Individuals also have differing perceptions of risk. Risk is always present but, in general, people who exploit opportunities tend to frame information more positively and respond to their positive perceptions. Opportunity exploiters tend to be more optimistic. This, however, may result in less than optimal decisions. Shane and Venkataraman (2000, 223) state that "people who exploit opportunities typically perceive their chances of success as much higher than they really are and much higher than those of others in their industry." Some people act on unrealistic rosy forecasts of the future. On the other hand, not engaging in risk precludes any chance of phenomenal success and wealth creation that can benefit not only founders but large numbers of associates.

Corporate Entrepreneurship

It is popular to paint an image of entrepreneurs as individualistic geniuses who found and develop billion dollar companies through their unique insights and perseverance. An alternative vision, however, is possible. This vision replaces the individual leader personification with the organization as creator of wealth and change. Organizations in reality are composed of people and there is no reason to believe that only people outside of established entities have the "right stuff" to innovate, develop new products, establish new markets, or create new ways of communicating. Large organizations as well as individuals are in pursuit of profit and wealth. Large organizations can encourage workers to create new products, they can set up small units dedicated to this task; they can offer bonuses and other incentives in order to maximize efforts of workers. Large organizations as well as small ones recognize that survival depends on fresh thinking, adaptability to the tastes of consumers, and Schumpeterian innovation. Innovation allows companies to survive the gales of creative destruction and enables businesses to generate a continuous stream of revenues. Corporate entrepreneurship, therefore, is not only possible but a reality. Large entities are not by definition trapped in the past, fearful of change, or filled with mediocre employees. Corporate entrepreneurism is not an oxymoron in that corporations do not necessarily destroy entrepreneurship but can foster it. Large bureaucracies do not have to deaden initiative where people find comfortable niches that do not challenge them. Despite the image of established corporations as lacking in imagination, a large literature has developed around the concept of "corporate entrepreneurship" or the reality of large organizations fostering innovative new enterprises.

Corporate entrepreneurship or "intrapreneurship" refers to the act of supporting employees who think and behave like entrepreneurs within an existing organizational structure. Employees are encouraged to identify opportunities and develop ideas that can lead to innovative new products, services, or businesses. In theory, corporate entrepreneurship produces ideas, which are disruptive in nature, rather than incremental. In addition, innovations tend to be "bottom up," led by employees, rather than "top down" and mandated by management. Specific corporate entrepreneurship programs provide companies with a means of overcoming sclerosis produced by hierarchical structures. For corporate entrepreneurship to be successful, it is important to identify and support talent within the organization. Talented employees must take risks, be open to new ideas, be passionate about goals, and be able to handle failure while moving forward (Kennedy 2018). The primary aim of corporate entrepreneurship is to ensure a consistent stream of new product that lead to future revenues. A secondary benefit is higher levels of employee satisfaction and lower levels of turnover.

Entrepreneurship is highly touted as the most viable strategy for success in today's corporations (Ireland 2009; Kuratko 2009; Kuratko et al. 2015). Entrepreneurship scholars are aware that to develop and nurture competitive advantages, firms must increasingly rely on corporate entrepreneurship.

Innovation is a common theme of corporate entrepreneurship. Innovation can occur from within the firm (corporate venturing) or innovation can occur when corporations wholly or partially purchase firms that have a record of accomplishment of innovation (Morris et al. 2011). The corporation owns innovations created within the firm. Companies that are purchased by larger entities typically are young ventures or early growth stage firms.

Stevenson and Jarillo (1990, 23) argue that corporations have different abilities to act entrepreneurially and assert that entrepreneurial behavior has to come from below. Spotting opportunities relates to efforts of company employees, training, and the amount of rewards that employees can acquire from their entrepreneurial initiatives. Firms that lessen negative consequences of failure are likely to exhibit a higher degree of entrepreneurial behavior. Managerial and technical capacity expand the ability of employees to exploit opportunities. Stevenson and Jarillo (25) conclude that it is possible to foster an "entrepreneurial culture" within firms. They state that practitioners of corporate entrepreneurship should address the environment of the organization and whether it fosters the detection of opportunities, whether the organization motivates employees to pursue opportunity, and finally whether encouraging entrepreneurship influences the outcomes.

RESOURCE-BASED ENTREPRENEURSHIP THEORY

It is difficult to do justice to the voluminous literature that posits the obvious that some people have inherent advantages, others do not. Those who already have resources or access to resources have less difficulty launching enterprises from their ideas, whether they are good ideas or not. Those with extensive networks of relationships among people have advantages over others. Personal relationships and networks contribute to success of new ventures. Finally, human capital or skill levels of individuals also contributes to an entrepreneur's success or failure.

Access to Financial Capital

Economists have tested the proposition that access to capital is an important determinant of entrepreneurship. Various econometric studies have tested this notion, producing mixed results. Holtz-Eakin et al. (1994, 334) found the size of an inheritance has a substantial effect on both the probability of becoming an entrepreneur and the amount of capital risked for the new enterprise. Not surprisingly, a body of research supports the proposition that the probability of entrepreneurship (as self-employment) increases with an individual's net worth (Meyer 1990). Inheritance or gifts relate to the probability of self-employment. All else being equal, people with greater family assets are more likely to become self-employed. This is consistent with data that indicates the desirability of self-employed. Those who are self-employed report higher levels of satisfaction than employees who work for others. A commonly cited explanation for why more individuals do not become self-employed is a shortage of capital. The largest single biggest concern of aspiring entrepreneurs is that of how to obtain capital (Blanchflower and Oswalt 1998, 50–51). Macroeconomic conditions also have an impact on capital availability. Periods of "easy credit" or lower interest rates are more conducive to self-employment and business creation in a variety of industries (Audretsch and Acs 1994; Shane 2003, 150; 1996).

Lack of capital remains an impediment. Because of difficulty in obtaining loans from formal institutions, many entrepreneurs self-finance business ventures by using equity in their homes. This demonstrates to outside investors a high level of commitment. Investors are more likely to risk funds when aspiring entrepreneurs make such a commitment to their dreams. Research indicates that a majority (approximately 70%) of entrepreneurs self-finance their new businesses (Aldrich 1999). This form of financing is more prevalent than financing from banks, family and friends combined (Blanchflower and Oswald 1998).

It makes logical sense that having access to personal resources or even one-time resources (such as lottery winnings) relates to self-employment. Many people have what they think are good ideas about how to make money, many people do not wish to work for difficult supervisors, many have dreams of gaining tremendous wealth, many dream of the autonomy and independence offered by self-employment. These individuals, however, need outside financing or access to personal capital to transforms their dreams of independence into reality. Survey data indicates that lack of capital is the number one reason that people who seriously consider self-employment do actualize their ambitions (Bates 1995; Blanchflower and Oswald 1998; Evans and Leighton 1989). Studies indicate that even the one-time cash infusion of winning a lottery has a noticeable effect on the probability of self-employment; people winning a moderate-sized lottery were more likely to become self-employed than those with smaller and larger winnings (Lindh and Ohlsson 1996).

Aspiring entrepreneurs face at least two significant limitations when attempting to self-finance perceived opportunities. Shane (1993, 171) states:

> First, many people lack the assets, income, inheritance, lottery winnings and even house values necessary to finance their entrepreneurial opportunities. Consequently, entrepreneurs are likely to face capital constraints, which limit their ability to actually exploit opportunities, if they only rely on self-financing.

Second, self-financing increases the risk of entrepreneurial activity because it requires the entrepreneur to bear all the potential downside loss.

Social Capital Perspective

Entrepreneurs often work in social networks to create, sustain, and grow their ventures. Research on entrepreneurship indicates that networks are useful tools for gaining access to resources. Networks not only help in gaining access to resources, they also facilitate information flows through social interactions. This can enhance an entrepreneur's ability to recognize opportunities. Weak or indirect ties are more important than strong or direct ties for accessing opportunity-related information. Direct ties are less valuable because they usually contain redundant information produced by a relatively small set of friends or family. In contrast, weak or indirect ties can link hundreds of individuals in disparate networks. Weak ties provide access to information that would not ordinarily flow through close friends or family members. Social ties that bridge unconnected social networks are particularly useful to entrepreneurs for gaining information. Greve and Salaff (2003) explain how entrepreneurs use social relations to get advice and gather resources to launch businesses. These resources are essential to aspiring entrepreneurs who have ideas, some knowledge, and some competence to run a business but lack financial support and access to distribution channels. Social network help in securing financial support. Weak and strong ties are complementary. In order to fit their needs, entrepreneurs can benefit from both people who are close and more distant to them. Contacts that lead to successful outcomes represent social capital that are a key component of entrepreneurial success. Contacts are possible from informal work relations and nonwork connections. Network relationships accumulate from professional associations, colleagues from earlier jobs, social organizations, religious, fraternal, and other organizations. Social networks provide a pathway for the transmission of information.

Sociological investigations have evolved beyond the simple observation that networks matter. Investigations explore how various types of networks affect entrepreneurship. One stream of this literature asserted that weak ties (acquaintances rather than close friends) are most important for assessing entrepreneurial opportunities (Granovetter 1973). Weak ties serve as bridges across otherwise disconnected social groups. Bridging relationships exposes actors to new information and opportunities they would not have encountered through strong ties. Bridging ties connect "structural holes" or empty spaces between groups of disconnected actors.

Social capital also enhances trust and preserves ongoing relationships. Connections develop implicit understandings of proper behavior of groups. Such information may not be available to those lacking in a network of social capital. Social ties might also help to attract investors who may be impressed by the social connections of aspiring entrepreneurs. Diversity of networks is an important aspect of weak ties. Nascent entrepreneurs with structurally diverse networks are more likely to encounter promising opportunities and have access to different types of information.

Aldrich and Waldinger (1990, 127) note that valuable information is typically obtained through both personal networks and via indirect ties to ethnic communities. The strength of networks differs by ethnic group with some groups having a hierarchical structure and a clear sense of family obligation, while others do not. Ethnic immigrants often gain access to co-ethnic contacts, learn on the job, and have access to role models. Those with ties to ethnic groups can also benefit from established institutions such as rotating credit associations. These associations serve as a popular means to raise capital (128).

Social capital can inhibit and foster business creation. Social capital acts to encourage entrepreneurship when aspiring entrepreneurs use their network connections to obtain needed resources. Social capital obstructs entrepreneurialism when closed social networks exclude prospective entrepreneurs from resources or impose mental conformity upon network participants. This discourages innovation that could disrupt status quo relationships. Social capital implies that what is important is "who you know" and not necessarily "what you know." This prioritizes one's social structure and complements human capital (what you know). While many who are successful claim that they "made it" on their own through hard work or individual brilliance, an abundance of social capital gives certain individuals a competitive advantage over others.

Human Capital Perspective

Shane (2003, 69–89) identifies human capital advantages that increases the likelihood for entrepreneurialism. One such advantage is that of education as those with more education have a greater predisposition to exploit entrepreneurial opportunities. This predisposition links information and skills to entrepreneurship. In theory, education should improve entrepreneurial judgment by enhancing analytical ability and understanding of the entrepreneurial process (Casson 1995). Numerous studies support the assertion that people with a higher than average level of education are more likely to pursue entrepreneurship opportunities. Studies utilizing U.S. census data indicate that this was evident for a wide variety of ethnic groups (Shane 2003, 70). This association between education and entrepreneurship is apparent not only in the United States but applies to other countries as well.

Education influences both decisions to start business and the performance of those ventures. Research indicates that firms founded by entrepreneurs (in the United States and other nations) with better education were less likely to fail. Education also helps to explain different growth rates of new businesses. Higher growth firms are associated with founders that possessed a higher level of education. Education also links to higher profitability and higher income from self-employment. These relationships are consistently confirmed by research both inside and outside the United States (Shane 2003).

Aside from education, career experience is a benefit to aspiring entrepreneurs. Shane (2003, 75) identifies five types of factors that relate to entrepreneurship: (1) general business experience, (2) functional experience, (3) industry experience, (4) start-up experience, and (5) vicarious experience. General business experience can polish skills in areas such as finance, sales, technology, planning, problem-solving, leadership, communications, and management. Empirical studies indicate that business experience reduces the likelihood of new business failure. The particular area of expertise is also relevant. People with knowledge in the functional areas of marketing, management, and product development were more likely to exploit entrepreneurial opportunities than people with expertise in finance and accounting do.

Industry experience provides information that outsiders do not possess. Many start new business in field of prior employment. This makes logical sense since people identify much of the information about starting a business through trial and error. Start-up experience is invaluable. Several studies support the value of "learning by doing." On-the-job experience can help entrepreneurs avoid costly mistakes and point entrepreneurs in the right direction. Finally, vicarious learning posits that people acquire information and skill through observation of others. In support of this perspective, several studies found that people whose parents were self-employed were more likely to become entrepreneurs themselves. Observing efforts of parents provide tacit knowledge of how to engage in the same activities.

Some authors posit that over time certain groups are able to capitalize on the human capital they possessed. For example, Hirschman (1982) contends that an ethnic group's achievements are a function of human capital and sociocultural orientations. Aldrich and Waldinger (1990, 122) note that immigrants are not equal in skill sets and possess different levels of human capital. For example, these authors contend that Senegalese traders have penetrated European and American cities (in spite of lacking co-ethnic clients, higher education, and occupational training) because they drew on their prior business experience. Some scholars maintain that a lack of business experience negatively affects Black Americans while prior business experiences aided the emergence of Chinese entrepreneurs. Despite human capital, some immigrant groups had difficulty in turning their previous education and experience into positions comparable to those they previously held. Some individuals who could not secure well-paying professional positions were often able to turn to entrepreneurship (123).

INTEGRATING THEORIES OF ENTREPRENEURSHIP

A wide array of theoretical perspectives supplement each other to present a holistic picture of why people become entrepreneurs, how they do it, and what conditions promote their behavior. In general, the field of entrepreneurship appears to divide into two main camps: (1) the human attribute perspective, and (2) the environmental perspective (Shane 1993, 2). Both shed light on this important subject, each by itself is inadequate as an explanation. To ascribe the entrepreneurial activity to the brilliance of individuals does not explain why certain areas as a whole appear to be devoid of development while other areas flourish. Do we assume that economic success is a function of geography alone? Do we assume that genetic makeup differs by location? Why do people from a specific ethnic group thrive economically in one place but not in another? Why are people of a given area economically prosperous in one era but not in another? It appears that exploration of more than individual traits and personality is necessary to explain entrepreneurial wealth creation. Environmental factors are relevant but to ascribe entrepreneurship solely to environment does not clarify why certain individuals fail and why others are successful in the same environment.

Multiple disciplines describe entrepreneurship. The perspective of economics describes the contributions of entrepreneurs to the marketplace, the field of psychology explains individual motivations and needs, sociology and anthropology discusses how culture and past practices affect proclivity toward entrepreneurship. One perspective alone cannot fully answer the questions of why some societies become wealthy through entrepreneurialism why some societies do not. One perspective alone does not explain why some people become entrepreneurs, what political environments are most conducive to entrepreneurship, or what cultural environment is most advantageous. Like the fable of the blind man and the elephant, each perspective provides some clues but does not accurately relay a valid picture of the whole.

Entrepreneurship is vital to wealth creation. Much of the previous as well as current prosperity is attributable to people assuming financial risks in the hope of profit. Entrepreneurship drives economic growth and innovation. It depends on people but also an environment in which people can act on their dreams and visions. An understanding of the types of people that become entrepreneurs, their motivations, and their actions is instructive. The disciplines of economics, sociology, management, finance, economics, public policy, anthropology, sociology, and psychology each provides insight.

Future entrepreneurship research should take a more holistic view of why individuals, cities, states, and nations become wealthy, stagnate, or decline. Research can explore why some societal contexts (sociological view) are associated with business creation while other contexts are not and whether cultural predispositions (anthropological view) matter. Personal traits, ability to identify opportunity, and ability to raise necessary capital are relevant, however, these individualistic factors may be of less important than the societal and cultural context factors. Individualistic factors may be irrelevant if aspiring entrepreneurs sow the seeds of great ideas on beds of rock.

A purely economic view that looks at business success or failure as a simple function of meeting or failing to meet market demand is incomplete. Studies should explore the legal, ideological, political, and cultural contexts in more detail to see what effect these external forces have on business and wealth creation. Do low tax, low regulation regimes foster business creation and wealth generation? Are jurisdictions with higher taxes, more regulations, and a more proactive government sector less likely to spur entrepreneurship? Are there personality commonalities between highly successful entrepreneurs? Insight into the overall environment that impact entrepreneurs can be useful. Knowledge of how the broad environment interacts with the individual can be a first step in recognizing and removing impediments.

Analysis of aggregate data is helpful but often fails to uncover subtleties of more in-depth exploration. Case studies such as described in the following chapter may be more beneficial in trying to ascertain why some folks become billionaires at an early age and others go bankrupt even though both groups share common traits. Case studies can identity what were the opportunities successful entrepreneurs identified and capitalized on. What personal characteristics did they possess? Did their cultural predispositions have any connection to their success? Did the political environment affect success or failure?

Answers to these questions are valuable for aspiring entrepreneurs as well as jurisdictions hoping to sustain or enhance their tax bases. From a public policy perspective, government officials who believe they have a responsibility to promote the general welfare should ask themselves whether they should intervene in the marketplace and if the answer is yes, they must inquire about how to best utilize their scarce resources. Should they enhance general education, lure businesses with incentives, work to create greater tolerance within their community, create more amenities, or do other things? Should they identify people that are more likely to be successful and subsidize their enterprises? Research into these question can be useful and can open up new areas of important inquiry. From the individual businessperson's perspective, awareness of what kinds of traits to develop, how to identify opportunities, how to raise resources and how best to manage organization is of value. Case studies that address these questions might uncover more insights.

America is replete with famous and infamous entrepreneurs who we vilify as "robber barons" or hail as visionaries that make life more comfortable, more enjoyable, safer and more productive for both themselves and others in society. In most cases, these individuals were not satisfied with accepting life as it is or carving out a slice of existing markets. Referring to an excerpt from George Bernard Shaw, John Kennedy, and Robert Kennedy, entrepreneurs are not people who "see things as they are and say, why" but "dream things that never were and say, why not." The following chapter describes in detail the backgrounds of contemporary American entrepreneurs that took risks, made profits, innovated, and fulfilled their visions.

Part II

ENTREPRENEURS AND THEIR ENVIRONMENT

Chapter 4

Contemporary Entrepreneurs

An ongoing debate in the entrepreneurship literature revolves around the question of whether the individual or the environment is more relevant to wealth creation. This debate relates to the ongoing disagreement of "nurture versus nature" and inherent traits making for success versus success arising from proper external conditions. It is likely, however, that a combination of factors provides a fuller answer. Personal factors such as intelligence, creativity, insight, motivation, perseverance play a role but at the same time, settings stimulate or suppress initiative. People can plant the seeds of individual efforts on either arid or fertile soil. Environments can keep people in poverty or thrust open opportunities. Over time, places prosper or decay due to the suppression or expansion of economic opportunity. Given freedom of movement, people will naturally flow to areas of greater opportunity. Migrations stimulate growth and are part of human history. The United States has benefited from such migrations as immigrants as well as native-born Americans have created great enterprises that produced personal wealth as well as wealth for the broader society. This chapter describes life circumstances and professional careers of the most successful wealth generators of our day. The methodology for choosing specific individuals for further review appear below.

METHODOLOGY OF INVESTIGATION

A review of *Forbes* listing of the world's wealthiest individuals provides a starting point for identification of the most successful living entrepreneurs. Many of these individuals were "self-made" in the sense that they did not inherit their wealth but created something entirely new that became the source of their wealth or identified an innovative means of employing existing technologies. These individuals did not generate their wealth due to theft or extortion (as in "kleptocracies") or as a sole result of family connections. In this sense, they are "self-made." The top twelve or "fortunate dozen" wealth generators are the subject of further review. The concept of "self-made" is not totally objective, some subjectivity remains. For example, many people admit they received help along their road to riches and many with inherited wealth claim they really would have succeeded through their own efforts. In this analysis, a number of the world's wealthiest individuals are absent from the listing of the "fortunate dozen." Those excluded include Jim, Alice and Rob Walton (children of Walmart founder Sam Walton); Bernard Arnault whose father was a construction magnate and used inherited wealth to purchase Christian Dior in 1985. While some argue that financiers merely move money around and do not "create," the financier Warren Buffet is included in the listing since he did not inherit great wealth, created a business, took risks, and reaped rewards. Business creation, risk, and reward are consistent with the classic elements of entrepreneurism.

Following identification of the "fortunate dozen" commonalities as well as differences between them are delineated. Demographic characteristics including gender, race, religion, marital history, and immigration status; environmental factors include region, and status of educational institutions. The extent to which each has been instrumental in generating great wealth is an empirical question that one can explore through case studies in this small population of living wealthy individuals.

FINDINGS OF INVESTIGATION

Each year *Forbes* provides an authoritative listing of the wealthiest people in the world. This listing includes "self-made" entrepreneurs as well as inheritors of wealth. According to Forbes (2020), as of March 2020, there were 2,095 billionaires in the world. The world's billionaires were worth $8 trillion at the time. Jeff Bezos was the world's wealthiest person in 2020 for the third year in a row, despite giving $36 billion worth of his Amazon stock to his ex-wife MacKenzie Bezos as part of their divorce settlement. Bill Gates was the second wealthiest individual. Only 241 women placed on the listing of more than 2,000 billionaires in 2020. More billionaires (614) resided in the United States than any other nation, followed by greater China (included Hong Kong and Macao) with 456. The list displayed some degree of change with 267 people dropping off from 2019 and 78 new additions hailing from 20 countries. Table 4.1 identifies the twenty-five wealthiest individuals in the world as of 2020.

Table 4.1 List of Twenty-Five Wealthiest Individuals in the World (as of June 2020)

Rank	*Name*	*Age*	*Net Worth*	*Country*	*Source/Company*	*Industry*
1	Jeff Bezos	56	160.1 B	USA	Amazon	Technology
2	Bill Gates	64	108.6 B	USA	Microsoft	Technology
3	Bernaud Arnault & Family	71	102.8 B	France	LVMH	Fashion and Retail
4	Mark Zuckerberg	35	87.9 B	USA	Software/Facebook	Technology
5	Warren Buffett	89	71.4 B	USA	Berkshire Hathaway	Finance and Investments
6	Steve Ballmer	64	68.9 B	USA	Microsoft	Technology
7	Larry Ellison	75	68.7 B	USA	Software/Oracle	Technology
8	Larry Page	47	64.3 B	USA	Google	Technology
9	Amancio Ortega	84	65.6 B	Spain	Zara	Fashion and Retail
10	Mukesh Ambani	62	64.6 B	India	Petrochemicals, oil & gas	Energy
11	Sergey Brin	46	62.6 B	USA	Google	Technology
12	Francios Bettencourt Meyers & Family	66	61.8 B	France	L'Oreal	Fashion and Retail
13	Michael Bloomberg	78	60.1 B	USA	Bloomberg LP	Media & Entertainment
14	Jim Walton	71	53.6 B	USA	Walmart	Fashion and Retail
15	Alice Walton	70	53.4 B	USA	Walmart	Fashion and Retail
16	Rob Walton	75	53.2 B	USA	Walmart	Fashion and Retail
17	Carlos Slim Helu & Family	80	53.2 B	Mexico	telecom	Telecom
18	Mackenzie Bezos	50	52.4 B	USA	Amazon.com	Technology
19	Ma Huateng	48	51.5 B	China	Internet Media	Technology
20	Julia Koch & Family	57	48.2 B	USA	Koch Industries	Diversified
21	Charles Koch	84	48.2 B	USA	Koch Industries	Diversified
22	Jack Ma	55	43.9 B	China	e-commerce	Technology
23	Phil Knight & Family	82	38.4 B	USA	Nike	Fashion & Retail
24	Beate Heister & Karl Albrecht, Jr.		37.6 B	Germany	Supermarkets	Fashion & Retail
25	David Thompson & Family	62	35.1 B	Canada	Media	Media & Entertainment

Source: Table made by author using data from Forbes (2020).

Table 4.1 provides much information. First, it is clear that the wealthiest individuals in the world have acquired tremendous wealth. The top twelve individuals alone as of March 2020 (a low point in the Dow Jones Industrial Average) had a combined wealth of more than $810 billion. As an illustration of how the wealthiest individuals prosper in favorable times, the combined wealth of the top twelve billionaire increased to more than $838 billion by June 2020 or an aggregate increase of more than $151 billion. Wealth accumulated over time. The average age of the twelve wealthiest individuals was sixty-three.

A review of table 4.1 indicates that individuals can accumulate fortunes within one's lifetime. Such wealth, in theory, should redound to governments and people residing in given areas in terms of a multiplier effect. The extent to which wealth "trickles" down to others, however, remains controversial and data indicates that there is not as much "seepage" as many people desire. According to data compiled by the Federal Reserve in the first quarter of 2020, the bottom 50 percent of Americans only retained 1.4 percent of the nation's aggregate wealth while the top 1 percent retained 31.2 percent. The names of non-self-made billionaires include persons who inherited substantial sums or became billionaires through divorce and appear in bold font in table 4.1. These individuals include Francois Bettencourt Myers (granddaughter of L'Oreal's cosmetics founder, Eugène Schueller); Mukesh Ambani, son of Reliance Industries founder; Bernard Arnault who used inherited wealth to purchase Christian Dior; Jim Walton, Alice Walton, and Rob Walton who inherited their wealth from Walmart founder Sam Walton. Charles Koch, Julia Koch, and MacKenzie Bezos all benefited greatly from inheritances or divorce.

The wealthiest twelve self-made billionaires identified in table 4.1 (Bezos, Gates, Zuckerberg, Buffett, Ballmer, Ellison, Page, Ortega, Brin, Bloomberg, Helu, Mas) founded and grew their own businesses. A review of these individuals reveals that the overwhelming majority (75%) reside in the United States. The remaining three self-made billionaires reside in Spain, Mexico, and China. Eight of the twelve "fortunate dozen" derive their wealth from technology, reaffirming its place as the dominant wealth creator of the early twenty-first century. The iconic companies of Amazon, Facebook, Oracle, Microsoft, and Google each played a prominent role making their founders billionaires. Seven of the eight technology entrepreneurs reside in the United States. Companies created by these entrepreneurs contributed significantly to the gross national product of the United States. In June 2020, the market capitalization value of just four U.S.-founded companies (Amazon, Alphabet the parent of Google, Microsoft, and Facebook) totaled almost $4.5 trillion. Consistent with Schumpeter's view of the new driving out the old, these companies were all relatively new creations. Amazon was founded in 1994,

Google in 1998, Facebook in 2004, and Microsoft in 1975. The rise of new technology-based companies puts a premium on the need to be at the cutting edge of expertise, creativity, and innovation.

Table 4.2 addresses the question of what characteristics appear to contribute to the fortunes of the most successful entrepreneurs. This table identifies gender, race, religion, marital history, immigration status, region, and status of educational institution for the twelve entrepreneurs.

In terms of gender, all twelve of the "self-made" entrepreneur billionaires are male. For the most part, the wealthiest females on the *Forbes* listing derived their wealth through inheritance or divorce. Religion did not play a large role in the lives of these individuals. The largest religious grouping are those that claim to be atheists, agnostic, not declared, or nonpracticing. Some individuals who assert they are nonpracticing (such as Ellison and Page) were raised in Jewish households. In regard to immigration status, only Sergey Brin was not born in the United States, however, a number of the twelve are first- or second-generation Americans. All twelve entrepreneurs were married at least one time. Many of the entrepreneurs experienced divorce.

Whether the nature of specific places affect wealth creation remains an important question. North (1990) supports the notion that general norms and

Table 4.2 Characteristics of Wealthiest Self-Made Entrepreneurs

Characteristics—Demographic	*Number*
Gender—Male	12
Gender—Female	0
Religion—Catholic	2 (Gates, Helu)
Religion—Jewish	4 (Ballmer, Brin, Bloomberg, Zuckerberg)
Religion—Nonpracticing, Agnostic, Atheist or Unknown	6 (Bezos, Buffett, Ellison, Ortega, Page)
Religion Buddhist/Taoist	1 (Ma)
Race—Caucasian	9
Race—Hispanic	2 (Helu, Ortega)
Race—Asian	1 (Ma)
Immigration status—Native born	11
Immigration status—Non-native born	1 (Brin)
Marital Status—Previously or currently married	12
Marital Status—Never married	0
Characteristics—Environmental	
Residing in USA	9
Residing outside USA	3
Prestige educational institution	10 (Bezos, Gates, Zuckerberg, Buffet, Ballmer, Ellison, Page, Brin, Bloomberg, Helu)
Non-Prestigious Institutions	2 (Ortega, Ma)

Source: Table made by author using data from Forbes (2020).

rules of a polity can affect economic outcomes. Concerning the twelve billionaires identified in table 4.1, nine of these twelve and the highest seven claim U.S. residence. It is unlikely that such an empirical configuration is the result of chance. Why this pattern exists is a matter of speculation, however, it appears that the economic environment of the United States and the "culture of place" at least partially explains recent wealth creation (Dolbeare and Medcalf 1993; Elazar 1984; Koven 1999; McClosky and Zaller 1984; Myrdal 1944; Tocqueville 1956).

Cultural studies have identified U.S. distinctiveness. In his 1835 classic *Democracy in America*, Tocqueville contrasted the aristocratic ethos of Europe with his perception of American society where hardwork and money making dominates as the prevailing paradigm. Tocqueville (1958) contended that in the U.S the common person enjoyed a level of dignity that was absent in European societies. He claimed that in the U.S. commoners did not defer to elites; he believed individualism and market capitalism dominated to an extraordinary degree. In contrast, Elazar (1984) described the three characteristics of morality, individualism, and tradition. Myrdal (1944) stresses the influence of immigrants and absence of a feudal period of history. Others look at values such as liberty, capitalism, property, equality, law, ideology, and democracy (Dolbeare and Medcalf 1993, 12; Koven 1999; McClosky and Zaller 1984, 1).

Educational institution whether through networks or knowledge appear to relate to wealth creation of the "fortunate dozen." Six of the twelve billionaires either graduated from or attended the Ivy League schools of Harvard (Gates, Zuckerberg, Ballmer, and Bloomberg), Princeton (Bezos), or the University of Pennsylvania (Buffet). Ellison graduated from the University of Chicago, Page and Brin from Stanford University. Carlos Slim Helu graduated from the National Autonomous University of Mexico (UNAM), a highly placed institution in world rankings. Only Ortega and Ma did not seem to benefit from the cachet of prestigious educational institutions. Ortega left school in Spain at the age of fourteen. Ma took the Chinese exam three times before attending the public Hangzhou Teacher's Institute, currently known as Hangzhou Normal University. Ma applied ten times to Harvard Business School without success.

In order to provide more in-depth information about the chosen entrepreneurs. The chapter provides extensive case studies of four entrepreneurs, chosen through random sampling. Case studies have the advantage of providing greater depth of understanding of complex issues. How to acquire massive fortunes certainly qualifies as such a complex issue. Case studies are a useful method particularly when a holistic, in-depth investigation is required. The general value of case studies is that they go beyond numbers to supply beneficial insights at the individual level. Case studies are particularly salient when a big sample population is difficult to obtain and researchers often utilize the case study method in studies of real-life situations (Zainal 2007). The four entrepreneurs Steve Ballmer, Larry Page, Warren Buffet, and Jack Ma were selected for in-depth investigation from random sampling. Following the four in-depth case studies, briefer biographies of the remaining eight entrepreneurs appear.

CASE STUDIES OF SELECTED ENTREPRENEURS

Steve Ballmer

Early Environment and Individual Traits

When Steve Ballmer was born in 1956, there was little in his environment to suggest that he would become one of the wealthiest individuals in the world. His father was a Swiss national who in 1946 used his expertise in languages to secure a job translating documents for the Nuremberg War Trials. Ballmer's father developed a reputation for misbehavior, was transferred to a relatively remote area of Germany, and eventually fired from his position. Nevertheless, he somehow managed to get passage to New York and headed for Detroit where he secured a job at the Ford Motor Company. Ballmer's mother was born in Detroit to Jewish immigrants from Eastern Europe. She worked at her father's auto shop at a young age. In 1952, Ballmer's father applied for U.S. citizenship and changed his name from Fritz to Fred (Maxwell 2002, 31).

Eventually Fred Ballmer and his family moved to a three-bedroom home in Farmington Hills, a suburb of northern Detroit. At the time, Farmington Hills was predominantly rural. After World War II, Farmington Hills became less rural, transforming itself into a relatively wealthy, mostly white enclave. The city consistently ranked as one of the safest in the United States. Neither of Steve Ballmer's parents attended college but his father always assumed his son would receive a college education. The younger Ballmer received a scholarship at the exclusive Detroit Country Day School, six miles from the Ballmer house. Friends of the Ballmer's were not surprised that Fred's son had begun to ascend the ladder of success (37).

Detroit Country Day School is located in Birmingham, Michigan, a town that raised and educated a disproportionate number of high achievers including Oscar award winner Robin Williams, Emmy award winner Tim Allen, journalist Michael Kinsley, Sun Microsystems cofounder Scott McNealy, and Steve Ballmer. Why the area spawned such a high number of distinguished achievers is a matter of speculation. One theory posits that it is due to the blend of well-funded academic, athletic, and social competition combined with high parental expectations, parental involvement, and a midwestern work ethic. The area is noted for being a very advantageous place for a business person to be raised since it included many benefits but residents weren't so rich that they spoiled their children (41). Today, many graduates from Detroit Country Day pursue degrees at the most selective Ivy League Universities (Detroit County Day School 2020).

Ballmer performed exceptionally well at Detroit Day. He graduated first in his class in 1973 and Harvard University admitted him to its Department of Mathematics and Economics. People viewed Ballmer as an exceptionally high achiever and he received a perfect score of 800 on the math section of the Scholastic Aptitude Test (SAT). A former classmate remembers Steve as always sitting in the front row, having a crew cut hair, and voracious in his appetite for learning. Ballmer's parents were supportive; his mother drove him all over the state for math competitions. Classmate recalls that when Steve came to Detroit Day, he was probably a year or a year and a half behind everyone in math but after two years at the private school, he was probably a year and a half ahead of everyone. Steve also was engaged in extracurricular activities and played football to fulfil the requirement for his scholarship (50). Although he came across as a nerd, fellow students considered him personable, down to earth, helpful, and easy to talk to. These qualities would serve him well in his later career at Microsoft. Ballmer went on to earn a BA degree from Harvard in 1977. At Harvard, he became an important part of various college activities and clubs. He was an equipment manager for the football team and worked on the student newspaper; he particularly excelled at selling ads (67).

After Harvard, Ballmer joined the consumer products giant Procter & Gamble in Cincinnati, Ohio. At the time, Procter & Gamble (P&G) was the leading consumer products marketing company in the world. Ballmer first joined the food products group of P&G as a brand assistant. The young Harvard graduate served as a sales trainee working with the sales force of the Duncan Hines brownie and muffin mixes. He managed his own sales section, made presentations to new clients, and gained experience in implementing ideas of brand managers. Ballmer claims that he left his position at P&G because its sales force lacked his passion about selling. After P&G, Ballmer entered the Stanford University Graduate School of Business, seeking an MBA degree. Before he could graduate, however, at the age of 24, he left Harvard to join his former classmate and close friend Bill Gates at the tech start-up Microsoft. Along with Gates, Ballmer helped to build the Microsoft Corporate giant.

A combination of environmental and individual factors influenced Ballmer's success. Certainly, his natural intelligence, drive, competitiveness, and sales skills helped in his future career. Unlike Bill Gates, Steve Ballmer's family did not possess significant wealth. Benefiting from scholarships, Ballmer's advancement was largely merit-based; he was known in his early years as a math prodigy. His parents were supportive of his efforts, he received encouragement from educators, and he was able to attend a top-ranked private preparatory school. Ballmer overcame early shyness, and in later years, his motivational speeches at Microsoft events became legendary. In terms of personality, some characterize Ballmer as the stylistic opposite of Gates. Ballmer is loud with his vocal cords once required surgical repair from excessive shouting. In contrast, many people view Gates as a petulant nerd.

Despite his modest family background, Ballmer benefited from a new-economy version of an old boys' network. He attended Harvard with Bill Gates and other future computing leaders such as Scott McNealy and Bill Joy of Sun Microsystems. Like many high-tech pioneers, Ballmer enjoyed a suburban childhood that whetted, rather than dulled, his drive to succeed. (Leibovitch 2000). Ballmer claims that he was not "techie" but was able to recognize and exploit the commercial potential of innovations. In his professional career, he excelled at identifying talent that would advance the interests of Microsoft. He ceaselessly promoted the product lines of Microsoft, and warding off competitive threats to the company's market shares.

Professional Career

Ballmer started at Microsoft in the summer of 1980 after asking his friend Bill Gates if there was an opening for a summer job. Gates convinced Ballmer to take a full-time job managing the company's operations. Over time, Ballmer would bond even more closely with Gates and demonstrate that he was an indispensable part of the company's success. Ballmer became Microsoft employee number 28 with the title assistant to the president; responsibilities included recruitment, accounting, legal, and related function. He particularly excelled at identifying potential talent to join Microsoft.

Ballmer proved to be an effective manager. One of his first acts was to control payroll by eliminating the massive overtime pay of programmers. As chief recruiter, he also helped to establish a culture that would attract super bright, super-motivated people. Ballmer's managerial skills also led him to reorganize Microsoft's partnership arrangement into a corporate structure. The corporate structure offered many advantages such as limits to liability in case of bankruptcy. The corporate rearrangement allowed Ballmer to obtain 8 percent of corporate ownership while Gates received 53 percent and cofounder Paul Allen 31 percent; others split the remainder. Ballmer also developed a stock option plan for employees (Editors, TheFamousPeople.com n.d.). The stock option plan allowed employees to purchase Microsoft stock at a reduced price but required them to stay at the company for at least five years. This became known as the employee's "golden handcuffs." Ballmer's stock in Microsoft became a significant source of his wealth. In 2019, Ballmer still owned approximately 300 million shares of Microsoft.

After Paul Allen's departure from Microsoft in 1983 for health reasons, Ballmer was instrumental in developing Microsoft's operating system, the core of the company's business. He also headed the campaign for branding Microsoft. When in 1986 Microsoft became a publically held company, Ballmer instantly became a multimillionaire; his shares at the close of trading on March 13, 1986, were valued at more than $47 million. Thirteen days before his thirtieth birthday, Steve Ballmer was a millionaire forty-seven times over (Maxell 2002, 115).

Microsoft's Office suite of applications, consisting of word-processing (Microsoft Word), spreadsheet (Microsoft Excel), and presentation software (Microsoft PowerPoint) drove profits. These tools of Microsoft have become essential for professionals today. Microsoft added to these core components in later years to include personal information management (Microsoft Outlook), note taking (Microsoft OneNote), and communication applications (Skype for Business and Microsoft Teams). Ballmer held various positions in the company; in 1992, he became executive vice president for Sales and Support. In 1998, he was promoted to president of Microsoft, and in 2000 was named as chief executive officer (CEO). As the CEO, Ballmer handled the company finances as well as daily operations. Under Ballmer's tenure as CEO, Microsoft developed its electronic game console system Xbox and the Zune family of portable media players. Corporate annual revenue increased from $25 billion to $70 billion, net income increased 215 percent to $23 billion. Ballmer stepped down from his position of CEO of Microsoft in February 2014 (Editors, TheFamousPeople.com n.d.).

Ballmer's accomplishments at Microsoft contributed greatly to his personal wealth and the overall success of the company. When he became CEO, Microsoft was fighting class action lawsuits in addition to an antitrust lawsuit brought on by the U.S. government and twenty states. In 2001, Microsoft settled the antitrust case in what many viewed as favorable terms. In Ballmer's time as CEO, Microsoft's total annual profit growth surpassed the performances of iconic CEOs such as General Electric's Jack Welch and IBM's Louis Gerstner. People praise Ballmer for protecting Microsoft's two core businesses (Windows and Office) from competitors. In terms of style, both Microsoft and Ballmer exercised aggressive behavior. One venture capitalist compared Microsoft to hockey star Gordie Howe who never won the award for the most gentlemanly player. Microsoft competitors complained about being hit with elbow after elbow. A former president of the University of Washington stated that it seemed that Microsoft always played with two feet on the foul line (Maxell 2002, 124).

Some accused Microsoft of stealing other people's code, crushing competition, stifling innovation, and protecting their favored position. People compared Ballmer's animated speeches to the John Belushi character in the classic film *Animal House*. Despite how crazy Ballmer's assertion appeared to be, people were advised to stay out of his way. Many including the *New York Times* questioned the legality of Microsoft's tactics. Microsoft was cited by the U.S. Department of Justice for unethical and sometimes illegal gamesmanship. Some began to refer to Microsoft as an "evil empire" that engaged in unfair competition and false advertising. According to the judge presiding over Microsoft's first antitrust trial, Microsoft enjoyed monopoly power based on their share of the market, the company established barriers to entry from competitors and used predatory tactics.

Ballmer remained a faithful team player for the company. Maxwell (2002, 170) claims that Microsoft's trial strategy was to deny, delay, and tell the big lie that they were not a monopoly. Maxwell stated, "nobody told the big lie better than Steve Ballmer." Microsoft appealed a court ruling to break up the company and reached a settlement with the government that critics of Microsoft called "toothless" with enough loopholes to drive a fleet of ships through (145). Maxwell speculated that it would be interesting to be able to see how much computer code Microsoft stole from others and it would be interesting to see how their codes made non-Microsoft applications run slower (251). Supporters of Microsoft, however, claim that they were just superior competitors in the free marketplace and any criticism of their behavior should be attributed to "sour grapes" by the losers in an open contest over wealth generation.

Despite his successes, by the end of Ballmer's tenure at Microsoft, many were calling for his removal. Critics accused Ballmer of missing the three big trends (search, social networking, and mobile) that revolutionized the computer industry and of not being as much in the vanguard of the latest cool technology as others such as Steve Jobs, Larry Page, Sergey Brin, and Mark Zuckerberg. Some describe his tenure as CEO as the luckiest "dorm assignment" in the history of the universe, cashing in on his personal friendship with Bill Gates. Many, however, were happy to see Steve Ballmer leave Microsoft. On the day he announced his retirement, Microsoft stock rose 7 percent. (Cassidy 2013).

Larry Page

Early Environment and Individual Traits

Biographers describe Larry Page's family as having come from just beyond the outskirts of the status quo (Brandt 2011). The family history is steeped in academics and the struggles of the labor movement. Larry Page's father, Carl

Page, was the first person in his family to graduate from high school in 1956. He studied engineering at the University of Michigan, and in 1965 earned a PhD in computer science from the University of Michigan. In 1967, Larry's father Carl Page joined the faculty at Michigan State University. Larry's mother taught computer programming at Michigan State; his older brother Carl Jr. served as an entrepreneurial role model and became a cofounder of a successful dot-com company. Larry's paternal grandfather was an auto-worker with leftist political leanings who helped organize the Flint Michigan Sit-Down Strike of 1937. His maternal grandfather was also a labor organizer who immigrated to Israel. Larry was born in 1973 in Lansing, Michigan.

From an early age, Larry was a "tinkerer" who developed an early fondness for computers. At the age of six, he had access to the family home computer. He attended a Montessori school, was active in Boy Scouts, enjoyed reading, and arguing about issues. He became an admirer of the eccentric inventor Nikola Tesla (1855–1943), played the flute, and studied music composition. Larry attended a renowned music summer camp and claimed that his musical education inspired his obsession with speed in computing. Larry followed his father's example, attending the University of Michigan to study computer engineering. His professors at the university remember him as always ahead of the others. While attending the university, he built his own printer, fitting the electronic and mechanical parts into a chassis made of lego blocks. Other activities include helping to design a solar-powered car that competed in an international contest. In 1995, Page received his undergraduate degree with honors from the University of Michigan and the school's Outstanding Student Award. He then decided to attend Stanford University for its outstanding computer science program, work in artificial intelligence and advances in robotics (Henderson 2012). Similar to others from academic families, Larry maintained his leftist roots and when his father died, he requested that friends donate to the Democratic Party instead of buying flowers.

Many consider Page's family upbringing as comfortably middle class. Unlike his partner, Sergey Brin, Page was conspicuously quiet; an adult friend described him as shy, a loner; strangers described him as asocial. Larry did not embrace his mother's Judaism, and like his father was agnostic. Page absorbed from his study of Nikola Tesla that it was not enough to invent things. In order to effect change, one needed to turn ideas into concrete realities such as producing marketable products. He did not want to die like the unsung Tesla. Page claims that probably from the age of twelve, he knew he would start a company. As an undergraduate at the University of Michigan, he took business classes and set his sights on attending Stanford University where famous careers were spawned by people such as William Hewlett, David Packard, and Jerry Yang (Auletta 2009, 33–34).

Page's brief stay at Stanford University proved to be extraordinary. He met his fellow cofounder of Google (Sergey Brin) and embarked on a scholarly research project that would make both of them among the wealthiest people in the planet. At the suggestion of his adviser, a pioneer in artificial intelligence, Page began to develop applications for the world wide web. The Department of Defense and a federal grant funded his initial research at Stanford to retrieve research papers. The great insight of Page and fellow graduate student Brin was that thanks to the world wide web they could share virtually any kind of data and make the data universally accessible (14).

Page and Brin were able to create a system where different databases would share information, create a massive index, and rank information by importance. The two graduate students bonded so thoroughly at Stanford that colleagues began to roll their names together as LarryandSergey. Larry's academic mentor encouraged both of them to follow their instincts and explore the future of online information retrieval. Their interests complemented each other. Larry's strength was in invention and computer science, Sergey's in data mining. As students, they created a search engine they named "Backrub" because of its ability to analyze back links that pointed to a particular website. They soon changed the name to "Google," a common spelling for Googol, or 10^{100}, a number that comported with their desire to build very large search engines (40).

Page and Brin were convinced that they created a better search engine than anything in the marketplace. Their development of what became known as the PageRank algorithm was a breakthrough in terms of being able to quickly search the entire world wide web and rank relevance of specific web links. Originally, they thought in terms of applying PageRank to the Internet as an interesting doctoral thesis; they later decided to take a leave of absence from Stanford and start their own business. University contacts helped. One of Page's professors, David Cheriton, arranged for Page and Brin to meet with Andy Bechtolsheim who was cofounder of Sun Microsystems and a legendary investor in technology start-ups. According to Vise and Malseed (2005, 45, 47), Bechtolsheim met with Larry and Sergey, appreciated their breakthrough, trusted the word of their professor who thought his students had a "great idea," and liked their plan to develop a fully searchable database. Bechtolsheim thought their plan to grow by word of mouth, had potential, and quickly made out a check for $100,000 to Google, Inc. Two weeks later the "Google boys" incorporated and opened the first bank account in the newly established company's name. The endorsement by Bechtolsheim facilitated fundraising from others. With investments of about $1 million, they were able to buy the computer equipment they needed to take the next steps on monetizing their innovation (48).

Professional Career

The rise of Google represents one of the great success stories of modern American business. As a testament to the achievements of Page and his cofounder, in 2006 both the *Oxford English Dictionary* and the *Merriam-Webster* dictionary added the word "google" to their dictionaries. According the *Merriam-Webster*, google is a verb meaning, "to use the Google search engine to obtain information . . . on the World Wide Web." Not everyone in their professional careers can claim that they made billions of dollars and that their company became so well known that its name had to be added to the lexicon of the English language.

As he launched his professional career, Page began to focus on delivering the absolute best search engine on the market. He was absorbed in product development. Only later at the urging of his venture capital investors did he and Brin begin to explore viable ways of generating profits. From the start of the business, it was clear that Page was incredibly smart, ambitious, had a healthy disregard for the impossible, and was highly confident that he had the "goods." A professor at Stanford describes both Larry and Sergey as invigorated by challenges and willing to tackle subjects that others did not want to touch. According to Vise and Malseed (2005, 50), the "Google boys" held on to their dream of changing the world. They embraced the idea of digitizing the entire universe and providing information free for everybody. They were able to "bulldoze" through the initial obstacle and transform their vision into reality.

Page and Brin shepherded their company through the early hazards of the business world. A few initiatives, however, stand out, including: (1) their desire to maintain control of company decisions, (2) their advertising model, and (3) the culture of the company. Their desire to maintain control enabled them to strike a favorable deal with investors that allowed them to hold large blocks of voting stock. Page and Brin negotiated with two of the leading venture capitalist firms of Silicon Valley. After Page and Brin threatened to look elsewhere for funding, each of two large venture capitalists and their firms agreed to put aside their desires for sole control and each invested $12.5 million while allowing Page and Brin to have majority control. The only provision demanded by the venture capitalists was that Page and Brin would hire an experienced executive to help transform the search engine into a profitable business. Page agreed to this provision, sensing that if he and Brin had the $25 million and voting control, they could push off any decision to hire a chief executive well into the future. Vise and Malseed (68) stated, "All indications were that the 'Google Guys' had a dream deal: the money they needed to build their beloved search engine, and the control they needed to call the shots."

In a formal announcement, Page stated that Google planned to aggressively grow by providing the best search experience on the world wide web. The announcement included additional information such as Google's impressive list of investors, its patent pending PageRank system, and its growth rate of 50 percent a month. It helped immensely that the two large venture capitalist firms believed that Page and Brin were very smart people, had a firm sense of conviction, had Stanford pedigrees, and a service that was demonstrably better than you could get anywhere else. They willing made large investments for shares in the company.

Page and Brin developed an advertising model that turned into a "cash cow" for Google. Google makes most of its money through online advertising. In Google's advertising system, advertisers bid on certain keywords that are entered in searches for clickable ads to appear in Google's search results. Advertisers pay per each click on their ads. Costs per click are determined by the competitiveness of keywords. The advantage of the advertising model is that it targets ads to users of searchers that are likely to be interested in specific products based on their keyword entry.

Finally, Page established a distinctive corporate culture that fostered innovation, loyalty, and future growth. Google sought to develop a culture of openness where everybody could freely contribute ideas to create a more comfortable and friendly working environment. Workers at Google enjoyed free food, a volleyball court, a swimming pool, a car wash, an oil change, a haircut, free healthcare, and many other benefits. Google's culture stressed experimentation, learning from mistakes, creativity, showing interest in the lives of employees, respecting individuality, and delivering great products to customers continuously. Google aspired to create an open working environment where employees felt at home and would want to go to the company to pursue their ideas (Tran 2017).

Google's Initial Public Offering represented another occasion where Page proved to be a savvy negotiator. At the urging of the two large venture capital investors, Google filed the necessary paperwork for an IPO in April 2004. Google insisted on receiving bids from investors electronically and allowed small investors to buy shares. Google resisted paying the traditional 7 percent brokerage fee and managed to pay significantly less. Page and Brin described in a letter to potential investors that they would offer two classes of stock, one class of stock for regular investors with one voting share, a second class of stock for themselves carrying ten votes per share. This would make a takeover of the company impossible without their approval. Page and Brin together owned 32 percent of Google's shares with CEO Eric Schmidt (who was hired in 2001) owning 6.1 percent (Auletta 2009, 107). At the time of the IPO, the "triumvirate" of Page, Brin, and Schmidt owned about a third of the company's stock but 80 percent of the votes (Scott 2008, 57). In the letter,

Page and Brin promised to be unconventional, not to be distracted by short-term targets, and have a structure that would likely leave the team of Page and Brin in place with significant control over decisions. These stock voting arrangements did not differ significantly than those of other companies (such as the New York Times, Washington Post, and Wall Street Journal) where owners desired tight control. After the IPO, Page and Brin became billionaires at the age of 31; approximately 1,000 out of Google's 2,300 employees became millionaires (Scott 2008, 41).

Page's initial passion was simply building the best search engine in the world; however, over time, he realized they had to generate more revenue. The company decided that rather than focusing on licensing a search engine, Google would profit from advertising, keep their search engine free, and sell targeted ads to businesses. Page and Brin decided they could sell the ads themselves since Google wrote its own software and built all their own computers. They developed a system "AdWords" to connecting the ads with specific searches. AdWords allowed advertisers to decide what word their product should be associated with and bid on the words in a complex auction process. By charging per click, online advertising became affordable to smaller businesses. Better targeting of ads to specific web pages also benefited advertisers. For example, people looking at a website about computers might find an ad from Dell or HP. Advertising became a Google money machine (Henderson 2012, 38).

Page also helped develop Google's distinctive culture. Google's culture entails numerous components. Page encouraged his engineers to think boldly (Auletta 2009, 203) while he and Brin Page supplied the "big" picture. Page was particularly involved in hiring decisions. He noted that Google hired people like himself and Brin who were brainy strivers who aced the SAT, brought home good grades, and wrote the essays that got them into the best schools. Google sought employees from Stanford, Berkeley, University of Washington, and MIT. Google still requested SAT scores and transcripts of grades even after evidence indicated that they do not relate to performance. Worried about "groupthink," Google occasionally allowed the "stray C or a non-Mensa SAT score" to be trumped by an accomplishment that indicated that someone was special (Levy 2011, 141). In Google's early years, a potential hire might go through a series of as many as twenty interviews. Evaluators would consider analytical ability, overall intelligence, technical skill, cultural fit, vita, and an overall summary of many traits. Page insisted on signing off on every employee hired at Google (142).

"Don't be evil" became Google's motto. Some felt that the motto reflected the soul of Googlers, implying that out in the world there are companies doing evil but people at Google had the opportunity to do "the right thing." Their motto suggested that Google was nobler than other companies. Page embraced "don't be evil" as a summation of his own hopes for the company. Levy (2011, 146) states that Google was about "two young men who wanted to do good, [who] gravitated to a new phenomenon (the Internet) that promised to be a history making force for good, developed a solution that would gather the world's information, level the Tower of Babel, and link millions of processors into a global prosthesis for knowledge. . . . Google would be a shining beacon for the way corporations should operate." Page and Brin made the expression "don't do evil" the centerpiece of their lucrative Initial Public Offering (146). The Google philosophy can be found on the corporate page of its website and provides insight into their culture that emphasizes focusing on users, doing one thing well, don't do evil, enjoy challenges, utilize small teams, organizing around people, calling out people for their bad behavior, and balancing work with life (Schmidt and Rosenberg 2014, 27–57).

Warren Buffett

Early Environment and Individual Traits

The Buffett family ancestry has deep roots in America, dating back at least to 1696. Generations of Buffett ancestors farmed in New York until 1867 when Sidney Buffet, unhappy with the low wages he received from his grandfather, migrated west. In 1869, Sidney Buffett opened the S. H. Buffett grocery in Omaha, Nebraska, where his son Ernest (grandfather of Warren) also worked. Known for his frugal ways and conservative political leanings, Ernest Buffett eventually opened his own grocery store. Ernest's son Howard (Warren's father) did not aspire to become a third-generation grocer, attended the University of Nebraska at Lincoln, and dreamed of becoming a journalist. Howard married a fellow University of Nebraska student (Leila Stahl), characterized as a hardscrabble country girl from a bleak, rural town in Nebraska. Leila and Howard married in 1925 in the middle of a cold Nebraska winter. On the advice of his father Ernest (who paid Howard's college tuition), Warren's father Howard turned down a newspaper job and accepted a position with a family friend at a local insurance company (Lowenstein 2008, 7). Howard became a deacon of a local church in the Omaha area; however, he was still interested in politics, openly praised Calving Coolidge's conservative views on small government and minimum regulation.

Warren's father left his job in insurance, and became a stockbroker in 1927, two years before the infamous 1929 stock market crash. Unlike fellow billionaires such as Page, Ballmer, Gates and others, Warren was a true child of the Depression. Born on August 30, 1930, Warren's family worried about putting food on the table. His mother skipped her church circle because she could not afford the twenty-nine cents to occasionally purchasing coffee for the group. She sometimes skipped meals rather than run up a bill at the family grocery. In 1931, Howard lost his job and savings when the Omaha Union State Bank closed. Within two weeks, however, he started his own stockbrokerage firm that quickly earned a profit. Outwardly, Warren's mother appeared upbeat, yet she suffered from bouts of "neuralgia" when she would verbally abuse Warren and his sister as worthless, ungrateful, and selfish. Leila Buffett often complained that her children enjoyed easy lives compared to her sacrifices. She would especially launch tirades against Warren's older sister Doris (Schroeder 2009, 44).

Despite the hard times of the early 1930s, Warren's father elevated his family into the more comfortable half of the middle class. When Warren was six years old, the family moved to a larger, brick house in a suburb of Omaha. While more prosperous than previously, Warren's mother always bought thrifty and practical gifts for her three children. The tough economic times appeared to have deeply affected Warren. Before he was five years old, he was deeply motivated to become very rich. At a young age, he sold individual cans of soda pop door to door, earning a five-cent profit on a pack of six cans. Warren also sold magazines, stuffing the coin sales in a money changer that he carried on his belt. At the age of ten, Warren sold peanuts and popcorn at the University of Omaha football games. He searched the local golf course for marketable balls that he organized by brand and price. Warren looked for winning tickets on the floor of the local racetrack that were erroneously discarded, he worked a paper route and expanded it. Warren's father took him to visit the New York Stock Exchange and he realized at a young age that he wanted money and money would make him independent. By eleven, Warren declared that he would be a millionaire by the time he reached the age of thirty-five (58, 61). At fourteen, he earned enough money from his various ventures to invest in forty acres of Nebraska farmland (23).

Warren idolized his father who taught Sunday school classes, sat on the local public school board, and became a role model for his three children. Warren and his two sisters were taught that they had a duty not just to God but also to the community. Warren's dad neither drank nor smoked; he dressed soberly in dark suits and his children lived in fear of disappointing him. When the Republican Party was looking for someone to run against the Democratic Party candidate in 1942, party leaders turned to Howard Buffett, an outspoken hater of Franklin Roosevelt. Howard defied the odds and with little money won the election to become a U.S. congressman. In office, Howard Buffett gained a reputation for maintaining high ethical standards and refusing offers of junkets. During his first term, he even refused a pay raise insisting on the lower salary of the time of his election. Warren inherited his father's scruples and concern for society (27).

Warren not only invested at an early age, he also learned from his missteps. At the age of eleven, Warren along with his older sister Doris bought a few shares of stocks. Warren felt responsible when the stock initially declined and when it recovered, he quickly sold netting a profit of $5. However, after he sold the stock advanced from $40 a share to $202 a share. Warren called the episode one of the most important in his life as he learned three lessons: (1) don't be fixated on the price you paid for a stock, (2) don't' rush to grab a small profit, and (3) don't be responsible for someone else's money unless you are sure you will succeed (Schroeder 2009, 61). When the Buffett family moved to Washington, DC, after Howard Buffett's election to Congress, Warren felt out of place having left his friends from Omaha. His grades did not start out well but improved over time. His classmates viewed him as friendly but shy; in his new high school, Warren felt as an outsider. Warren nevertheless worked numerous jobs and saved his money. He also became an admirer of Dale Carnegie and dedicated himself to following Carnegie's rule of how to win friends and influence people. Eventually he made more friends, and joined the high school golf team. Reading Carnegie's popular book *How to Win Friends and Influence People* honed Warren's wit and improved upon his flair for salesmanship (92). Before long Warren was making more money than his teachers selling refurbished golf balls, sets of collectible stamps, putting pin ball machines in barber shops, and running a car-buffing business.

Warren graduated sixteenth out of a class of 374 in June 1947. The caption on the yearbook reads, "Likes math . . . future stockbroker" (Lowenstein 2008, 28). After high school, Warren briefly attended the prestigious Wharton Business School at the University of Pennsylvania. He did not take well to his classes and in 1949, at the end of his sophomore year, he transferred to the University of Nebraska. Buffett applied to Harvard for graduate school but was denied admission. He explored other programs and began studies at the Columbia University Business School. One of the professors at Columbia, Benjamin Graham, was to become a major influence on Buffett's life. Graham was a leading figure in securities analysis and traveled from his Wall Street office every Thursday to teach a course on stock valuation. Warren eventually became Graham's star student and even offered to work for him without pay; he became the only student to receive a grade of A+ in Graham's twenty-two years of teaching at Columbia.

Lowenstein (2008, 43–44) stated that Buffet "was fanatical about following in Graham's footsteps" and "saw Graham in idealized terms—a 'hero' like his father." Graham taught his students to look for big gaps in the price you are willing to pay for a stock and its "inherent" value identified through the liquidated value of its assets. Graham reasoned that "intrinsic" value would surface the way a barrel, trapped under winter ice, pops to the surface in a spring thaw. Schroeder (2009, 132) states that Warren's reaction to Graham's method of investing was like "a man emerging from the cave in which he had been living all his life, blinking in the sunlight as he perceived reality for the first time." Buffet was ready to launch upon his own illustrious career as an investor.

Professional Career

Warren Buffett's offer to work for Graham was initially rejected. He then returned to Omaha and began to work for his father as a young stockbroker. His initial sales were to his aunt and college friends. His stay at home was brief, when Professor Graham offered him a job in New York City, Warren and his new wife Susie immediately relocated and he began employment at the Graham-Newman investment company. Warren's investments proved to be profitable for the company and he quietly invested on his own. In 1956, Graham retired and relocated to California. Warren then left New York, relocated to Omaha, organized a pool of investors, and established the company of Buffett Associates Ltd. (Lowenstein 2008, 58). From this inauspicious start, Buffett amassed one of the largest fortunes in the world. Although the son of a congressman, graduate of a prestigious business school, and star pupil of one of the most famous authors in business investing, Warren started with a relatively small stake of capital. He initially organized a pool of funds totaling $105,000. Buffett warned investors that he would not reveal anything about where he would invest the money. He would only provide a yearly summary of results. By the end of 1957, Warren was managing five partnerships totaling in the range of $500,000 (62).

Buffett followed his mentor Ben Ginsberg's advice in looking for undervalued stocks that held untapped wealth or held potential for future appreciation. Before long, Warren was able to purchase controlling interest in companies, appointed himself chairperson or member of the board of directors of those companies and put capable managers in charge of running operations. His mangers cut costs, closed plants, and slashed inventory. The companies subsequently became profitable. Buffett's early record of return on investment for his partnerships is impressive. Figure 4.1 compares the returns on Buffett's early partnerships with the returns on the Dow Jones Industrial

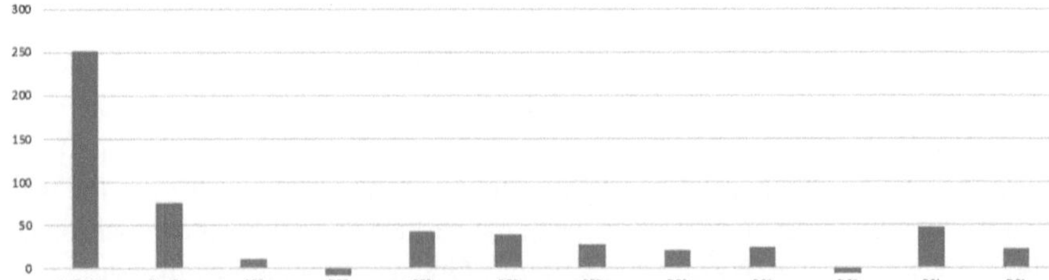

Figure 4.1 Buffett vs. Dow 1957–1961 (in percentage). *Source*: Created by author using information from Lowenstein (2020, 69).

Average (Lowenstein 2008, 69). The figure indicates that Buffett's return clearly outpaced those of the Dow with a five-year return of 251 percent compared to 74.3 percent for the Dow. In addition, Buffet and his partners never lost money in any given year compared to Dow Jones Industrial Average losses of negative 8.4 percent in 1957 and negative 6.3 percent in 1960.

As indicated in figure 4.1, from the start Buffett and his investment partnerships reaped sizable returns. His personal goal was to beat the Dow by an average of ten points a year. Buffett made big investments in stocks such as Berkshire Hathaway, American Express, and Disney. He recognized untapped value in Disney's film library, he identified a relatively low price for American Express, and believed that Berkshire Hathaway was terribly mismanaged. By 1963, Warren became Berkshire Hathaway's biggest stockholder. He continued to buy stocks, eventually identifying individuals willing to sell large blocks of stock and before long acquired a controlling interest in the company. Buffett quickly placed a handpicked manager in charge of the company as president. Under new management, the company started earning a profit; he then applied profits to invest in other ventures.

Buffett engaged in a strategy of placing big bets on select companies such as Berkshire Hathaway. Returns on investments in the second five years of his partnerships consistently outpaced the Dow. In some years, gains were spectacular. For example, in 1966, the Buffett partnerships gained 20.4 percent while the Dow declined by 15.6 percent. Over the ten-year period (1957–1966), the Buffett partnerships grew in value by 1,156 percent compared to an advance of 122.9 percent on the Dow Jones Industrial Average. Wary about the direction of the market, Buffett liquidated his partner's assets in 1969. Buffett's reputation as a savvy investor grew. Lowenstein (2008, 95) observed that investors "were starting to worship Buffett. . . . He was the unassuming genius who drank nothing but Pepsi Cola and could beat the pants off Wall Street year after year."

In 1970, Warren became chairman and CEO of Berkshire Hathaway Inc. and began writing humorous, down to earth, and anecdotal letters to shareholders. As head of Berkshire Hathaway, Buffett made many lucrative investments. In the 1970s, he invested in companies such as the *Washington Post*, the *Buffalo Evening News*, and American Broadcasting Company (ABC). Buffett helped finance the acquisition of ABC by Capital Cities for a 25 percent stake in the combined company, Capital Cities/ABC (Kleinfield 1985). The sale of ABC surprised media analysts, since ABC was four times bigger than Capital Cities at the time. In the 1980s, Berkshire Hathaway purchased large stakes in the investment bank Salomon, Inc. and the Coca-Cola Company. Coca-Cola turned out to be one of Buffett's most lucrative investments. Other investments include the investment bank Goldman Sachs (in 2008 at the height of the financial crisis for a relatively low price), Bank of America (2011), Freddie Mac (1988), Burlington Northern Santa Fe railroad (2009), and See's Candy (1972). One of Buffett's most lucrative purchases was Coca-Cola. By 2017, the Coca-Cola stock Buffett purchased in 1988 increased in value by more than 1,000 percent, not including dividends (Frankel 2017). Buffett's company, Berkshire Hathaway netted more than $3 billion from a $5 billion investment/bailout of Goldman Sachs in 2008 (Mohammed 2020).

In his later years, Buffett turned to philanthropy. In 2010, he joined Bill Gates in forming a campaign to recruit wealthy individuals for philanthropic causes. In 2018, Berkshire Hathaway joined JPMorgan Chase and Amazon to form a new healthcare company for their U.S. employees. Buffett called the rising cost of healthcare a "tapeworm on the American economy" and expressed the view that in time costs could be controlled while enhancing patients' satisfaction and outcomes (Warren Buffett 2020).

People gave Buffett the moniker "Oracle of Omaha," and he became a cult-like figure as "financial groupies" annually arrived in Omaha for his yearly meeting with stockholders. Buffett, however, did not fit the stereotypical image of the Wall Street tycoon. Lowenstein (2008, xii) states that he could explain finance like a general store clerk discussing the weather and unlike portfolio managers whose mindset was that of a trader, Buffett risked capital on long-term growth of a few select businesses. As the plainspoken midwesterner, he represents the antithesis of the Wall Street archetype. According to Lowenstein (2008, xiii), Buffet with his "commonsensical cracker barrel wit" answered to a "deeply American need for authentic heroes. . . . The uncorrupted commoner from the Midwest or West who stands up to the venal Easterners, be they politicians, bankers, big businessmen, or others." Lowenstein concluded (xiv) that Buffet is in the mold of "the self-made man from the midcountry—a Lincoln a Twain a Will Rogers."

Jack Ma

Early Environment and Individual Traits

Jack Ma is a study of determination and grit, a Chinese Horatio Alger story from someone who started out in life with the albatross of heavy disadvantage. Ma Yung (later known as Jack Ma) was born in 1964 in Hangzhou, the capital of Zhejiang Province in the southeastern part China. He grew up in a time when China was isolated from Western culture and market economies. Ma acquired the nickname of "Jack" from a pen pal he met while working as an English-speaking tour guide. Ma's parents were professional performers of storytelling and ballad singing. His grandfather, however, was associated with the losing side in China's civil war between Mao's victorious Communist Party and the Nationalists (Kuomintang) Party under Chiang

Kai-shek. Ma's family became the subject of hatred due to their Nationalist associations. They became associated with the "five blacks," or categories of reviled people that included landlords, rich peasants, counterrevolutionaries (Ma's family), evildoers, and rightists or conservative revisionists who held "incorrect views." The Chinese Communist Party (CCP) persecuted members of the five outcast groups through methods such as beating and torture. Jack in his early years was regarded as a rebel, stubborn, naughty, and incorrigible (Shiying and Avery 2009, 2).

Despite his short and scrawny stature, Ma adopted a pugnacious attitude; few among his teachers, neighbors, and family thought he had much of a future. Ma, however, was good at languages, determined, and was able to polish his English skills by listening to broadcasts over the radio. He practiced his English with foreigners he met. At the age of thirteen, Ma rode 17 miles on his bicycle to give tourists English-speaking tours. He aspired to attend college but various obstacles stood in his way. He was highly proficient in his English skills, however, relatively unskilled in math since he never attended a first-rate middle school or grade school. The first time Ma took China's college entrance exam he failed due to his poor math score. After two attempts, Ma finally passed the exam and in 1984 at the age of twenty, he entered Hangzhou Normal College, an institution that prepared students for the teaching profession. Still carrying a stigma, leaders eventually allowed him to "join the ranks of the revolution" to "reform himself" (11–12).

Ma did not find his classes at the Normal College to be difficult and upon graduation was the only student assigned to be a teacher in an institution of higher education. He spent the next five years teaching English at the Hangzhou Electronics Technical College and began teaching night classes to friends who were involved in foreign trade. Night instruction enabled Ma to establish a network of associates and learn more about foreign trade and global business. At the Technical College, Ma was a dynamic teacher and performer (14). In his teaching and professional life, he was viewed as a performer with street smarts who spoke to the heart of issues in simple language. One of Ma's perceived strengths was his willingness to defy conventional rules. His early professional life is marked with failures but a steady refusal not to let those failures deter him. The qualities of grit and determination served him well as he embarked upon his business career. Often Ma was able to conceptualize scenarios that others might miss through his ability to think outside the box (Shiying and Avery 2009, 182).

Professional Career

In January 1994, at the age of thirty, Ma left his teaching position and established the company Hangzhou Haibo Translation Agency. The government granted his company permission to register as a business that specialized in translations. Initially, the company floundered, and to shore up income, Ma sold flowers, clothes, and books on the street. By 1995, however, the company began to earn a profit and Ma did not have to raise income through street sales of various items. Ma also continued teaching his night classes to businesspeople. Before long, the Hangzhou municipal government chose Ma to go to the United States and serve as both an interpreter and mediator in business negotiations. On his trip back to China, Ma was able to contact a U.S. Internet service provider and he developed the idea of starting a company in China that sold an array of Chinese products over the Internet. While in America, Ma had his first web page constructed for his translation company with prices and a telephone number listed.

Ma initially was not knowledgeable about the Internet but grasped the idea that it represented a great opportunity to put information about Chinese enterprises on the world wide web and sell products throughout the world. In 1995, he raised some money and established the company China Yellow Pages. His idea was to establish a business-to-business (B2B) e-commerce network where associates in the United States would be responsible for uploading content for websites. Ma's role would be to attract business advertisers of various products from China. Few businesses at the time understood the Internet and they therefore were reluctant to advertise on an unknown outlet. Eventually, Ma convinced a hotel in Hangzhou and a law office to have Ma's company put up information on the Internet. Before too long, China Yellow Pages expanded to twenty-seven cities throughout China and began to be profitable. Ma's company eventually severed relations with its U.S. collaborators and began to develop its own websites for advertising products. China Yellow Pages later merged with a larger company that had good political connections. However, Ma had some disagreements with the new owners of the company. These disagreements led Ma to transfer his shares of the enterprise to employees and he departed from the company in 1997 (38).

At the request of the government, Ma then set up a company to develop a website for the Ministry of Foreign Economic Relations and Trade (MOFERT). He drew a salary and held 30 percent of the shares in the company; however, he felt stifled working for the ministry in the capital of China, Beijing. Ma decided to move back to his home city, joined by his entire team. Ma considered his experience with the ministry MOFERT a failure but lessons learned would help him achieve success with his new entrepreneurial venture, Alibaba (Shiying and Avery 2009, 41–42). The germ of Ma's idea in starting Alibaba was to serve the 30 million or so small- and medium-sized enterprises in China with a business-to-business (B2B) system. Ma understood that small enterprises in China were severely disadvantaged in dealing with huge purchasers such as Walmart and could benefit from trade with each other. He recognized that Asia was the largest supplier for exports to other parts of the world and among the many small companies in Asia, most did not have channels to reach a broad market. Use of the Internet through Ma's Alibaba company would open up sales by small Chinese companies to buyers in America and Europe. In February 1999, Ma launched the Alibaba e-commerce company declaring that the Internet could make small companies an invincible force (50).

Ma set up Alibaba with three goals in mind: (1) to last for 102 years, (2) to provide e-commerce services to China's small- and medium-sized companies, and (3) to set up the world's largest e-commerce company. As Alibaba grew, it attracted outside investors. By 2001, Alibaba had the largest B2B website membership in the world. In 2004, Alibaba became the largest public offering (IPO) of all time to open on the New York Stock Exchange. In 2005, Taiwan-born technology leader and then the CEO of Yahoo! Jerry Yang invested $1 billion and handed over all of Yahoo! China's operations in exchange for a 40 percent stake in the company (Cheng 2017).

Yang's investment helped catapult Alibaba into the big leagues. The $1 billion infusion of capital enabled Alibaba to build its consumer-to-consumer (C2C) portal, Taobao.com. The Taobao portal was not profitable for the first several years, as Alibaba had to spend large sums to outpace eBay. The company eBay, which once dominated China's consumer-to-consumer Internet market with a 70 percent market share, had to retreat in 2006 after seeing sales dwindle. Alibaba's platforms were then able to control the vast majority of China's online shopping markets in terms of value of goods sold, especially after factoring in transactions via mobile phone apps. Two factors aided in Alibaba's success: (1) an early entry into meeting demand for consumption and (2) its huge user base has made it a valuable partner for others (Cheng 2017). In 2009, as lead investor in a group of investment banks, the U.S. firm Goldman Sachs invested $5 million, a short time later the Japanese holding company Softbank Group invested $20 million.

Some asset managers caution against investing heavily in Alibaba. They note that there could be a rise in bureaucratic crackdowns as Alibaba and other Chinese e-commerce companies expand into online finance. Others see Alibaba as coming under attack from powerful interests in Chinese political circles who fear Alibaba's impact on China's shopping malls and department stores. Those same sources, however, note that President Xi, who visited Alibaba's offices and met with Ma when Xi was party chief of Zhejiang from 2002 to 2007, has played a hand in protecting the company from overzealous bureaucrats. Alibaba insists that the company is not a threat to large retailers pointing out that Alibaba is helping many retailers transition to the online economy. In 2017, Ma announced that gross merchandise volume on Alibaba's platforms have already crossed the half-a-trillion-dollar mark.

Alibaba's international business-to-consumer platform continues to make inroads into markets outside of Asia. They have become the top e-commerce platform in Russia (Cheng 2017).

Alibaba's business model is based on charging fees from China suppliers rather than from advertising or receiving a percentage of transactions. Important services provided by Alibaba include verification of buyer credentials, a safe method of making payments, help in creating websites, and the ability to respond quickly to customer inquiries (Shiying and Avery 2009, 197). Eventually, Alibaba was able to move beyond its initial B2B emphasis and branch out to providing consumer-to-consumer services (C2C), business-to-consumer services (B2C), electronic payment services, shopping search engines and cloud computing services. Despite its size, Alibaba does not put a great deal of money into advertising and does not pay high salaries. The company attempts to attract talent by developing team spirit and a "happy" corporate culture with a flat hierarchy (108).

Jack Ma's general attitude toward wealth and business helped to sustain his professional success. He sees himself as an entrepreneur rather than a garden-variety businessperson. In his mind, a businessperson focuses on making money whereas an entrepreneur takes on the more important mission of bringing about positive change. He believes that entrepreneurs create value for society. Ma sees himself as someone who wants to change the history of China's e-commerce. He stated, there are many people who understand how to make money but not many who can push society to make itself better. He noted that to make a great company you have to improve upon society (Shiying and Avery 2009, 186). Ma built a formidable company. As of 2020, Alibaba Group Holding Limited comprised more than 117,000 employees, with a net income of approximately $20 billion, and total assets of approximately $185 billion. In 2008, Alibaba exceeded $500 billion in its valuation on the New York Stock Exchange (Jao 2018). In Fiscal Year 2016, Alibaba surpassed Amazon and eBay combined in online sales, profits topped those of all U.S. online retailers combined. Analysts estimate Alibaba's Internet platforms control close to 80 percent of China's online shopping in terms of gross merchandise value of goods sold. Alibaba hopes to grow along with a rising middle class of consumers in China and emerging markets outside of Asia. Previously, Chinese President Xi Jinping was a strong booster of Alibaba. Some analysist, however, caution that China's tech sector is highly protected and Alibaba may have a harder time succeeding overseas than domestically in the Chinese market. The government of China largely restricts foreign Internet companies, such as Google, Twitter, and Facebook in China. Alibaba may face similar political obstacles as it tries to expand in foreign markets (Cheng 2017).

In October 2020, Ma publicly criticized Chinese regulators for stifling innovation by being too risk averse. He noted that to innovate one must take risks. Subsequently, Chinese regulators blocked the planned Initial Public Offering of Alibaba's financial affiliate, Ant Group. The IPO would have been the world's biggest stock market listing. The Ant Group is China's biggest online payments platform, offering everything from investment accounts to insurance, credit scores, and even dating profiles. Following Ma's 2020 statements, China also launched an antitrust investigation into Alibaba. Chinese officials said it would investigate the company's practice of requiring merchants to sign agreements that prevent them from selling products on rival platforms. The State Administration for Market Regulation (SAMR), China's top market regulator, instituted new guidelines that it said are intended to prevent Internet monopolies (He 2020).

Some speculate that an underlying rationale for tighter regulation was that the rapid growth of Chinese tech giants diminished the influence of state-owned banks that in turn diminished the power of the Chinese Communist Party. Alibaba pledged to cooperate with antitrust investigators. China's harder line on Jack Ma and Alibaba coincides with increasingly negative perceptions of the e-commerce billionaire. Some call Ma a "villain," an "evil capitalist," and a "bloodsucking ghost." Perceptions of diminished economic opportunity fuel growing discontent toward Ma and other billionaires. While China had more billionaires than the United States and India combined about 600 million of its people earned $150 a month or less in 2020. Young people, who have borrowed from a new generation of online lenders like Ma's Ant Group, have debts they increasingly resent (Yuan 2020).

The Communist Party seems willing to tap into popular resentment. The party vowed to prevent what it termed the disorderly expansion of capital. Following the cancellation of the Ant Group public offering, Xi Jinping, China's top leader, toured a museum exhibit devoted to an industrialist who helped build up his hometown, and opened hundreds of schools. With members of the business community, Xi pointed to the industrialist as a role model and urged the people at the meeting to rank patriotism above all else. Some pro-market people in China worried that the country might be drifting toward the hard-line of the 1950s (Yuan 2020).

Observers of China say Ma was lying low as authorities turned up the heat on his businesses. They note that it is not unlike Beijing to dole out punishment for prominent Chinese figures who clash with the interests of the Chinese Communist Party. For example, the actress Fan Bingbing dropped out of sight in 2018 before reappearing in 2019 to apologize for tax evasion. Real estate tycoon Ren Zhiqiang was jailed for eighteen years on corruption charges after he allegedly criticized President Xi Jinping's handling of the coronavirus pandemic (Wang 2021).

BRIEF BIOGRAPHIES OF REMAINING SUCCESSFUL ENTREPRENEURS

Jeff Bezos, Bill Gates, Mark Zuckerberg, Larry Ellison

Jeff Bezos

Jeffrey Jorgensen (later known as Jeff Bezos) was born on January 12, 1964, in Albuquerque, New Mexico, the son of a 17-year-old high school student and a bike shop owner. Following his parent's divorce, Jeffrey's mother married Cuban immigrant Miguel Bezos and Jeffrey Jorgensen became Jeffrey Bezos. As a youth, Bezos lived in Houston, Texas, and Miami, Florida. Displaying scientific interests and technological proficiency, Bezos became a high school valedictorian and a national merit scholar. He attended Princeton University and graduated summa cum laude, earning a bachelor of science in engineering (BSE) with an emphasis in electrical engineering and computer science. Following graduation, Bezos worked at a telecommunications start-up company, in the banking industry, and a newly created hedge fund. In 1994, with $300,000 in funding from his parents, Bezos established his signature company Amazon out of a garage in Seattle, Washington. He began Amazon as a vendor of books through the Internet.

Early critics argued that Amazon would not survive once the large book chain stores such as Borders and Barnes & Noble launched their own websites. However, adopting the slogan "Get Big Fast," by 1997, Bezos's company had one million customer accounts. In that year, Amazon raised $54 million in an IPO; in 1999, *Time* magazine named Bezos Person of the Year. Over time, Amazon branched out to more than selling books. In 1998, Amazon began to sell music and videos over the Internet; in 1999, it began to sell items such as consumer electronics, video games, software, home improvement items, toys and other goods.

Amazon attracted a loyal clientele with personalized services such as special recommendations for products to purchase. It morphed into a technology company in addition to its original focus on consumer sales. In 2002, Amazon launched Amazon Web Services (AWS) to sell data about Internet traffic patterns. It expanded its AWS services later by renting out computer processing power; it also began to rent data storage over the Internet. AWS became Amazon's most profitable division. Rather than depend on shippers, Amazon began to maintain its own inventory and manage product supplies for businesses. As the company grew, it began to sell its own Kindle e-book readers.

In addition to Amazon, Bezos began to invest in other companies. In 2000, Bezos founded Blue Origin, a spaceflight start-up company. In 2013, he purchased the *Washington Post* and began to reconstruct its digital media and mobile platforms. With an increase in online readership in 2016, the paper was profitable for the first time since the acquisition. In 2015, Bezos announced that an orbital launch vehicle was under development at Blue Origin. In that year, Blue Origin launched a space vehicle that successfully landed back at its launch site in West Texas. Bezos has spoken freely about his hopes to colonize the solar system, and has been selling Amazon stock each year to capitalize Blue Origin. His public persona and personality has been described as that of a brilliant but mysterious and cold-blooded corporate titan (Wingfield and Bowles 2018).

Bill Gates

Bill Gates is best known as the cofounder of Microsoft Corporation. Gates was born on October 28, 1955, in Seattle, Washington. His family possessed a rich business, political and community service background. His great-grandfather was president of National City Bank of Seattle (1911–1929) and director of the Seattle Branch of the Federal Reserve Bank of San Francisco. His grandfather was a bank vice president and his father a prominent Seattle lawyer. Bill Gates's mother Mary Maxwell Gates was involved in philanthropy and became the first woman to serve as president of the Seattle area's United Way. Later, Mary Gates served on the board of the national United Way with IBM CEO John Open. She became the first woman to lead Seattle's United Way. Using her personal connections, Gates's mother helped her son secure a contract with IBM to build an operating system for IBM's first personal computer. At the time, Microsoft was only a small software company. Bill Gates is the fourth of the family name but is known as William Gates III or "Trey" for three (Manes 1994, 15).

At the young age of thirteen, Bill Gates enrolled at Seattle area prep school and wrote his first computer program. He met his future partner Paul Allen at the prep school, graduated in 1973, scored 1,590 out of 1,600 on his SAT and entered Harvard University. Gates met fellow student Steve Ballmer at Harvard and left college after his second year. Upon leaving, Gates declared that he learned all he could from Harvard and moved to Albuquerque, New Mexico, to set up Microsoft with his friend Paul Allen. The company began writing programming languages for the first commercially popular personal computer (Maxwell 2002, 65). Over time, aided by their relationship with IBM, Microsoft was transformed from a small business to the leading software company in the world. Sales of the software (MS-DOS) made Microsoft a major player in the industry. In 1981, Gates became president and chairman of the board of Microsoft with Paul Allen as vice president and vice chairman. In early 1983, Allen left the company after being diagnosed with cancer.

Some people characterize Gates's management style as verbally combative often berating senior managers and program managers. According to economist James Henry, almost everyone had an opinion of Microsoft and it was always negative. In a 1990 article that appeared in *Business Month*, Henry states that Gates gained his wealth by being tediously technical, less innovative, and a ruthless dealmaker who freely "borrowed" from partners and grew fat as a parasite growing on their success. Henry concluded that Gates now has such a large stake in the status quo and that it holds up progress by creating entry barriers to innovation in order to protect its profit margins (124). In the 1998 antitrust case (*United States v. Microsoft*), Gates gave testimony that several journalists characterized as evasive. In 2006, Gates announced that he would transition out of his role at Microsoft to dedicate more time to philanthropy.

Mark Zuckerberg

Born in 1984, Mark Zuckerberg, at the age of twenty-three, became the world's youngest self-made billionaire. As of 2019, he was the only person under fifty in the Forbes ten richest people list, and the only person under forty in the Top 20 Billionaires list. Zuckerberg was raised in a small town of Westchester County about 21 miles from Midtown Manhattan. His dentist father and psychiatrist mother encouraged young Mark's interest in computers and when he was eleven hired a tutor who referred to Mark as a computer prodigy. At his local high school, Zuckerberg excelled in his classes and after two years, transferred to the prep school Phillips Exeter Academy. He entered Harvard in 2002 with a reputation as a competent programmer and by his sophomore year he developed the software "CourseMatch" that enabled users to select classes based on choices of other students. Later he created a program that allowed users to look at photos of two people and choose the person that they thought looked more attractive. While at Harvard, several students asked Zuckerberg for assistance in developing a website named "Harvard Connection" to connect Harvard students. Zuckerberg then developed his own site that evolved into his company Facebook. Zuckerberg dropped out of Harvard by the end of his sophomore year to run Facebook. The Harvard students that requested Zuckerberg's assistance sued Zuckerberg claiming that he stole their idea and stole the execution of the idea. Zuckerberg later settled the lawsuit. Messages sent by Zuckerberg while at Harvard do not indicate theft but portray him as conniving and insensitive (Vargas 2010).

Soon after launching Facebook in 2004, Zuckerberg and a few friends moved to California and leased space in Palo Alto. They received early funding from venture capitalist and founder of PayPal, Peter Thiel. Zuckerberg and his associates turned down offers by major corporations to buy the company. By 2006, Facebook had become a worldwide phenomenon, available in Canada, the United Kingdom, as well as the United States. In 2008,

Facebook became available in several languages, including French, German, and Spanish as its worldwide popularity grew. Facebook easily outpaced the growth of one of its competitors, MySpace, a company owned by media mogul Rupert Murdoch. In 2010, Zuckerberg reported that Facebook reached the 500 million-user mark. In that same year, *Vanity Fair* magazine named Zuckerberg number one on its list of the Top 100 most influential people of the Information Age. After Facebook's Initial Public Offering (IPO) of stock in 2012, Zuckerberg's net worth was estimated at more than $19 billion.

Facebook's success created some controversy. Zuckerberg was criticized for the proliferation of fake news posts on his site leading up to the 2016 U.S. presidential election. Zuckerberg also came under fire when it was revealed that a data firm with ties to Donald Trump's 2016 campaign had used private information from Facebook profiles. In 2018, Zuckerberg announced plans to improve methods for defending Facebook users from outside users. Zuckerberg was also accused of stifling competition to Facebook by acquiring competitors such as Instagram and its WhatsApp.

Larry Ellison

Larry Ellison was not born into wealth. In 1945, at the age of nine months, his single mother sent Larry from her home in the Bronx, New York, to live with an aunt and uncle in Chicago. He did not meet his biological father (an Italian American United States Army Air Corps pilot) until he was forty-eight years old. Ellison describes his aunt and adoptive mother as warm and loving in contrast to his distant adoptive father who took the name Ellison to honor his point of entry into the United States, Ellis Island. Larry and his adoptive father in essence were sons of Ellis Island. Ellison was raised in a Reform Jewish home by his religious parents but he remained a religious skeptic. He attended a public high school in Chicago and after graduation enrolled at the University of Illinois at Urbana-Champaign. After the death of Ellison's adoptive mother, he dropped out of the University of Illinois and worked at a variety of part-time jobs. Ellison then attended the University of Chicago intending to pursue a degree in physics and mathematics. He was expelled after the first semester and in 1966 moved to California at the age of twenty-two.

When Ellison arrived in Berkeley, California, with little money, he moved from job to job without achieving great success. He became interested in computers and eventually landed a job as a programmer where he worked on the first IBM compatible mainframe system. In 1977, Ellison along with two colleagues founded the company Software Development Labs to engage in contract programming for other companies. Ellison was inspired by a paper written by computer scientist Edgar F. Codd. He recognized the commercial potential of Codd's approach to organizing large amounts of data for storage and retrieval. Ellison and his cofounders were able to secure a contract with the Central Intelligence Agency to build a database management system they called Oracle. Ellison renamed the company after this system and in 1986 the company went public under the name Oracle Corporation. A total of $31.5 million was subsequently raised in an IPO. Oracle became the leader in database management. Oracle was able to grow through multibillion-dollar acquisitions of companies such as PeopleSoft and Sun Microsystems (Larry Ellison 2019).

Ellison's business did not follow a straight upward trajectory. In 1990, Oracle posted its first negative earnings report and the company was headed toward possible bankruptcy. Ellison radically reorganized the staff and shifted his focus to product development. The company quickly rebounded and by 1992 was the leading developer of database management software. Oracle stood out as a survivor of the early 2000s recession that wiped out many tech companies. By 2010, Oracle provided software extensively to the largest corporations in the world. Ellison became one of the wealthiest people on the planet, he began to collect expensive cars and airplanes. Ellison gained a reputation as one of Silicon Valley's most divisive figures, both admired for his success, and deplored for his sometimes ruthless business methods and conspicuous consumption (Gregerson and Hall 2020).

Amancio Ortega, Sergey Brin, Michael Bloomberg, Carlos Slim Helu

Amancio Ortega

Born in 1936, the youngest of four children, Amancio Ortega was raised in León, a province in the northwestern part of Spain. Ortega left school at the age of fourteen and began work as a shop hand for a local shirtmaker. He later managed a clothing store that catered to a wealthy clientele. Ortega's success and wealth largely emanates from his ability to manufacture inexpensively and competitively priced high-end garments. He applied this business model when founding the company Confecciones Goa in 1972 to sell quilted bathrobes. In 1975, Ortega opened his first Zara store. Zara became an internationally famous chain and the flagship of the holding company Inditex. Ortega is known as a pioneer in "fast fashion" and altered the retail fashion industry by speeding the time in which clothes move from fashion runways to retail shops. Zara's garments are based on runway attire but sold at prices that moderate-income people could afford.

Virtually all of Inditex's garments are based on the "fast fashion" concept where trendspotters attend fashion shows, choose the best ideas, manufacture the garments at low cost, and deliver the garments to retail stores within a few weeks. Unlike many clothing manufacturers, Inditex does not outsource virtually all production to low-cost areas. A significant amount of the company's garment production occurs in Spain and surrounding countries. The holding company Inditex includes the popular Zara stores as well as seven other fashion-related enterprises (Chen 2008).

All of Inditex's brands follow the Zara template of trendy and decently made clothing but inexpensively sold in beautiful, high-end-looking stores. Inditex went public with an IPO in 2001 when it sold 26 percent of the company to investors putting the value of the company at around 9 billion Euros or 10.2 billion dollars. In 2007, Inditex launched the Zara Home online retail store. In 2008, Inditex became the world's largest fashion retailer with approximately 4,000 stores in 70 countries. In September 2011, Inditex brought Zara's e-commerce platform to the United States. In general, Inditex avoids magazine advertising, with print campaigns only occurring on billboards in certain regions. The company chooses to invest in prime locations for optimum visibility.

Zara developed a highly responsive supply chain that enables delivery of new fashions to their stores as soon as a trend emerges. Zara can deliver new products twice a week to its many stores around the world. Because of its speed in delivered new products, Zara is not forced to anticipate trends but can evaluate trends first, then follow. The company adopts a "just in time" management system with the objective of having inventory readily available to meet demand. Zara relies on highly automated Spanish factories, where robots work around the clock cutting and dyeing fabrics and creating unfinished "gray goods." Gray goods are typically defined as branded goods that are sold without the consent of the owner of the trademark. This strategy proved to be very successful (Petro 2012).

In 2011, Ortega stepped down as chairman of Inditex. He is considered to be a very private person and according to his communications department, he never gives interviews, nor does he attend award ceremonies or parties. Ortega's success has been attributed to personality traits, such as flexibility, commitment to hard work, and profound self-confidence. He adopted a flat organizational structure, ate lunch in the company cafeteria with fabric experts and buyers, and never visited resorts for millionaires. An online biographer stated, "Unprivileged childhood conditions and no MBA degree obtained have apparently made Amancio the man he is: possessing an entrepreneurial spirit, deeply involved with all the business routine while keeping a low profile" (Amancio Ortega Gaona Biography n.d., webpage).

Sergey Brin

To a large extent Sergey Brin's professional story is the story of Google and has already been told through the narrative of his cofounder Larry Page. Sergey's family background bears similarities with that of Page. Both Larry and Sergey attended a Montessori school, both had academic parents, both were considered computer prodigies, and both attended Stanford in the school's computer science program. To a greater extent, Brin's narrative represents the quintessential immigrant success story. Sergey was born in Moscow in 1973. His family immigrated to the United States when Sergey was six to escape anti-Semitism in Russia. Sergey lived with his family in Maryland, moving there when his father secured a position as a professor of mathematics at the University of Maryland. His well-educated mother worked for NASA on projects related to climate and weather forecasting. A brilliant student, Sergey started college in 1990 at the University of Maryland and graduated in three years with honors in mathematics and computer science. He then pursued his graduate studies at Stanford where he met Larry Page. They then worked together on a project that became the genesis of their famous search engine, Google. Initially, Sergey believed the project would make for a great dissertation topic and did not anticipate that it would make him fabulously wealthy (Scott 2008, 5).

Brin embraced a management philosophy of offering a pleasant environment to workers that would motivate and retain them. With the encouragement of Sergey, Google began to provide yoga classes, massages, bars, free ice-cream machines, organic food prepared by two chefs, a ping-pong table, a swimming pool, and two pianos. Sergey believed that providing employees with free healthy meals powered good thinking, good work, would cut down on time away from the office, and would enable employees to build a sense of community. Google built a state-of-the-art kitchen and hired a former chef for members of the Grateful Dead band (49). These amenities contributed to Google's worker-friendly environment for its talented and creative workforce.

Brin's intellectual contributions to the computer science field are also significant. He authored more than a dozen articles in top-level academic journals and has been a lecturer in various academic forums. He often speaks to the press about search engine technology and the IT industry in general. In a 2015 letter to stockholders, Sergey emphasized that Google was not just a search engine or an advertisement seller, but also a research and development company that allowed people to live healthier and happier lives. Mentioned in the letter were projects such as a glucose-sensing contact lens, means to store photos/videos, and self-driving cars. In his personal life Brin enjoys yoga, he is often on roller skates, sometimes plays roller hockey and prefers to wear jeans, sneakers, and a sports jacket (Sergey Brin biography 2020).

Michael Bloomberg

Michael Bloomberg's enormous wealth derives from his company Bloomberg L.P. He built Bloomberg L.P. around a computer that revolutionized the way security data is stored and disseminated. The company became a monolith in providing business information around the world. Aside from the core business model that is based on providing information over a computer terminal, Bloomberg News produces content for a variety of terminals, for television programming, radio, web, and mobile platforms. Bloomberg was born in 1942 and grew up in a suburb of Boston. His father was a Jewish immigrant from Poland who became a bookkeeper; his mother was a secretary.

Bloomberg graduated from Johns Hopkins University in 1964 earning a BS degree in electrical engineering. He later attended Harvard University where he obtained an MBA degree in 1965. Bloomberg then worked at an entry-level position for the investment bank Salomon Brothers. Within fifteen years Bloomberg became a partner. When Salomon was acquired by another firm in 1981, Bloomberg received a substantial buyout and used the money to create a financial data services company. The firm evolved in Bloomberg L.P. that became the source of Bloomberg's immense wealth. The Bloomberg Terminal is fundamental to the success of the data services company. This terminal delivers up to the minute financial information (Editors of the Encyclopedia Britannica 2020).

The Bloomberg Terminal connected users to a network of information, analytics, and people quickly and accurately. By 2019, it sat on the desks of at least 325,000 influential decision-makers supplying real-time information that could be obtained from any Internet-connected PC or mobile device. The terminal supplies independent research analysis from more than 1,500 sources, as well as comprehensive information at the industry and company levels. Most large financial firms have subscriptions to Bloomberg Professional Services. Terminals are leased at relatively high prices in two-year cycles. The key to Bloomberg L.P.'s success was the insight that Wall Street companies would pay a high price for in-time business information, delivered on computer terminals in a variety of usable formats. Beginning in 2012, the Bloomberg Terminal had a greater annual revenue than Thomson Reuters, the company that founded the market information business. The Bloomberg Terminal has become the standard in the financial industry. It can supply huge amounts of information about companies, make financial calculations, enact trades, and compare potential investments. Bloomberg Terminals can even provide fine-grain information such as the locations of oil tankers and wildfires (Stewart 2019).

Bloomberg left his company when he was elected mayor of New York City. He served three terms and during his tenure as mayor (2002–2013), he brought his technocratic management approach to city government. Bloomberg succeeded in applying a statistical, metrics-based management approach to city government, and granted departmental commissioners broad autonomy in decision-making. He implemented a "bullpen" office plan in city government, similar to a Wall Street trading floor, where dozens of managerial staff are seated together in a large chamber. The design is intended to promote accountability and accessibility. During his administration the city ran a budget surplus, increased funding for affordable housing, established public charter schools, raised standards in the city's public schools, invested in infrastructure, and rezoned large tracts of land. All of these efforts helped to enhance new commercial and residential construction.

Bloomberg sought to enhance entrepreneurship by supporting small businesses and strengthening industries such as film, television, bio-science, technology, and tourism. New York City experienced significant private-sector job growth even in the wake of a national recession. Bloomberg's passion for public health led to bans on smoking, anti-poverty efforts, and initiatives to fight climate change. During his tenure as mayor of New York, life expectancy in the city increased, poverty declined, and the city's carbon imprint was reduced. New York City's welfare rolls fell 25 percent, and between 2000 and 2012 New York became the only big city in the country not to experience an increase in poverty (Michael Bloomberg Biography n.d.). Some programs such as New York City's stop and frisk policy became controversial and in 2014, Bloomberg returned to Bloomberg L.P. as chief executive officer.

Carlos Slim Helu

Carlos Slim Helu (also referred to as Carlos Slim) acquired extensive holdings in the fields of communications, insurance, construction, energy, mining, retailing, publishing, and finance. He was born on January 28, 1940, in Mexico City to a family of Lebanese Christian immigrants. His father amassed a significant amount of money in real estate and taught Carlos valuable business lessons such as the importance of keeping accurate financial records. At the age of eleven, Slim purchased stock and at the age of seventeen, he worked at his father's construction company. Carlos later attended the National Autonomous University of Mexico and graduated with a degree in civil engineering. He also took economics courses in Chile and after earning an engineering degree in 1996 began a career as a stock trader. Profits from private investments grew and allowed him to start his own stock brokerage firm.

In the 1960s and 1970s, Slim invested in and founded a variety of businesses in the construction, soft drink, printing, real estate, bottling, and mining fields. He later expanded into industries such as auto parts, aluminum, airlines, chemicals, tobacco, cable manufacturing, paper, tires, cement, retail, hotels, telecommunications, and financial services. In the 1960s and 1970s, Slim began to turn around struggling soft drink and printing companies. He purchased numerous businesses at bargain prices in the aftermath of the

1982 crash and under his leadership they became profitable. Stock values of companies increased significantly. The anchor of Slim's success was his ownership of the former national telephone monopoly, Teléfonos de México (Telmex). This ownership allowed Slim to broaden his investment portfolio into American technology and telecommunications and also extend his interests in Mexican companies.

Slim benefited from close ties to Mexico's ruling party and their leaders. With his good connections to political leaders, he was able to purchase controlling interest in Telmex. The giant mobile telephone division of Telmex became a separate company in 2001 and enjoyed spectacular growth, eventually Telmex becoming one of the largest telecommunications companies in the world. In addition to Telmex, Slim was able to purchase some of Mexico's largest flagship companies. His acquisition of Telmex is illustrative of his ability to capitalize on opportunities. Over time Slim dominated the economy of Mexico and by 2015 his net worth was estimated to be about 6 percent of Mexico's gross domestic product. His empire of more than 200 companies operated across many industries and countries. In 2009, his conglomerate became the largest shareholder in the *New York Times* newspaper (Braswell 2015).

Slim attempts to combat any perception that his wealth is built on anticompetitive practices and government favors rather than his own business acumen. However, *The Wall Street Journa*l once labeled him "Mexico's Mr. Monopoly." He has been the target of anti-monopoly laws, and a focus of Mexico's attempt to regulate monopolies in telecommunications and broadcasting. Consistent with Warren Buffett's investment strategy, Slim adheres to "value investment" practices of buying stakes in companies that are grossly undervalued. In the 2000s, Slim purchased large stakes in U.S. retailers. Previously, he acquired stakes in well-known companies such as Firestone Tires, the Hershey Company, Denny's and British American Tobacco. Slim's three older sons serve in key positions in his companies. They are involved in the day-to-day running of his empire. Slim is a Maronite Catholic and prominent backer of Legion of Christ, a Roman Catholic religious institute. He has been publicly skeptical of pledges by Gates and Buffett to give away at least half of their fortunes. According to his spokesperson, Slim devotes significant amounts of money to nonprofit foundations concentrating on Mexico City's arts, education, healthcare; sports; and downtown restoration.

UNSUCCESSFUL VENTURES

It is widely reported that most small businesses do not succeed and clearly few business creators become billionaires. According to data from the Bureau of Labor Statistics, between 2007 and 2017, approximately 20 percent of small businesses failed within the first year, 30 percent of businesses failed by the end of the second year, by the end of the fifth year, about half failed and by the end of the decade, only 30 percent of businesses remained for a failure rate of 70 percent. Success or failure is affected by both internal capacity of entrepreneurs and outlier events. For example, the Covid-19 pandemic has created harsh economic conditions for many industries, including bars, restaurants, nightclubs, and other businesses that depend on close physical interaction. Small business failure rate varies significantly from industry to industry. In general, healthcare businesses and organizations tend to have a lower-than-average failure rate since the demand for healthcare services is high and steadily increasing. At the other end of the spectrum, failure rates for warehousing and transportation businesses are high; presumably, because of high start-up costs and a competitive marketplace (Carter 2021).

Analysis of 368 start-up failures revealed a variety of reasons for start-up failures (CB Insights 2019). Tackling problems that are interesting to solve rather than those that serve a market need was cited as the number one reason for business failure. Other top-cited reasons include: failure to find markets and failed pivots, failure to establish a diverse team with different skill sets, failure to pay attention to the competition, and difficulty in pricing a product high enough to cover costs but low enough to attract customers. The stories of high-profile unsuccessful ventures are legendary, two of which are those of Chris Gronet/Solyndra and Kenneth Lay/Enron.

Chris Gronet/Solyndra

The founder of Solyndra, Chris Gronet, possessed a solid Silicon Valley résumé, including a bachelor's degree in materials science and a doctorate in semiconductor processing from Stanford. As a doctoral student in the mid-1980s, Gronet worked on a semiconductor manufacturing process that involves quickly heating silicon wafers to extraordinarily high temperatures. Along with his mentor at Stanford, Gronet filed several patents and founded a start-up company called G-Squared Semiconductor. The goal of the company was to manufacture equipment for solar energy. The company was acquired in 1991 for an undisclosed sum, and Gronet stayed on as a general manager until 2002. He later joined the company U.S. Venture Partners as an entrepreneur-in-residence. In 2005, Gronet began spending time at the Colorado offices of the National Renewable Energy Laboratory, the government's premier lab for renewable energy research and development. He was able to gather insights about how solar panels could be manufactured by using different materials such as copper, indium, gallium, and selenium (CIGS) rather than silicon. Solar energy workers at the government renewable energy center described him as a very good scientist who is also an easy person to work (Hull 2011).

Gronet believed that instead of manufacturing a flat solar panel, energy could be tapped by etching CIGS material onto a glass tube and insert it into a second outer tube that would be hermetically sealed. He formed a company originally named Gronet Technologies that eventually was renamed Solyndra. Gronet personally pushed for a $535 million loan guarantee from the Department of Energy in order to build a 300,000-square-foot manufacturing facility. Solyndra was awarded the loan guarantee and the company quickly became the poster child for both the stimulus funding and the promise of green jobs. President Barack Obama visited Solyndra in 2010 and Gronet gave him a personal tour. However, in 2011, Solyndra filed for bankruptcy, throwing more than 1,000 employees out of work and igniting a debate about the role of government in supporting clean-energy companies. Former Solyndra employees described Gronet as driven and aggressively ambitious. They fault him for delusional thinking in his view that his product was superior to all others. Former employees claim that he fell dangerously in love with a solar technology that was expensive to make and had limited commercial appeal. Gronet resigned from the Solyndra board of directors shortly before the company declared bankruptcy (Hull 2011).

A variety of external factors contributed to the demise of Solyndra. These external factors included a dramatic drop in the price of silicon, a significant rise in the supply of natural gas as a result of fracking, and China's ascent in the solar industry. The financial models for solar energy were built on assumptions that the price of fossil fuels including natural gas would continue to rise. Those models began to fall apart as a natural gas boom transformed the energy landscape. China's efforts to dominate the solar energy field also contributed to making Solyndra noncompetitive. National banks and provincial government in China helped to lower the price of solar panels by giving local solar energy manufacturers generous subsidies. The national government of China compelled utilities to buy electricity from solar developers at above-market rates to offset their production costs and sell low-priced Chinese solar panels abroad (Eilperin 2012).

Ken Lay and Enron

Ken Lay was born in a small town in Missouri. His father was a Baptist preacher and Lay grew up in poverty. Later in Lay's childhood, his family relocated to Columbia, Missouri, and he attended the University of Missouri where he studied economics. After receiving bachelor of arts and master of arts degrees from the University of Missouri, he earned a doctor of philosophy degree in economics from the University of Houston. Lay worked at Humble Oil as an economist from 1965 to 1968. He climbed the corporate ladder in the energy industry and in 1982, Lay joined Transco Energy Company. He held various positions in the company until 1984 when he became chairman and CEO of the renamed Houston Natural Gas Company. When an Omaha-based natural gas transmission company bought Houston Natural Gas, in 1985, Lay gained control of the board, became the CEO, and renaming the company Enron. At Enron's peak, its shares were worth $90.75 just prior to declaring bankruptcy on December 2, 2001, shares traded at $0.26 (Segal 2021). Lay was one of twenty-nine Enron executive that sold their Enron stock as the company plummeted toward bankruptcy. Lay and other insiders received $1.1 billion by selling 17.3 million shares from 1999 through mid-2001 (Wayne 2002).

In 1990, Lay lured Harvard graduate Jeffrey Skilling away from the consulting firm McKinsey and Company to work at Enron. Skilling was later promoted to president and chief operating officer. With the help of Skilling, Lay transformed Enron into a trader of energy contracts, acting as an intermediary between natural gas producers and their customers. Enron eventually dominated the market for natural gas contracts. Over time, the culture of the company changed to emphasizing aggressive trading. The company began to focus on closing as many cash-generating trades as possible in the shortest amount of time. It began to engage in speculative trades for a wide variety of commodities including electricity, coal, paper, and steel.

As Enron began to face increased competition in the energy trading business, the company's profits shrank rapidly. In response to declining profits, Enron began to rely on dubious accounting practices, including a technique whereby the company was able to write unrealized future gains into current income statements. This provided an illusion of higher profits. Troubled assets were transferred to off-the-books limited partnerships in order to minimize perceptions of financial problems. Nevertheless, the severity of Enron's problems began to become apparent in 2001 as outside analysts began to dig into the details of Enron's publicly released financial statements. Things began to unravel as the federal Securities and Exchange Commission (SEC) began investigating Enron's dubious financial practices (Bondarenko 2019).

In 2006, Lay was convicted of one count of conspiracy, two counts of wire fraud, and three counts of securities fraud. He was also convicted at a separate trial of bank fraud and making false statements to banks. After the trial, FBI director Robert S. Mueller stated that the verdict spoke loudly about the right of investors and employees to be told the truth by their corporate leaders. Representatives of the U.S. attorney general's office proclaimed that the verdict declared that no one including the heads of Fortune 500 companies was above the law. An official Department of Justice (2006, webpage) press release declared that Lay and other executives

> engaged in at various times between at least 1999 and 2001, to deceive the investing public, the U.S. Securities and Exchange Commission and others about the true performance of Enron's businesses. . . . It had the effect of inflating artificially Enron's stock price. Prior to sentencing, Kenneth Lay died of a heart attack in Colorado.

EXPLANATIONS FOR ENTREPRENEURSHIP: AN EMPIRICAL INQUIRY

The precise nature of factors that are linked to business creation remains an enduring question. It is possible to investigate linkages between business creation and other factors using government data from sources such as the U.S. Census Bureau, the U.S. Small Business Administration, Kauffman Foundation (derived from U.S. Census data), the World Atlas and other sources. At the state level, data on new employers in 2020 (Ewing Marion Kauffman Foundation 2021), and per capita existing businesses in 2020 (U.S. Small Business Administration [2020]) provide measures of entrepreneurial growth and historical levels of entrepreneurship. These measures were compared to state human capital measured by percentage of state residents with bachelor degrees in 2018 (World Atlas 2021), tolerance measured by percentage of foreign born in 2019 (U.S. Census Bureau 2019), quality of governance, measured by desirability of state viewed from the Tiebout perspective of population change between 2010 and 2019 (U.S. Census Bureau 2021), and business climate measured by corporate tax rate (Tax Foundation 2021).

Pearson correlations were calculated for both of the entrepreneurship measures (the number of new businesses according to Kaufmann Foundation data and number of existing businesses derived from Small Business Administration publications. Correlations were calculated between these measures and state-wide indicators of education, governing quality, tolerance, and business climate. None of the relationships indicated statistical significance with the strongest relationship ($p = .127$) existing between new business creation and population change. This suggests that at the state level, popular explanations for business creation such as tolerance, education, population growth, and tax rates are not supported at the state level by the empirical data. The data also suggests that among the various explanations given for new business creation, a place's overall attractiveness measured through population growth may hold the greatest relevance. Future empirical analysis that compared the merits of various strategies can shed greater light on this question.

COMMONALITIES OF ENTREPRENEURS

The twelve successful entrepreneurs selected for investigation share many traits but differences also exist. First, by definition, all are incredibly wealthy and have had great success in their business endeavors. Second, they are all male, mostly white male. Third, for the most part they seem to possess incredible ambition, perseverance, and most achieved high academic success. Many of the discussed entrepreneurs attended some of the finest schools in the world. Fourth, with some exceptions (Ma, Ortega, and Slim) they were either born in the United States or came to America as immigrants. There does not seem to be strong regional concentrations. Four of the identified entrepreneurs were born or were raised in different areas of the East Coast (Bloomberg, Brin, Ellison, and Zuckerberg), some in the Midwest or Plains states (Ballmer, Buffett, and Page), one in the Northwest (Gates), and one in New Mexico (Bezos).

Many of the "fortunate dozen" billionaire entrepreneurs capitalized one way or another on the burgeoning field of computer science. Brin and Page created a search engine that fundamentally improved the ability to quickly find almost any information. Gates developed software that allowed users to more easily operate personal computers. Ballmer used his basic knowledge of computers to become an early employee and enthusiastic cheerleader for Microsoft. Ellison enhanced data storage and memory capacity. Bezos, Ma, Bloomberg, and Zuckerberg all applied advances in computer technology and the Internet to link users with desired information. Bezos and Ma made purchasing products easier through their e-commerce world wide web sites, Zuckerberg facilitated connections between friends or relatives. Bloomberg allowed users of his Bloomberg Terminal to access up to the minute financial information. These entrepreneurs leveraged computer savvy to ultimately satisfy consumer demands for their products. Ortega, Buffett, and Slim took different routes to becoming wealthy. At first sight, Ortega appears to be a traditional merchandiser yet he was an innovator in quickly moving "high-end" fashion to moderate-income consumers. Buffett and Slim sought underpriced companies and were instrumental in improving their efficiency.

Another commonality of the entrepreneurs is that with few exceptions (Gates and Slim), the cohort was not born into significant wealth. Many were raised in middle-class or lower middle-class household that stressed education and hard work. Many were immigrants themselves (Brin) or early descendants of immigrants (Bezos—Cuban stepfather; Ballmer—Swiss father, Belarusian mother; Bloomberg—grandparents from Poland and Lithuania; Slim—father

Lebanese; Ellison—biological father, Italian American). Some were raised in Jewish households. This cohort of fabulously wealthy entrepreneurs were often highly demanding of their workers yet believed in flat organizational structures where employees were relatively free to advance new ideas and pursue their own lifestyles.

Each of the twelve successful entrepreneurs discussed in this chapter added something of value to society, either by creating usable products or improving efficiencies of existing businesses. They recognized that they had something to offer to consumers and that people will pay a premium for services that make life easier for them. Improvements such as better search engines and easy-to-use word processors should be viewed as a continuation of historical innovation. Just as Henry Ford became wealthy when automobiles replaced horses and buggies, Gates, Page, and Brin became wealthy when word processors replaced typewriters and search engines replaced treks to the library. Individual traits such as academic achievement, perseverance, and self-confidence appear to be related to the success of the wealthiest individuals in the world. Geographical concentrations in U.S. entrepreneurs in places such as Silicon Valley also suggests that the environment of place played a role in the creation of successful companies.

In contrast to the twelve successful entrepreneurs, Kenneth Lay did not grow up in middle class or affluence. He attended much less prestigious universities. Rather than developing a unique product of innovation, his corporation Enron developed a business model focused on high-risk speculation in future prices of commodities. Short-term profit became a goal in a high-pressure work environment. Gronet's background in terms of education and product focus resembled that of other Silicon Valley entrepreneurs. However, Solyndra differed in their dependence on government financing rather than venture capital. The company was unable to adapt to changing conditions and did not continuously innovate or alter its orientation away from its original innovation.

The fundamental value of this chapter is to provide a human face on prominent entrepreneurs. Insight into their backgrounds, habits, idiosyncrasies, and predispositions adds an element that raw numbers on factors such as company size or company growth cannot relay. The following two chapters move away from discussion of the personal element and begin to describe the effect of the overall environment on entrepreneurial behavior.

Chapter 5

The Educational and Legal Environment for Development

The previous chapter explored narratives of the lucky few individuals who acquired enormous wealth through entrepreneurial activity. Many of these individuals were either born in the United States or immigrated to the United States. Was this accidental or did U.S.-specific factors play a role in the development and attraction of individuals that would become enormous wealth creators? This chapter explores the educational and legal environment in the United States. The chapter argues that the creation of very successful enterprises was not a matter of luck or chance but that these enterprises were fostered by established favorable rules, the U.S. educational system and the U.S. legal system. Individual narratives do not prove that one place is superior to another in wealth creation. They, however, suggest that place of residence is not irrelevant to entrepreneurship because entrepreneurs exist within a broader environment or ecology that can either discourage or encourage certain types of behavior.

The United States has been a magnet for generations of adventurers and risk takers. It has been and apparently still is a fertile place for people seeking their fortunes. Many native-born Americans as well as immigrants have found their pot of gold at the end of the proverbial rainbow by starting small businesses. Many of these small businesses have evolved into massive enterprises. These massive enterprises in turn benefited others who served as well-paid employees of giant companies. Some small entrepreneurs have struggled but managed to survive and attain modest success, a success they previously only dreamed of attaining. Anecdotal stories as well as actual numbers of successful entrepreneurs in the United States suggests that location was not unrelated to outcomes. Entrepreneurs benefited from an educational infrastructure that allowed them to soak up previous knowledge, explore and make discoveries at the cutting edge of innovation. Legal systems allowed people to form businesses with minimal entry requirements, such as complex rules and intrusive regulations. Many assert that the general business climate, the tax structure and the political environment was conducive to risk taking since it allowed entrepreneurs to retain the fruits of their efforts.

INSTITUTIONAL ENVIRONMENT FOR ENTREPRENEURSHIP

The institutional perspective of development has attracted a good deal of attention in recent years (Galiani and Sened 2014; North 1990). Institutions have been described as both formal (laws, constitutions, property rights) and informal (sanctions, customs, traditions, and codes of conduct). These forces underpin societies and cultures of a place. According to Nobel Prize-winning economist Douglas North, many economists overlook the importance of institutions that are required to create efficient markets. This chapter describes the environment for entrepreneurism in the United States with regard to education and law. These institutional features support the broader ecology of place.

The success of U.S. entrepreneurs suggests that characteristics of the United States have placed it in a very favorable position in regard to entrepreneurship and wealth creation. Wealth creation in the United States appears to have benefited from the nation's social, political, educational and legal environment. This is a matter of speculation, however, many of the "top self-made" billionaires in the world reside in the United States. Is this coincidence or driven by other forces? Statistics tells us that the likelihood a randomly selected country would contain so many of the top billionaires is extremely unlikely. Environment plays a role; the seeds of innovation and creativity can be thrown on fertile or barren ground. Norms, customs, values, and history establish ecological systems that shape entrepreneurial behavior that in turn influences growth or decline. The evolution of the nation's educational and legal structures help establish institutional norms and are reviewed in greater detail in this chapter.

UTILITY OF A POSITIVE EDUCATIONAL ENVIRONMENT

Education is often cited as a bridge toward the "American Dream" and as a ladder for economic opportunity. For generations, education has been a gateway to middle-class employment and upward mobility. At the aggregate level, empirical data supports the correlation between education and income.

According to data from the U.S. Bureau of Labor Statistics, in 2019 median weekly earning for persons with a doctoral degree was $1,883 while those with professional degrees enjoyed weekly earnings of $1,861. In contrast, median weekly earnings for persons with less than a high school diploma was $592. The unemployment rate of those with less than a high school diploma was 5.4 percent compared to 1.1 percent for persons holding a doctoral degree (Bureau of Labor Statistics 2020). These disparities should come as no surprise and is consistent with the dominant view that education enhances prospects for higher earnings.

According to the Bureau of Labor Statistics, occupations that typically do not require a college degree for entry earn roughly 42 percent of the annual average for occupations that typically require at least a college degree (Cross 2018). Access to better education has also improved. U.S. Census Bureau data indicates that in 1940 only 24.5 percent of persons in the United States age 25 and older completed high school while only 4.6 percent completed four years of college or more. By 2014–2018, 87.7 percent completed high school and 31 percent completed college. In theory, access to a more extensive education should result in higher productivity and higher earnings. Educational attainment at the highest levels with attendance at some of the most prestigious universities in the world in theory should also enhance innovation. Innovation in the view of economist Joseph Schumpeter drives capitalist development. As the old goods and services are replaced by the new, those jurisdictions that can create the new goods and services will be rewarded while those that are not at the cutting edge of innovation will stagnate and digress. The quality and historical evolution of a place's education system therefore is of paramount importance.

EARLY HISTORY OF U.S. EDUCATIONAL SYSTEM

Education in Colonial Times

In colonial time, education was viewed as essential for developing the character of individuals. This was especially true for the Puritans of the Massachusetts Bay Colony. The Puritans of New England valued education, both for the sake of religious study and for the sake of citizens who could participate in town meetings. A 1647 Massachusetts law (commonly referred to as the "Old Deluder Satan Act") mandated that every town of 50 or more families support an elementary school and every town of 100 or more families support a school where a few boys could learn Latin in preparation for college, the ministry or law. Virtually all New England towns made an effort to provide some schooling for their children. Young people whose education was neglected could be removed from their parents or masters. Wealthy children studied with private tutors while middle-class children could learn to read from literate parents. Many poor and middle-class white children, as well as virtually all Black children, went unschooled (Knight 1922).

The emphasis New England Puritans placed on literacy influenced the relatively high literacy rate of the entire Thirteen Colonies, in comparison to European nations of the times. Puritans especially held on to the view that children should be taught at home, in the church, and in a school, referred to as the "Holy Triad" (Jeynes 2007, 4). While schooling was emphasized in New England relative to other colonies, the Puritans also contended that if a child's home life was not correct then their education would not be put to proper use. Therefore, what a child learned at church and school had to be put into practice in everyday life. The church was responsible for teaching the Bible and along with religious principles, the church generally controlled all education. Colonists believed that the school was accountable for molding children into virtuous individuals, which was perceived as the ultimate goal of education (5). Every school the Puritans founded, including Yale and Harvard, focused on spiritual truths and teachings.

Education also played an important role in other colonies. The Mid-Atlantic colonies with its more diverse population (consisting of Dutch, English, Irish, Scottish, and German colonists) were more varied in their religious beliefs and did not develop a common school system such as the system of the New England colonies. In the Mid-Atlantic colonies each group often developed their own schools which promoted their own culture, religion and traditions. For example, the Quakers who settled in Philadelphia, the city of "Brotherly Love," emphasized tolerance of others.

In the southern colonies, the wealthy plantation owners developed their own system of education to prepare their sons for further schooling. Children from poorer households received a minimal education and slaves from Africa only learned what was necessary to attend to the needs of their owners. Sons of the wealthy were generally tutored with the objective of preparing them for college on the European continent. By the 1600s, colonist began establishing their own institutions of higher learning. In 1636, Harvard College became the first post-secondary school on the North American continent. In 1693, the College of William and Mary was founded in Williamsburg, Virginia. Dame schools were also common in the colonies. These schools were usually established by women and charged a modest fee. Education at dame schools concentrated on reading, writing, and calculation (Colonial America 1999).

The influence of New England settlers on the development of U.S. education cannot be minimized. Some of the most significant educational accomplishments were made in the first few decades after the arrival of the Pilgrims, in 1620, and the Puritans, in 1630 (Jeynes 2007, 1). These accomplishments included establishing Harvard College (1636), Boston Latin School (1635), the nation's first secondary school, and compulsory education. This foundation provided the underpinning for a schooling system that would one day become the envy of the world. The colonial emphasis on education was influenced by Puritan ministers, many of whom were graduates of Oxford and Cambridge universities. Puritan leaders strongly believed that ministers should be trained for work in the new colony. To the Puritans, serving God was of utmost importance, and education was a means to that end (6). The highest emphasis was placed on reading, so that children could read the Bible as soon as possible. The fact that the Puritans kept records of the number of volumes owned by the leaders demonstrates the emphasis that they placed on literacy.

The years from 1635 to 1637 were crucial in the history of American education and governance. In those years, advances by the Puritans and Pilgrims set the stage for future achievements. Legislation such as the Old Deluder Satan Act of 1647 asserted that Satan wanted people to be ignorant, especially of the Bible. Therefore, the Act concluded that it was the responsibility of each community to ensure that ignorance did not prevail among the youth. Six major principles were enunciated in the legislation: (1) universal education of youth is essential to the well-being of the state; (2) the primary obligation for education rests with the parents; (3) the state can justifiably enforce this obligation; (4) educational opportunity must be provided, even if it is at public expense; (5) the state has the right to establish a minimum educational standard; and (6) tax money may be used to fund education (Martin 1894).

In later years, the U.S. education borrowed heavily from other models, especially the Prussian model of education. This model was adopted by reformers such as nineteenth-century Massachusetts secretary of education Horace Mann. Mann's adaptation of the Prussian model of "common schools" quickly gained acceptance, especially in northern states. The concept of common schools is rooted in efforts to fund schools in every community with public dollars and incorporate public schooling.

LATER INFLUENCES ON THE U.S. EDUCATIONAL SYSTEM

Prussian Model of Education

The Prussian model of education was adopted by American public schools and universities in the late eighteenth century. The 1806 defeat of Prussia at the hands of Napoleon provided the basis of the educational reform. After the Napoleonic wars, Prussia adopted their reforms in an effort to regain their former glory; enlightenment ideas were embraced by Prussia in line with those of other European nations. Friedrich von Humboldt was a leading advocate of the Prussian model. Over time this model became synonymous with the Humboldt Model of education and was adopted in the United States by education reformers such as Horace Mann.

The core principle of the Humboldt Model is to integrate the arts and sciences with research to achieve both comprehensive general learning and cultural knowledge. The intent of Humboldt's model is to go beyond vocational training and recognize that there are certain kinds of knowledge that are required for the cultivation of the mind and character. Humboldt contended that people cannot be good craft workers, merchants, soldiers or businesspeople unless they are well-informed human beings and citizens. He argued that if the foundation of character is laid in schooling, vocational skills are easily acquired later and people can move from one occupation to another. As an official in the Prussian government, Humboldt reformed Prussia's education system according to humanist principles and founded the University of Berlin in 1810. Berlin University became well regarded for appointing distinguished scholars to both teach and conduct research. The philosophy of the university departed from pre-Napoleonic views as well as the Napoleonic model of centralized, bureaucratic control. In contrast, the Humboldt Model featured autonomy and academic freedom (Anderson 2016). Berlin University was regarded as the world's preeminent university for the natural sciences during the nineteenth and early twentieth century. The school is linked to major breakthroughs in physics and other sciences by professors, such as Albert Einstein. The university was renamed Humboldt University of Berlin in 1949.

In Humboldt's Prussian model, both teaching and research were combined in contrast to the French model that separated teaching and research. The Prussian model emphasized the principle that students should be taught by professors actively engaged in research and should themselves share in the search for truth. This reflected the German ideal of liberal education as a self-directed and harmonious unfolding of the individual personality. Humboldt distinguished between schools, where teaching was dogmatic, and universities, where science and learning should be pursued freely for their own sake. He believed that once students arrived at universities they should shape their intellectual lives in the context of a community of learning. For this to occur, freedom of learning and teaching were essential. Under the Prussian model, fixed curricula did not exist, professors were free to follow their own scientific path, and students were free to construct their own patterns of learning. Knowledge was to be established by rigorous investigation and criticism, independent of national bias, politics, or religion. After the German empire was founded in 1871, academic freedom was protected in state constitutions.

Humboldt adopted a broad vision for education as a builder of character. The Prussian model was flexible without fixed curricula, defined years of study, or regular examinations. Professional examinations for medicine, law, the civil service, and teaching existed and were run by the state. The universities were able to award PhD degrees as a sign of academic achievement. Unity of teaching and research put the professor at the heart of the university; German professors became powerful and respected figures. The concept of the seminar, along with the PhD, was the feature of Prussian education most copied elsewhere. The seminar represented a group of students working with the professor on related research topics. In the sciences, the equivalent to the seminar was the laboratory or institute where professors trained researchers. The origins of the modern research laboratory are often seen as derivative of the Prussian model (Anderson 2016).

Humboldt sought to create an educational system based on unbiased knowledge and analysis. Prussian universities achieved broad autonomy and allowed professors' the right to select university administrators. Professors were chosen from a list submitted by faculties. State control was tempered. After 1871, universities were the responsibility of the separate German states not the responsibility of the central government. The German education system became renowned for its contribution to science and its education system abetted industrial expansion. Disciplines such as physics and chemistry contributed directly to industry, however, universities were generally hostile to applied science, technology, or commercial subjects, which were taught in technical high schools.

The legacy of Humboldt and the Prussian model that he promoted contributed greatly to the system of education in the United States today. By the 1830s, the Prussian model was characterized by free primary schooling for poor citizens, professional teacher training, a basic salary for teachers, recognition of teaching as a profession, an extended school year, funding to build schools, supervision to ensure quality instruction, curriculum inculcating a strong national identity, and science and technology instruction (Origins of Prussian Education System 2004–2020). The Prussian model required that all young citizens, both girls and boys, be educated by mainly municipality-funded schools from the age of five to thirteen or fourteen. Education reformers in the United States embraced Prussian education principles such as tax-funded schools and compulsory primary education. They also followed Prussian education reforms such as state certification requirements for teachers.

The Prussian model consisted of an eight-year course of primary education providing not only basic technical skills needed in a modernizing world but also music and religious (Christian) education. Working in close cooperation with the churches, the Prussian model tried to impose a strict ethos of duty, sobriety, and discipline. Over time, other features of the Prussian model emerged, including age-based grade levels, letter grades, professional hierarchies, permanent student records, and minimum number of school days.

Critics of the Prussian model claim that in reality it did not achieve Humboldt's goals of autonomy and character building since it suppressed innovative thinking while promoting subservience to the state. Paradoxically, the idea of the Prussian model of education is often used interchangeably with the "factory model" of education. Despite these reservations, education reformers such as Horace Mann perceived great merit in the Prussian model and aggressively sought to implement it in the United States. In 1843, Mann traveled to Germany for the purposes of learning more about the Prussian model. He focused on implementing two aspects of Prussian education upon his return to the United States: (1) the creation of schools to train public school teachers and (2) the creation of well-appointed, safe, and well-resourced schoolhouses.

Education Reformer: Horace Mann

In the 1830s, American education reformers began to argue successfully for a greater governmental role in the schooling of all children. In 1837, Horace Mann (often referred to as the Father of the Common School) left his career as a Massachusetts lawyer and legislator to assume the duties of secretary to the newly established Massachusetts Board of Education. Mann's commitment to common schools was grounded in his belief that political stability and social harmony depended on universal education. He argued that support for nonsectarian common schools was a religious as well as a civic duty. Mann's message to the working classes was that education is the great equalizer of conditions. This message still resonates with many Americans today. Mann's message to the wealthy was that their security and prosperity depended upon having literate and law-abiding neighbors who were competent workers and who would, via the common school, learn about civic responsibility and the sanctity of private property. He contended that education was the absolute right of every human being (Cremin 1957, 87).

Reforms advocated by Mann helped to bring about state-sponsored public education, a statewide curriculum and the principle that local property taxes should finance public education. By the year 1870, all states in the United States enjoyed free elementary schools and the U.S. population boasted one of the highest literacy rates in the world. Encouraged by Mann's reforms, by the close of the 1800s, public secondary schools began to outnumber private schools. The term "common school" (a public, often one-roomed school) was coined by Mann. It refers to school's aim to serve individuals of all social classes and religions. Students often went to the common school from ages six to fourteen with the duration of the school year often dictated by the agricultural needs of particular communities.

Mann's work revolutionized the Massachusetts' school system which in turn influenced the direction of other states. U.S. common schools became tax funded, did not charge tuition, and were open to all white children. Each district was typically controlled by an elected local school board and a county school superintendent who was usually elected to supervise activities of several school districts. Mann published his views in a journal that he founded in 1838. He hoped that by bringing children of all classes together, they could share a common learning experience. In theory, such an education strategy would give the less fortunate an opportunity to advance in society.

Mann's ideas were initially resisted. He met with bitter opposition by schoolmasters who disapproved of his reforms and by religious figures who railed against the exclusion of religious instruction in public schools. Mann opposed harsh discipline, preferring positive reinforcement to physical punishment. He fully embraced Prussian model reforms which included age grading and allowing students to progress within their grade. When students completed all courses of the secondary school, they were awarded a certificate of completion (Education Reform: The Example of Horace Mann, n.d.). The reforms of Horace Mann helped to establish a school system that fostered political stability and allowed the massive numbers of immigrants that came to the United States in the late nineteenth and early twentieth centuries a means of assimilation and upward economic advancement.

Mann's lasting contribution to America is his commitment to the young of all social and economic classes. He was fundamentally dedicated to the improvement of future generations through a common education. Upon leaving his law practice he stated, "Let the next generation be my client." He asserted that he had taken himself "to the larger sphere of mind and morals." Because he perceived the present generation as "unmalleable," cast in iron, he preferred to expend energy upon young children who he perceived as "wax" that could be molded (Winship 1937, 69). Mann is considered to be a quintessential symbol of American education, the father of the public school, an object of reverence as well as revulsion among historians, an architect of educational reforms originating in the middle decades of the nineteenth century. He was convinced that the fate of children, the nation and the world depended on nurturing the young. In his annual reports as secretary to the Massachusetts Board of Education and through the contents of the journal he founded, Mann demonstrated an intense concern with children's environments. He consistently expressed the sentiments that children were vulnerable and therefore they required protection (Finkelstein 1990).

Mann supplied moral leadership for educational reforms. His message centered on the following six fundamental propositions: (1) universal popular education was necessary since a republic cannot remain ignorant and free; (2) education must be paid for, controlled, and sustained by an interested public; (3) such education is best provided in schools that embrace children of all religious, social, and ethnic backgrounds; (4) education, while profoundly moral in character, must be free of sectarian religious influence; (5) education should preclude harsh pedagogy in the classroom; and (6) education can be provided only by well-trained, professional teachers. Mann encountered strong resistance from clergymen who deplored nonsectarian schools, from educators thought his ideas undermined their classroom authority, and from politicians who viewed more centralized boards of education as an infringement on local authority. Mann's views nevertheless prevailed and provided a guide for American education (Cremin 2020).

Educational Reformer: John Dewey

Many proclaim John Dewey as the "Father of Progressive Education." His influence on the advancement of U.S. education helped to found a pedagogical movement that others would build upon. Dewey is associated educational reforms of the early twentieth century that moved away from the traditional, literature-based education into a more socially conscious curriculum. The traditional curriculum focused on memorization and mental discipline while Dewey preached a pedagogy of practical relevance. Following the prescriptions of Aristotle, Dewey was a strong proponent of learning through doing. Dewey and other progressive reformers hoped to repurpose schools with a more universal and practical bent. Learning by doing became a watchword of Dewey's progressive model of education. In addition to learning by doing, Dewey believed in education as a means to inculcate social responsibility and foster democracy. He pushed for course instruction to include projects, field work, and inquiry, rather than memorization and recitation (Hopkins 2017).

Dewey's teaching philosophy emphasized finding meaning and solving practical problems. Progressive reformers such as Dewey maintained that students should perceive knowledge naturally with teachers serving more as facilitators in the process of scientific discovery. Dewey opposed excessive bureaucracy in education because of its tendency to force students to conform to rigid routines. He opposed doctrinaire teachings that he believed made a person passive, lacking inquisitiveness. Dewey also promoted individual and intellectual freedom through education; he viewed freedom to discover knowledge as a safeguard against harmful manipulation. According to Dewey's non-traditionalist ideas, a sound education would strengthen democracy. He advocated academic freedom as an essential means to check the power of the status quo. Dewey cofounded the American Association of University Professors (AAUP) in 1915 for the purpose of protecting and preserving academic freedom of university professors.

Dewey also championed the development of professional standards. He endeavored to use schools to educate the wider community. This goal is seen today in mission statements of various universities and land-grant universities which were created to provide education to society as a whole rather than providing education exclusively for the upper-class elites. Dewey's influence is witnessed in today's provision of greater access to higher education. His ideas are incorporated in the teaching, research, and extension goals of land-grant universities that seek to create new knowledge which can be imparted on stakeholders outside of academia. He prescribed applying knowledge to contemporary social problems. Dewey's influence on education is infused within American higher education today. The concepts of social responsibility, practical relevance, learning through experience, and teachers as facilitators is present throughout college curriculum (Hopkins 2017).

Dewey encouraged students to think for themselves. He maintained that students would then be more likely to become active citizens who could help to shape a better society. He viewed education as essential for social progress. For Dewey, education would activate citizens to play a more active part in their communities and society at large. He wanted students to develop critical thinking skills in order to safeguard against those who wished to impose heavy-handed top-down leadership. Dewey also encouraged students to find compatible vocations; he believed such a discovery would lead to happiness.

Dewey has been described as the most influential philosopher in regard to education. However, some assert that application of his philosophy is becoming more infrequent due to contemporary emphasis on preparing students for passing standardized exams and state assessments. Nevertheless, it appears that some schools in the United States and throughout the world still embrace Dewey's basic concepts. These schools place strong emphasis on the importance of enhancing their communities, building strong relationships, developing higher-level thinking skills for practical application, and following student's interests when planning instruction. Some contend that students who are exposed to Dewey's pedagogy will likely be critical thinkers and significant contributors to local communities and to society in general as they mature and become adult citizens (Williams 2017, 100).

Central to Dewey's beliefs was his advocacy of a child-centered education in which the children themselves determined what was learned in the classroom. He contended that what the child enjoys learning should constitute that which is taught by the teacher. He believed that in the long term, teaching children what they enjoyed maximized the amount that they would learn. Such thinking stood in sharp contrast to the traditional approach that prioritized the ability of teachers and adults to know best what children need to know in order to function well in society. Dewey contended the goal of education is to make children into lifelong learners. He believed that teacher should attempt to do everything in his or her power to make that happen (Jeynes 2007, 219).

The foundation of universal and practical education advocated by early educational reformers such as Dewey contributed to what some consider an U.S. comparative advantage. The educational base of the United States not only fostered republican and democratic ideals but also paved the way for continuous innovation, self-sufficiency, wealth creation, and national security. Education, particularly higher education, represents one of several "export" industries in the United States in that students from all over the globe vie for placement in scores of prestigious American institutions. International students pay top dollar for the right to benefit from a system that has spawned numerous humanists, scientists, entrepreneurs, and innovators. The educational system of the United States helped to ensure political stability in periods of economic travail and security in times of peril.

INFLUENCES OF GREAT DEPRESSION, COLD WAR, AND SPUTNIK ON EDUCATION

Impact of Great Depression on U.S. Education

Crisis is a great motivator of change; this aphorism is witnessed in U.S. education as the external shocks of depression and fear of scientific inferiority produced significant transformations in U.S. education. As a response to the fiscal restraint of the Great Depression, schools learned to operate with greater efficiency and student achievements increased. The Cold War and the launching of the Russian satellite Sputnik represents a second external factor that caused the United States to make alterations in its instructional priorities (Jeynes 2007, 243).

Despite funding cuts, overall student academic achievement rose during the Great Depression. It is a matter of speculation regarding why this occurred during this period of time. Various explanations have been proposed as contributing to the change. First, research indicates that in times of economic uncertainty students often work harder. During the Great Depression, the number of books that students read soared as students were more appreciative of their educational opportunities. During this period of uncertainty, the amount of time students spent reading was high. Second, during the Great Depression, lower income individuals, particularly immigrants, came to belief that the road out of poverty was neither charity nor revolution, but education (Cremin 1962, 59). During this time, there was a sense that the U.S. school system represented a path toward economic salvation. Third, the Great Depression attracted many bright people to the teaching field because they began to reevaluate their priorities. Events of the Great Depression caused Americans to reassess life and in this assessment their estimation of education rose. Many people concluded that they wanted to make a difference in the world by becoming teachers. This resulted in more qualified people entering the field. Finally, teacher salaries remained fairly stable during the Great Depression, attracting very capable people to the discipline. Statistics indicate that schools experienced budget cuts during the Great Depression, but did not cut spending on teacher salaries. In 1932, salaries for teachers and principals in many eastern states stood at 98 percent of the 1929 level. In contrast, in the nation as a whole, by 1933, personal income had fallen 45 percent from its 1929 level. With this steep drop in personal income in the nation as a whole, the relative salary level of teachers looked very attractive (Jeynes 2007, 246).

Education during the Great Depression uncovered some tensions between education reformers and parents. Many reformers looked at the economic crisis of the 1930s and concluded that perhaps capitalism had failed and that a new social order was needed. Reformers noted that the 1930s represented an ideal time to promote a progressive agenda with new ideas about pedagogy. In contrast, however, most families thought of education as a means of ensuring the future survival of their children. During this period parents were concerned with practical matters of earning a living. As a consequence, the progressive movement faced resistance from pragmatic parents. In some school district, parents complained that the progressive approach emphasized activities and projects, when in order to ensure future employment, the parents wanted to return to an emphasis on reading, writing, and arithmetic. The experience of the Great Depression suggests that resource limitation can actually work to the benefit of schools and that during times of fiscal strain the U.S. school system actually flourished. Jeynes (2007, 249) concluded that "the Great Depression was a challenging era in education. Nevertheless, despite the obstacles, schools served their purpose by giving people hope and a means by which the next generation could rise above the limitations of the times."

Impact of Sputnik on U.S. Education

The launching of the Soviet satellite, Sputnik represented a second great challenge to the U.S. education system. In 1957, Americans were stunned by the Soviet Union's launch of Sputnik, the first of a series of unmanned orbital satellites into space. This event sparked fear that the Soviet Union could drop nuclear bombs on U.S. cities and that America's technological advantages had been eliminated. A race for supremacy of space and the necessary scientific knowledge to triumph in that race quickly ensued (Montgomery 1994). This nascent space race was motivated by national security concerns and fears that the militarily strategic "high ground" would be lost. The quality of U.S. science education and education in general became a pressing focus. Many military experts and scientists concluded that the Soviet Union's satellite launch meant that they not only achieved superiority in space explorations but had also attained a decided advantage over the United States in their attempts to build intercontinental ballistic missiles (ICBMs), which could travel thousands of miles to reach their targets. Western leaders also feared that the Soviet Union might want to establish a military base on the moon.

Sputnik called for an immediate examination of the U.S. failure to become the first to explore space. Reasons cited for Sputnik's success were numerous. Some cited the large number of aeronautic engineers in the Soviet Union and their understanding of documents written in German and French. When this was revealed, social scientists and political leaders immediately blamed the U.S. education system for the country's space race failure. There was a call to examine the U.S. educational system and correct any deficiencies. Investigations revealed that the percentages of American high school students taking advanced math, science, and foreign language courses had been in steady decline for years. The percentage of high school students taking foreign language courses had peaked in the 1910s and had steadily declined to only about half of that percentage in the 1950s. Critics believed that high schools had loosened requirements for nearly every major field of study.

The perceived threat of the Soviet Union's satellite launch led directly to action to improve the U.S. educational system. Politicians agreed to support legislation that would increase both educational standards and funding. Funding was used largely to strengthen standards. The National Defense Education Act (NDEA) of 1958 called for significant increases in education spending targeted to three main areas: (1) providing help to schools for purchase equipment to aid in the teaching of math, science, and foreign languages; (2) supplying graduate fellowships in disciplines related to national defense; and (3) establishing a fund to train teachers of foreign languages, math, and science. The bill had an immediate impact in terms of tougher standards and more money.

A longer-term impact of Sputnik was the change in Americans' attitudes toward federal intervention in education. Traditionally, states and local areas played dominant roles in education, however, over time the influence of the federal government on education grew. Jeynes (2007, 263) concluded that "the federal government's response to the event [Sputnik] would forever change Americans' attitudes toward federal intervention in education." Two facts favored the establishment of federal support for schools. First, the huge numbers of baby boomers that emerged after World War II created the perception that current school facilities would be inadequate to meet the demands of the next generation. Second, more people viewed obtaining a good education as necessary for experiencing success in life. People realized that superior technology often determined who was the premier world power and that in the dangerous nuclear era, the United States could not afford to fall behind the Soviet Union technologically. SAT scores rose after 1958 as more federal aid poured into schools and tougher standards were adopted. By the mid-1960s, it was fairly clear that the United States had caught and surpassed the Soviet Union in the space race.

INNOVATION AND HIGHER EDUCATION

The concept of higher education as a driver of innovation and wealth creation is alive and well. The track record of company formation and growth indicates that many prosperous enterprises evolved from embryonic research that began at leading universities. Many graduates or student attending institutions such as Harvard, MIT, Stanford, and others leveraged their knowledge in forming immensely profitable companies. Scientific discoveries became a catalyst for economic growth and product innovation. In line with Schumpeter's writings (1976), innovation drove capitalism as the old was constantly being replaced by the new. Those at the cutting edge of innovation monetized ideas, created benefits for consumers, expanded government tax bases, and individually became wealthy. Innovators in biotechnology and computer science particularly benefited from what Schumpeter termed the "gales of creative destruction." The technologically advanced knowledge base was developed at the elementary and secondary levels and further refined in the nation's institutions of higher learning. The U.S. benefited from generations of investment in education, discovery, and scientific inquiry. These advances were transformed into marketable products by ambitious entrepreneurs.

Economic development theory supports the importance of new product development spurred by innovation. Raymond Vernon's (1966) research suggests that technological sophistication can be a driver of new product development that in turn leads to high profits, wealth creation, high wages, and general economic growth. Fundamental to Vernon's theory is the need to create and maintain sophistication in research and development. American universities have traditionally played a key role fostering basic scientific research. New products such as cures for disease or "invisible" aircraft or protection against deadly viruses derive from a base of knowledge that cannot be formed in a vacuum. A few examples of how universities can impact wealth creation either through instilling knowledge or partnering with businesses demonstrates the ability of individuals to leverage knowledge into income. Companies such as General Electric, Siemens, Rolls-Royce, and IBM have collaborated with universities for years, while a variety of younger companies including Amazon, Facebook, Google, and Uber are also using universities as a key element of their innovation and new venture strategies. Even smaller, more regionally oriented companies have come to believe that universities contribute to ecosystems to support and shape regional economies (Frølund et al. 2018).

Universities serve varied functions. These functions include creating knowledge for the next generation of solutions, serving as an extended "workbench" to solve short-term problems, and providing a flow of newly minted talent to business. Universities now are essential partners with business in creating innovation ecosystems. Silicon Valley, Kendall Square in Cambridge, Massachusetts, and Block 71 in Singapore represent visible innovation ecosystems where universities are stakeholders in private sector companies, government entities, and venture investments. While relationships in the past between universities and business have been largely ad hoc, there is evidence that relationships can become more long term and strategic. The ad hoc approach views university collaborations as focused on specific R&D needs of companies. Collaboration partners are most likely chosen based on networks between individuals at universities and those seeking their input on specific projects. The ad hoc approach has been described as an "extended workbench." In the ad hoc approach, university collaboration is limited rather than formalized into larger plans that could benefit both corporate and university parties. As a result, opportunities for broader engagement are lost.

In contrast to the extended workbench model, companies can also enter into longer-term strategic agreements with universities. Relationships are no longer simply based on personal connections between an academic and a corporate researcher but increasingly, companies select universities based on their expertise in an area of strategic importance and their familiarity with the company. Companies have started to make agreements with universities to create transparency, accelerate the deployment of projects, and encourage interfaculty collaboration on topics of shared interest. Such approaches were established in the 1980s between Harvard Medical School and Hoechst A.G., Washington University and Monsanto, MIT and Exxon; and between the University of Oxford and Rolls-Royce. Comprehensive agreements offer benefits to universities in that they enable individuals from corporate labs to become embedded on-site at the university. The agreements also provide a stable source of funding for universities and allows for more multifaceted interactions. The change from incremental problem-solving to strategic partnerships is important because it signals that universities are places not just to solve predefined problems but also to tackle ambitious challenges that have an open-ended, exploratory emphasis (Frølund et al. 2018).

University partnerships are increasingly important for companies that wish to link with the broader innovation ecosystem. Large corporations benefit from and seek university input. Familiarity with a university can also become an entry point for companies to develop broader links into the innovation ecosystem. This is beneficial to multiple parties. Businesses seek insights for product development from university researchers. Universities value the support corporations can provide in terms of providing money for research labs, research centers, and entrepreneurship programs. From the perspective of local, state, and national jurisdictions, strong institute of higher learning can lead to economic development and stronger tax bases. Businesses seek input from research centers in the belief that specific research can help the businesses innovate in expanding their product base. The establishment of a strong educational infrastructure therefore is essential to creating and sustaining the economies of places. U.S. performance at the highest levels of research is well regarded, however, there are concerns when the performance of the total U.S. population is considered.

COMPARATIVE U.S. EDUCATIONAL PERFORMANCE

The overall performance of U.S. students by international standards has been relatively good, but not exceptional. The United States ranked twenty-fifth out of seventy-eight nations that were assessed by the Organization for Economic Cooperation and Development (OECD), in 2018–2019 for math, science, and reading of fifteen-year-old students. According to the OECD's PISA (Program for International Student Assessment) study, students in the United States trailed the performance of students in nations such as China, Singapore, Macao, Hong Kong, and Estonia but recorded scores significantly higher than the lowest-ranking nations (PISA 2018; WorldWide Ranking n.d.). Table 5.1 identifies the twenty-five highest-ranking nations in terms of average scores on math, science, and reading.

The PISA scores revealed large divergences in the performance of individual students. In terms of reading, the top U.S. students ranked high in international comparison but at the same time, a relatively high proportion of U.S. students scored at the lowest levels. Scores between the top and bottom performers continued on a bifurcated path. Top performers tended to come from wealthier families. Very few students from poor families scored at the highest reading levels (Camera 2019). The relatively good performance of the highest-performing students is reflected in the reputations of U.S. colleges and universities. By international standards, the United States performs relatively well but not exceptionally when considering average performance of all students. However, U.S. universities still rank high on international comparisons.

Table 5.1 Highest Average Math, Science, Reading Scores, PISA (2018)

1	China (Beijing, Shanghai, Jiangsu, Zhejiang)
2	Singapore
3	Macao, China
4	Hong Kong
5	Estonia
6	Japan
7	South Korea
8	Canada
9	Taiwan
10	Finland
11	Poland
12	Ireland
13	Slovenia
14	United Kingdom
15	New Zealand
16	Netherlands
17	Sweden
18	Denmark
19	Germany
20	Belgium
21	Australia
22	Switzerland
23	Norway
24	Czechoslovakia
25	United States

Source: Table made by author using data from PISA (2018) World Rankings (2018).

According to the *Times Higher Education World University Rankings 2021*, the U.S. is home to many of the finest universities in the world. Table 5.2 identifies the 25 highest ranked universities-based assessments of more than 1,500 universities across 93 countries and regions. Rankings are based on thirteen performance indicators that measure an institution's performance across the four areas of teaching, research, knowledge transfer, and international outlook.

As indicated in table 5.2, in 2021, the United States claimed seven places in the top ten of the world rankings of universities. The California Institute of Technology, Stanford, and the Massachusetts Institute of Technology, ranked second, fourth, and fifth respectively. When the top twenty-five world universities were considered, the United States placed sixteen schools among the top twenty-five. The United Kingdom was the nation with the second largest number of top twenty-five universities with four. When more specialized programs that conceivably drive technology-related growth were considered, U.S. universities also ranked highly. Table 5.3 identifies the top twenty-five-ranked universities in the world in the discipline of computer science.

When considering only the discipline of computer science, six U.S. universities placed in the top ten on the world ranking (Stanford, Massachusetts

Table 5.2 Highest Ranked Universities in the World (2020)

1	University of Oxford (UK)
2	California Institute of Technology (USA)
3	University of Cambridge (UK)
4	Stanford University (USA)
5	Massachusetts Institute of Technology (USA)
6	Princeton University (USA)
7	Harvard University (USA)
8	Yale University (USA)
9	University of Chicago (USA)
10	Imperial College of London (UK)
11	University of Pennsylvania (USA)
12	Johns Hopkins University (USA)
13	University of California-Berkeley (USA)
14	ETH Zurich (Switzerland)
15	UCL (UK)
16	Columbia University (USA)
17	University of California, Los Angeles (USA)
18	University of Toronto (Canada)
19	Cornell University (USA)
20	Duke University (USA)
21	University of Michigan-Ann Arbor (USA)
22	Northwestern University (USA)
23	Tsinghua University (China)
24	Peking University (China)
25	National University of Singapore (Singapore)

Source: Table made by author using data from The World University Rankings (2020a).

Institute of Technology, Carnegie Mellon University, Harvard University, Princeton University, and the California Institute of Technology). It is interesting to note that Stanford University, ranked second in the world in computer science, was able to attract the two founders of Google, Larry Page and Sergei Brin. This is a very small sample but it is suggestive of the enormous potential of highly regarded universities in cutting-edge disciplines. The educational infrastructure in the United States that created so many highly ranked universities also contributed to the creation of highly profitable enterprises. This fact relates to the idea that high-quality education (particularly in the sciences) can lead to the formation of new industries based on innovation. Innovation and new product development serves as a corollary to high-paying jobs, high profits, and wealth creation for jurisdictions.

The association between education and economic development, better health, and national security has been long recognized. For example, in response to an inquiry by President Franklin D. Roosevelt, Vannevar Bush, former head of the U.S. Office of Scientific Research and Development (OSRD) argued that extending the boundaries of science would allow the

Table 5.3 Highest Ranked Universities in the World for Computer Science (2020)

1	University of Oxford (UK)
2	Stanford University (USA)
3	ETH Zurich (Switzerland)
4	Massachusetts Institute of Technology (USA)
5	University of Cambridge (UK)
6	Carnegie Mellon University (USA)
7	Imperial College London (UK)
8	Harvard University (USA)
9	Princeton University (USA)
10	California Institute of Technology (USA)
11	National University of Singapore (Singapore)
12	University of California, Los Angeles (USA)
13	Nanyang Technological University (Singapore)
14	Cornell University (USA)
15	Tsinghua University (China)
16	Georgia Institute of Technology (USA)
17	Hong Kong University of Science and Technology (Hong Kong)
18	Technical University of Munich (Germany)
19	UCL (UK)
20	Ecole Polytechnique Federale de Lausanne (Switzerland)
21	Columbia University (USA)
22	University of Michigan-Ann Arbor (USA)
23	University of Toronto (Canada)
24	University of Edinburgh (UK)
25	University of Texas-Austin (USA)

Source: Table made by author using data from The World University Rankings (2020).

creation of new technologies, which in turn would spur new industries, create jobs, generate wealth, and maintain U.S. power. Bush contended that new products, new industries, and more jobs relate to continuous additions to knowledge of the laws of nature, and the application of that knowledge to practical purposes. He maintained that this can only be obtained through basic scientific research.

Scientists often exhort the value of knowledge creation. They reason that progress against disease depends upon a flow of new scientific knowledge, military success depends on technology, and scientific breakthroughs will lead to more jobs, better products and profitable businesses. Basic research is seen as essential, commercial applications then build off of the basic research. In a 1945 report to President Franklin D. Roosevelt entitled "Science the Endless Frontier," Vannevar Bush contended that in order to expand the base of scientific knowledge, "the U.S. must have plenty of men and women trained in science, for upon them depends both the creation of new knowledge and its application to practical purposes" (Bush 1945, Summary of the Report). Bush's report recommended increasing the numbers of people who are trained in science because of their importance in the creation of new knowledge and its application to practical purposes. He reasoned that in order to increase those trained in science, colleges, universities, and research institutes must be strengthened. Bush noted that advances on any scientific frontier depends on the number of highly qualified scientists. To recruit more scientists that would protect U.S economic, health, and military security, he called government provision of undergraduate scholarships and graduate fellowships. This would expand opportunities to talented individuals in every part of the population. According to the report of Vannevar Bush, with few exceptions, those without the means of buying a higher education go without advanced schooling. He reasoned that increasing scholarships could help equalize opportunity. The report proposed that ability, and not the circumstance of family fortune should determine who shall receive higher education in science. Scholarships would support the idea of meritocracy and, in theory, should motivate individuals toward higher effort.

The rankings on quality of universities suggests that education represents a comparative economic advantage of the United States. Education should therefore be viewed as one of the number of key "institutions" that support the nation's economic success. Other factors besides education also influence the environment that potential entrepreneurs must navigate. The legal environment that underpins the U.S. system of justice represents a second factor of significant importance. Logic indicates that laws can either promote or suppress motivation, entrepreneurship, individual wealth accumulation, and aggregate economic growth. Factors such as red tape, property right protections, the ability to apply basic research, and the extent of corruption is a society all contribute to entrepreneurial success or failure.

ENTREPRENEURSHIP, REGULATION, PROPERTY RIGHTS, AND TAXATION

Regulatory Impediments to Business Creation

Institutions are defined as "the rules of the game" which determine the incentive structure in the society. Formal institutions include legal systems and bureaucratic structure. Informal institutions refer to customs and norms. These institutions are fundamental to decisions such as whether to or not to engage in entrepreneurship. Burdensome legal regulations can exert both indirect and direct costs to society. Indirect costs include inhibiting potential entrepreneurs from starting their business and diverting resources that are spent on complying with business regulations from more efficient uses. Direct costs of regulation include compliance costs that firms need to spend in order to operate. In addition, regulations exact costs on governments who oversee the operations of businesses (Nystöm 2010, 3).

Inhibiting entrepreneurs exacts hard to measure but real costs on jurisdictions. Places that foster entrepreneurs could conceivably benefit immensely from the creation of massive businesses such as Google, Facebook, Apple, and others. Places that hinder business location (such as New York City with regard to Amazon) deter development. Increased attention recently has been given to both the cost of administrative burdens (sometimes referred to as "red tape" associated with running a business) and the benefits of shifting public policies away from strict regulation. Empirical studies support a relationship between time, cost and number of procedures associated with starting a new firm and the number of businesses created (Klapper et al. 2006). Time associated with starting a new business was also associated with the number of firms in technology-related areas (Ciccone and Papaioannou 2006). In general, most empirical studies find that business regulations have a negative effect on the amount of entrepreneurial activities in an economy (Nystöm 2010, 2).

Regulations may make it incredibly difficult for new businesses to form. Djankov et al. (2002) found that countries differ significantly in the way in which they regulate the entry of new businesses. For example, authors note that to meet government requirements for starting to operate a business in Mozambique, an entrepreneur had to complete 19 procedures taking at least 149 business days and pay more than $200 in fees. In contrast, an entrepreneur in Canada can finish the process in two days and complete everything with two procedures. Djankov et al. (2002) concluded that in most countries in the world, legal entry for an entrepreneur is extremely cumbersome, time-consuming, and expensive. Stricter regulation of entry was not associated with higher quality products, better pollution records, better health outcomes, or more competition. Stricter regulation of entry was associated with sharply higher levels of corruption, and a greater relative size of the underground economy. High levels of regulation appear to incentivize corrupt behavior that evades regulation. Constraints on operating legitimate businesses can lead to an expansion of bartering and working off the books. Countries with open access to political power, constraints on the executive, and political rights were characterized by less burdensome regulation of entry. In 2002, the United States ranked sixth out of eighty-nine countries in terms of total number of entry procedures, time, and cost for creating businesses (Djankov et al. 2002, 18).

The relative ease of business creation in the United States represents an advantage over other nations. Screening of new business applications can also deter or foster business. In theory, screening aims to keep out "unattractive" projects or entrepreneurs. There are large cross-country variation in terms of the number, time, and cost of screening procedures. Regulations can protect the public from undesirable enterprises or it can limit free-market competition. Public choice theorists view regulations as a tool of the incumbent industry that are designed with the intent of limiting competition and raising profits. Stricter regulation leads to high barriers to entry which gives advantages to established firms. A second variant of public choice theory views regulation from the perspective of potential gains for politicians and bureaucrats. Politicians can use regulations to extract campaign contributions and bribes. Officials with the power to deny permits facilitates collecting bribes in return for government approvals.

From the public choice perspective, regulations are highly pernicious. Regulations can be used by despotic regimes in order to maximizing bribes to bureaucrats and profits of political cronies. Djankov et al. (2002, 28) state that dictators "use distortionary policies to favor their friends and to abuse their opponents. . . . Insecure dictators extract what they can from the economy as fast as they can both to prolong their tenure, and to enrich themselves and their supporters while still in power." Regulatory restrictions are imposed when the public is less aware of business and political abuses. Representative government and limited government that do not aim to extort payments are associated with lighter regulations for business entry. Djankov et al. (2002, 35) concluded, "Entry is regulated more heavily by less democratic governments, and such regulation does not yield visible social benefits. The principal beneficiaries appear to be the politicians and bureaucrats themselves."

It is evident that the legal and bureaucratic structure of a jurisdiction can either make it more difficult or easier for businesses to form and prosper. According to the World Bank, the United States ranks relatively high on a measure of ease of doing business. The United States ranked sixth out of 190 countries when countries were scored on the following ten measures of ease of doing business: (1) starting a business, (2) dealing with construction permits, (3) getting electricity, (4) registering property, (5) getting credit, (6) protecting minority investors, (7) paying taxes, (8) trading across borders, (9) enforcing contracts, and (10) resolving insolvency. The U.S scored particularly high in regard to resolving insolvency (2nd) and getting credit (4th). Countries deemed to have greater ease of doing business included: New Zealand, Singapore, Hong Kong, Denmark, and South Korea. The countries of Somalia, Eritrea, and Venezuela ranked lowest (World Bank 2020, 4).

Gaps in ease of doing business between developing and developed countries was wide. The World Bank found that an entrepreneur in a low-income economy typically spends around 50 percent of the country's per capita income to launch a company, compared with just 4.2 percent for an entrepreneur in a high-income economy and it takes nearly six times as long on average to start a business in the economies ranked in the bottom fifty as in the top twenty. Legal protections are weakest among low- and middle-income economies. Economies that scored the highest in legal protections adopt widespread use of electronic systems and online platforms to comply with regulatory requirements (vii). Nations of the sub-Saharan Africa region ranked poorly in regard to legal rights and ease of business creation. The potential for regulations to have deleterious economic effects are widely accepted. The World Bank (2020, 2) states,

> Governments in many economies adopt or maintain regulation that burdens entrepreneurs. Whether by intent or ignorance, such regulation limits entrepreneurs' ability to freely operate a private business. As a result, entrepreneurs resort to informal activity. . . . Foreign investors avoid economies that use regulation to manipulate the private sector.

In addition to ease of entry for new businesses, other factors also affect decisions to start a business. Regulation burdens exact a real cost, tax structure may hinder investment. In addition, levels of corruption may be the most salient factor when considering to launch a private sector venture. As alluded to previously, when virtually all of one's profits are subject to extortion by government employees or others there is little incentive to invest or put in great efforts while pursuing one's dreams. Protection of private property remains one of the touchstones of market systems. Low levels of corruption and regulation protect property rights while high levels of corruption and state control undermine such rights.

Private Property Right Protections

Protecting private property is a fundamental tenet of free-market capitalism. Philosopher John Locke posited that the primary purpose of government is to protect property rights. He believed government should permit people to enjoy the fruits of their labor. Locke viewed this as essential to self-preservation and happiness. He expressed the view that government is morally obliged to serve people, namely by protecting life, liberty, and property. Locke concluded that protection of private property was absolutely essential for liberty to survive. His philosophy was embraced by U.S. founding fathers such as Thomas Jefferson, James Madison, John Adams, and Benjamin Franklin. In addition, more contemporary writers such as Milton Friedman provide a vigorous defense of private property rights. Friedman, the 1976 Nobel laureate, clearly asserted that businesses were private property and owners should decide what to do with their property. He viewed corporate executives as employees of the owners who have responsibilities to conduct their business in accord with the desires of the owners. The wishes of the owners were assumed to be making as much money as possible while conforming to the basic rules of society (Friedman 1970).

According to Friedman, the primary functions of government should be limited to: (1) protecting citizens from crimes against themselves or their property, (2) military defense, and (3) enforcement of contracts. He noted that enforcing contracts, preserving the rule of law and protecting private property rights are at the core of both prosperity and liberty. Property rights are perceived to be the most basic of human rights and an essential foundation for other human rights. Friedman warned against government attempts to rearrange the economy, legislate morality, or help special interests since he believed those efforts would come at a cost in terms of inefficiency, lack of motivation, and loss of freedom (Blackwell 2014).

The United States is considered to be a strong private property nation with cultural and historical tradition that displays respect for private property. The United States has a relatively weak legacy of government intervention into the constitutional rights of property owners. Its federalist system orients a good deal of discretion toward local governments. In contrast to the United States, European governments are perceived to have adopted a structure of a strong state and a weaker set of private property (Jacobs 2009, 63). The value of private property was clearly enunciated by U.S. founding fathers such as John Adams, James Madison, and Thomas Jefferson. For Jefferson, the idea of the yeoman farmer with ownership rights was essential to the very existence and viability of democracy. Jefferson argued that because the yeoman farmer owned land and could produce food and fuel they could be independent of others. They were free to exercise their political views as a free citizen within a democratic government. Founding fathers such as Jefferson believed that the very act of ownership created the conditions that allowed democracy to exist (54).

How well the United States adheres to the prescriptions advocated by private property defenders such as Friedman has been empirically explored. According to the International Property Rights Index (International Property Rights Index 2019), the United States ranked 12th out of 129 countries in property rights protections overall and led the world in copyright and patent intellectual property protections. The Property Rights Index measured the strength of physical property rights, intellectual property rights, and the legal and political environments that enforce them. Large disparities were found between countries in terms of property right protection. In general, nations with property rights protections enjoyed higher incomes. Countries in the top quintile of the index were found to enjoy a per capita income sixteen times greater than those at the bottom.

Confidence in the safety of property and confidence that people can purchase, sell, and value their properties in a free marketplace is viewed as highly constructive for entrepreneurship, reducing corruption, increasing civic participation, and raising long-term investment in research and development (International Property Rights Index 2019). In general, countries scoring high on the index of property rights protection were from Western Europe, Commonwealth nations, the United States or parts of Asia such as Japan and Hong Kong. Countries scoring low on the index were from less developed places such as Yemen, Haiti, Venezuela, Angola, and Bangladesh.

The International Property Rights Index notes that institutional quality is highly relevant as a catalyst for prosperity. Creators of the index claim that the literature of the new institutional economy contributes greatly to an understanding of property right protection. The index identifies the importance of rules in reducing transaction costs and promoting efficiency. It states that property rights are an essential element for a free society based on the idea of citizens being able to control their own lives and build their own destiny. The index observes that there is an extensive and rich literature that reports the relationship between institutions and social welfare and particularly between property rights and social prosperity. The International Property Rights Index publication states, "property rights nurture economic growth and social development. Property rights promote innovation and productivity and have been the most effective mechanism to guarantee civil rights and civil liberties" (Levy-Carciente 2019). The index was developed to serve as a barometer for the status of property rights around the world and includes assessments of: (1) the legal and political environment, (2) physical property rights, and (3) intellectual property rights.

Tax Structure

In theory, tax structure can also be related to entrepreneurship and economic development. It is assumed that owners of businesses wish to maximize the returns for their effort and therefore would be attracted to places where governments extract a lower proportion of their net revenue. Many in the United States decry the "bite" that government takes out of their profits. However, relative to other nations taxes in the United States are relatively low. According to the Tax Policy Center, in 2018, taxes at all levels of U.S. government represented 24 percent of gross domestic product (GDP), compared with an average of 34 percent for the other thirty-five member countries of the OECD. Among the OECD countries, only Chile, Ireland, and Mexico collected less tax revenue than the United States as a percentage of GDP. Taxes exceeded 40 percent of GDP in seven European countries, including France, Denmark, Belgium, Sweden, Finland, Austria, and Italy.

Taxes have been identified as an impediment for entrepreneurs (Watson and Kaeding 2019). Taxes can influence the risks entrepreneurs take, the incomes they earn, and their fixed costs. Higher tax rates on entrepreneurs drive up the return needed to move forward on an investment. Corporate income tax rates were found to be associated with lower levels of entrepreneurship. Lower corporate income tax rates increase firm entry by increasing the return to risk. Countries benefit more from lower corporate income tax rates if they make it more difficult to hide income through accounting manipulation. Personal income taxes may also inhibit entrepreneurship since the progressivity of individual income taxes reduces an entrepreneur's expected after tax rate of return.

Research indicates that "superstar inventors," those who create a disproportional amount of innovation as measured through patents and inventions, are sensitive to individual and corporate income taxes. Tax policy, however, is only one of many considerations prospective innovators must consider when deciding where to locate. Inventors are less sensitive to tax rates in areas where there is an abundance of innovators living and working closely together in business clusters. This helps explain why cities such as San Francisco and New York City maintain growth despite their relatively high overall tax burden (Watson and Kaeding 2019, 10). Innovators often look at other factors such as agglomeration (other innovators in the area) and access to universities.

ROLE OF UNIVERSITIES IN BUSINESS CREATION AND INNOVATION

Universities contain talent pools of scientists and educators that may be either ignored or leveraged by entrepreneurs in attempts to create wealth. Recognizing that universities have untapped talent led the U.S. government to enhance the incentives for university researchers to explore profit making and assist business creation. Legislation played a key role in advancing university-business linkages. The Bayh-Dole Act of 1980 represents U.S. legislation that was created in an effort to leverage the talent in universities in order to address perceptions of decline in U.S. economic competitiveness. The Bayh-Dole Act facilitated the creation of research partnerships between universities and businesses with the objective of rapidly bringing innovations to market. The Patent and Trademark Law Amendments Act of 1980, better known as the Bayh-Dole Act, deals with protection of intellectual property arising from federal government-funded research. The legislation permits universities that receive federal funding, as well as other organizations that receive federal funding to gain ownership of an invention. Previously, ownership rights that derived from federal funding were assigned exclusively to the federal government. The Bayh-Dole Act facilitates partnerships between university researchers and others who wanted to create private-sector value based on government-supported innovations. It encourages the commercialization and utilization of innovations that derives from university-based research.

The Bayh-Dole legislation was passed at a period of time when it was feared that U.S. industry had lost its international competitiveness to Europe and Japan. Examples of the loss of competitiveness abounded, from the loss of U.S. leadership in both mature industries (such as automobiles and televisions), and emerging industries (such as memory chips, and new industries). Many emerging industries were becoming dominated by Japanese companies but based on American and European innovations. The fear of economic decline forced U.S. leaders to reexamine their policy that inventions resulting from federally funded research belonged to the government. Policy makers began to realize that such a posture could harm commercial development arising from university research. The Bayh-Dole Act represents a culmination of the view that important discoveries were not being adequately monetized. The Act attempted to alter this situation by providing incentives to businesses that could then partner with universities. It has been asserted that the Bayh-Dole bill was the most inspired piece of legislation to be enacted in America over the past half-century. The bill was intended to reverse the situation where the wealth of scientific talent at American colleges and universities that were responsible for numerous scientific breakthroughs was going to waste as a result of bureaucratic red tape and government regulations (Stevens 2004).

The Bayh-Dole bill has been credited with aiding high technology economic development; its success in the United States led to adaptation of similar policies in nations such as Germany and the United Kingdom. These policies recognize the need for private industry to receive some of the advantages from patent rights even if research was government sponsored. The Act encouraged private sector application of government research. Not tapping into available talent in universities was viewed as an impediment to growth yet other factors such as corruption also play a significant role in entrepreneurship.

CORRUPTION AND ENTREPRENEURSHIP

Corruption can be a serious impediment to entrepreneurship. Aspiring entrepreneurs who cannot pay the bribes that are often necessary to secure the necessary paperwork are at a distinct disadvantage. Corrupt bureaucrats and political leaders are often in positions to protect allies from competition or extract the maximum payoff from others based on their political positions (i.e., rent seeking). Corruption can occur at all levels of government, national, state, local, and neighborhood. Those seeking payments include bureaucrats, national dictators, and regional officials. Corruption can occur at the local level as a myriad of permits are often needed for approval and entrepreneurial efforts can often be deterred by any one of many corrupt officials who "gum up" or slow down the process for approval of new businesses. An inefficient regulation system tends to go hand in hand with the seeking of payoffs. According to a World Bank Report (2020, 8), countries that score poorly on Transparency International's Corruption Perceptions Index placed more impediments in the path of aspiring entrepreneurs.

The Transparency International's Corruption Perceptions Index ranks countries and territories by their perceived levels of public sector corruption. In 2019, the United States ranked 23rd out of 180 countries and territories in terms of perceived levels of public corruption. The corrupting role of big money in political party financing and the undue influence it exerts on political systems was cited as the leading U.S. problem. Across the board, there was a popular perception that rich people buy elections, both among countries that were perceived as highly corrupt and others that are perceived as less corrupt. Keeping big money out of politics was viewed as essential for serving the public interest and curbing opportunities for corrupt deals. The Nordic nations in particular stood out for their low levels of perceived corruption (Transparency International 2020).

Corruption has an insidious effect since it decreases the expected profitability of investments. The decrease in profitability is attributed to various factors. First, the payment of bribes to corrupt government bureaucrats adds to the costs and uncertainty of doing business. Second, corruption requires entrepreneurs to devote resources to manage bribes instead of using resources for other purposes. Third, since bribery is illegal, potential investors cannot be certain that government promises will be fulfilled or the firm's reputation will not be harmed. When the business sector is characterized by high levels of corruption, the prestige of being an entrepreneur decreases which in turn can lead to suppressing the level of entrepreneurship. Various empirical evidence studies support the contention that corruption has a negative effect on entrepreneurship (Avnimelech et al. 2011). Sobel (2008, 7) examined data from forty-eight U.S. states and concluded that better institutional structures produce higher rates of venture capital investments, a higher rate of patent filings, a faster rate of sole proprietorship growth, and a higher birth rate for new companies.

The impact of legal structure on entrepreneurship cannot be minimized. Good institutions promote what has been termed "productive entrepreneurship" or actual value-seeking opportunities in contrast to unproductive entrepreneurship based on political connections. Rates of return on entrepreneurship in turn are shaped by the quality of social, political, and legal institutions. Avnimelech et al. (2011, 6–7) posit that when institutions provide norms such as honesty, property rights, equitable justice, contract enforcement, and limits on government's ability to tax, the profitability of unproductive entrepreneurs (that may have relied upon corrupt practices) diminishes. Productive rather than unproductive ventures are more likely to prosper. Under a sound institutional structure, creative individuals are more likely to engage in the generating new wealth through risk taking and innovation.

Practically speaking, corruption can be a business and entrepreneurship killer. Fukuyama (1995) argued that some societies are able to develop cultural norms, such as hard work and mutual trust, more than others. Such positive cultural values foster economic growth, the absence of such values retards growth. For Fukuyama, cultural values direct behavior. Fukuyama focuses on the element of trust, which he defines as the expectation of regular, honest, and cooperative behavior, based on commonly shared norms. Social capital arises from the prevalence of trust in a society and the acquisition of characteristics such as loyalty, honesty, and dependability.

Numerous empirical studies support a relationship between corruption and entrepreneurship. Driouchi and Gamar (2015) assessed the relationship between the Global Entrepreneurship Development Index (GEDI), and the Corruption Perception Index (CPI) for 2013–2014. Results indicated that lower levels of corruption fostered entrepreneurship while higher levels were a deterrent. Other studies also show that better controls on corruption was related to increases in innovation and entrepreneurship (Anokhin and Schulze 2009). This relationship is attributed to an increase in the reliability and enforcement of the laws that guaranty a fair market.

Corruption has been shown to be a primary factor for business creation in both rural and urban areas of Nigeria (Festus et al. 2014). When the tourism sector was examined, higher levels of corruption was linked to declines in entrepreneurship (Poprawe 2014). Most publications view corruption as a deterrent to entrepreneurship. However, some studies suggest that corruption may have a positive effect in opening up some market to people who are willing to pay bribes. These markets may previously have been closed to them by government red tape or unwillingness of government officials to damage their relationships with status quo actors. Bribery in effect then saves time and provide opportunities to access new markets (Driochi and Amar 2015).

EVIDENCE OF FAVORABLE U.S. ENVIRONMENT FOR BUSINESS CREATION

Operationalizing the environmental factors that leads to business creation and exponential growth is not an easy task and should stimulate future research. Some metrics indicate that over time, the United States has enhanced its research capability and currently possesses one of the greatest pools of basic research talent in the world. Lists of Nobel Prize winners in physics indicate that U.S. physicists received zero Nobel awards between 1900 and 1920, however, between 2000 and 2020 (including multiple individuals working on the same project and joint citizenship) there were twenty-eight U.S.-based recipients. In terms of Nobel recipients in Chemistry, between 1900 and 1917 there was one U.S. recipient. Counting joint authorship and joint citizenship between 2000 and 2020, there were thirty-three American recipients of the Nobel Prize in chemistry. Of the top ten university in terms of Nobel laureates in 2021, seven of the ten were U.S. universities. In descending order, these universities included: Harvard, Columbia, the University of Chicago, Massachusetts Institute of Technology, the University of California-Berkeley, Stanford, and Yale. The other three universities (Cambridge University, Oxford University, and the University of Paris) are located in the United Kingdom and France. U.S. colleges and universities attract large numbers of international students. During the 2018–2019 academic year, more than one million international students attended U.S.-based institutions of higher learning. China (33.7%) and India (18.4%) accounted for the largest proportions of international students (Moody 2019).

Numbers of patents applications are another indicator of innovation. The World Intellectual Property Organization (WIPO), which oversees a system for countries to share recognition of patents noted that the United States had filed the most applications in the world between 1978 and 2018. However, in 2019, China replaced the United States in the top patent filing position. China's patent filings represented a 200-fold increase in just twenty years. China's success was attributed to a very deliberate strategy on the part of China's leaders to advance innovation. According to the WIPO, China's Huawei Technologies, the world's biggest maker of telecoms equipment, was the top corporate patent filer for the third consecutive year. The head of WIPO speculated that China's advances in patent applications may be due to its model of using state subsidies to a greater extent than Western economies (Nebahay 2020).

The extent to which overall business environment also affects new business formation is an open question. Forbes (2021) ranked states on business climate by assessing factors such as business costs, labor supply, regulatory environment, economic climate, growth prospects, and quality of life. These ordinal rankings were compared to ordinal rankings on previously discussed figures for new business creation (Ewing Marion Kauffman Foundation 2021; U.S. Small Business Administration 2020). The value of the Spearman who rank correlation ($p = .535$) did not identify a significant relationship between the Kauffmann Foundation rankings of state business climate and business creation. As discussed in the previous chapter, data at the state level failed to identify a statistically significant relationship between a measure of entrepreneurship and other metrics. Insights into how the Googles, Facebooks, Amazons, and Apples of the world arise may be better understood through detailed case studies.

Entrepreneurship does not occur in a vacuum. It is advanced or retarded by the institutions that are present in a given location. Two such institutional influences on entrepreneurship are the quality of education in a place and its legal structure. "Cutting-edge" research particularly in fields such as engineering, medicine, and computer science can lead to the creation of massively profitable enterprises that in turn supports their broader economy. The educational experiences of U.S. entrepreneurs such as William Gates, Mark Zuckerberg, Larry Page, Steve Ballmer, Michael Bloomberg and others suggests that pursuit of higher learning and knowledge of new technologies is often related to business success. The data regarding small business creation, however, does not support a linkage between business creation and possible explanatory variables. This suggests that linkages are not apparent in regard to small businesses. At the higher end of the value chain and in regard to businesses that evolve into massive corporations, case studies combined with reports from respected international organizations suggest that the educational and legal environment of the United States present aspiring entrepreneurs with distinct advantages.

Many of the most successful entrepreneurs seem to have benefited from the U.S. educational and legal systems. A legal structure that can protect profits and provide the infrastructure for cutting-edge research has great advantages. Transparent rules, enforcement of contracts, laws that protecting fair competition, and laws that assure freedom from expropriation, instill faith that effort will be rewarded and that wealth can be created. The legal structure combined with a strong educational infrastructure represent two specific institutional factors that contribute to a favorable environment for entrepreneurs. Other factors, however, exist and are addressed in the following chapter.

Chapter 6

The Social and Political Environment for Development

In addition to the educational and legal environment discussed in the prior chapter, other key components of the American ecosystem that have contributed to the nation's prosperity and entrepreneurial spirit are the social and political environments. The social environment of the United States is one of both toleration of difference and intergroup friction. The history of the United States reveals enduring conflict between ethnic, religious, and racial groups going back to the colonial period. At the same time, the United States exhibited more tolerance of "others" than many other places and became a magnet for immigrants throughout the world. These immigrants contributed greatly to U.S. development, not only through business creation but also in adding to the culture, the variety of food, serving in the military and other actions.

SOCIAL ENVIRONMENT

History of Intolerance and Tolerance in the United States

The history of religious intolerance and persecution based on religious beliefs is well documented. Original Puritan settlers displayed great antipathy toward those of other religious persuasions. For example, the Massachusetts legislature, enacted, in 1658, a law that all Quakers who were not an official inhabitant of the Massachusetts colony but living within its jurisdiction should be apprehended without warrant and imprisoned. On conviction, Quakers were banished and could be sentenced to death. In 1659, 1660, and 1661, three English Quakers, as well as a Quaker from Barbados were condemned to death and executed by public hanging. Other Quakers were sentenced to death in Boston, but had their punishments were commuted to that of being whipped out of the Massachusetts colony from town to town.

Between February 1692 and May 1693, more than 200 people were accused of witchcraft, 30 were found guilty, 19 of whom were executed by hanging. In 1834, a Catholic convent was burned to the ground in Boston by an anti-Catholic mob. In Philadelphia, anti-Catholic and anti-immigrant sentiment fueled riots in 1844; houses were torched, Catholic churches were destroyed and at least twenty people were killed. In 1838, the governor of Missouri expelled all Mormons from the state, militiamen killed seventeen church members, and in 1844, a mob in Illinois murdered Mormon founder Joseph Smith and his brother Hyrum while they were in jail. In 1855, Protestant mobs in Louisville, Kentucky, attacked German and Irish Catholic neighborhoods. At least twenty-two people were killed, dozens injured, and many properties were destroyed by fire.

The Know-Nothing Party (also known as the American Party) became home to anti-immigrant and anti-Catholic hatred. At its height in the 1850s, the Know-Nothing Party included more than 100 elected congressmen, eight governors, a controlling share of half-a-dozen state legislatures, and thousands of local politicians. Know-Nothing Party members supported the deportation of foreign beggars and criminals; a twenty-one-year naturalization period for immigrants; mandatory Bible reading in schools; and the elimination of all Catholics from public office. Playing on xenophobia in the United States, the Know-Nothing Party reached its height around 1856 but rapidly declined thereafter as many of its members joined the newly formed Republican Party and supported Republican candidate Abraham Lincoln for president in 1860. In general, members of the Know-Nothing Party distrusted new immigrants who they believed would undermine traditional Protestant values such as self-reliance, temperance, and hardwork (Boissoneault 2017).

Racial conflict in America is also well documented. Following the Civil War, many states and localities enacted Black Codes that detailed when, where, and how formerly enslaved people could work, and for how much compensation. Under the Black Codes, many states required Blacks to sign yearly labor contracts; if they refused, they risked being arrested, fined, and forced into unpaid labor. All the former Confederate states passed strict vagrancy and labor contract laws. The labor contract laws were designed to punish anyone who offered higher wages to a Black laborer that was already under contract. Many former Confederate soldiers worked as police officers and judges in former states of the Confederacy. During the Reconstruction era, organizations such as the Ku Klux Klan terrorizing Black communities and engaged in lynching of Black citizens. The Jim Crow era forbid African Americans from entering public parks, theaters, and restaurants. Bus stations, train stations, water fountains, restrooms, building entrances, elevators, and cemeteries were segregated. Laws forbade African Americans from living in white neighborhoods. Lynching become prevalent and in the summer of 1919, race riots broke out in many cities including Washington, DC; Knoxville, Tennessee; Omaha, Nebraska, and Chicago, Illinois.

Poverty of the Great Depression deepened racial resentment. States in the North as well as the South restricted the rights of African Americans. Some states required African Americans to own property before they could vote, schools and neighborhoods were segregated, and businesses displayed "Whites Only" signs. Many suburban developments enacted legal covenants that excluded Black families, and African Americans often found it difficult or impossible to obtain mortgages for homes in "red-lined" neighborhoods (History.com Editors 2020a). Racial and religious antipathy do not represent the whole range of social antagonisms in the U.S. environment. Class and nationality differences also fueled resentments. Labor-management conflict was particularly intense in the late 1800s and early 1900s.

SOCIAL ENVIRONMENT OF THE UNITED STATES AND IMMIGRATION

Despite this undeniable checkered past in terms of tolerance and acceptance of others, evidence suggests that the United States was at least somewhat welcoming to immigrant groups. Throughout its history, the United States attracted relatively large numbers of immigrants, at first largely from Western Europe, later from Eastern and Southern Europe and in more recent times from Latin America and Asia. Immigration allowed for a more heterogeneous social environment and enriched the U.S. culture in a variety of manners. Some credit immigrants for their work ethic, religiosity, family cohesion, and relatively low crime rates. Others point to immigrant contributions in the diversity in cuisine, music, and culture. Many immigrants such as Andrew Carnegie (Scotland), Levi Strauss (Bavaria), Sergey Brin (Russia), and Elon Musk (South Africa) went on to found massive corporations that employ thousands of workers at relatively good-paying jobs.

As stated by Milton Rose Friedman (1980, 1), in *Free to Choose*, ever since the first settlement of Europeans in the New World, America has been a magnet for people seeking adventure, fleeing from tyranny, or trying to make a better life for themselves and their children. They noted that when immigrants arrived in America, they did not find streets paved with the proverbial gold, nor did they find an easy life but they did find freedom and an opportunity to make the most of their talents. Applying their talents through hard work, ingenuity, thrift, and luck, most of them succeeded in realizing enough of their hopes and dreams to encourage friends and relatives to join them. Ethnic enclaves were established, more immigrants came, and while prejudices may not have been erased, they were softening enough for different people to live together in relative peace. In contrast to ancient societies, that sought to seal themselves off from "outsiders" and so-called barbarians, American society became a beacon of hope for the world's huddled masses who yearned to be free.

The extent to which a social environment of relative tolerance and acceptance of difference contributed to economic growth in the United States is unclear. The social environment represents only one of numerous factors that influence complex decisions such as whether to migrate or stay in place. The question of what factors affect development is not novel as others have explored the issue in detail (Berggren and Elinder 2010). An array of scholars have looked at factors such as trust (Buchanan and Tullock 1962), political institutions (Barro 1996), and stocks of social and human capital (Glaeser et al. 2004). In addition to these specific factors, it is useful to consider the broad "ecology" or environment of place. This broad environment includes not only demographic or wealth characteristics of place but also public functions. Public functions such as providing quality education, affording legal protections for private property, and providing a political structure that protects individual freedom are essential features of the ecology of place. A social environment of relative tolerance, tacit indifference, or visceral hostility can nourish or suppress development. The social environment of the United States in terms of its ability to accept others and tolerate intellectual as well as other forms of diversity is addressed in this chapter.

Some of this discussion harkens to the nurture versus nature dilemma. The nurture position contends that the environment plays a key role in one's success by allowing people to reach their full potential. Arguably, people such as movie star Arnold Schwarzenegger (Austria), Google founder Sergey Brin (Russia), denim jeans founder Levi Strauss (Bavaria), baseball star Mariano Rivera (Panama), and entrepreneur Elon Musk (South Africa) would not have been as successful if they stayed in their native countries. It is doubtful Steve Jobs would have formed the billion-dollar company Apple if his biological father Abdul Fattah Jandali did not flee the turmoil of the Middle East to move to New York. The role of environment does not dismiss the natural talents of a Steve Jobs, Mariano Rivera, or Sergey Brin. However, the success of these individuals lends support to the view that the host environment of the United States was highly instrumental for their success.

Tolerance in the United States and Entrepreneurship

In a widely acclaimed book, Richard Florida (2012, 233) states, "the places that are most open to new ideas and that attract talented and creative people from across the globe broaden both their technology and talent capabilities, gaining a substantial economic edge." Tolerance is viewed by the urban scholar Richard Florida as one of the three key ingredients (tolerance technology and talent), for a new model of economic development. According to Florida, the fact that some places are better than others at generating, attracting, and holding onto talent has everything to do with how open, diverse, and tolerant they are. Florida's research indicates that places that are welcoming (to immigrants, artists, gays, bohemians, socioeconomic integration, and racial integration) are more likely to experience high-quality economic growth. He contends that just as it is important to have low entry barriers for industry, it is also important for a place to have low entry barriers for people, to be a place where newcomers are accepted quickly and that they are accepted into all sorts of social and economic arrangements (234).

Various studies identify a connection between open, culturally diverse environments, and innovative activities for both immigrants and the U.S. born (Liu et al. 2014; Saxenian 1994). The relevance of tolerance in promoting economic development is empirically supported by Florida in the book, *The Rise of the Creative Class*. In *The Rise of the Creative Class*, Florida proposes that new ideas are generated in places where different approaches and lifestyles are tolerated. Tolerance or openness to diversity "provides an additional source of economic advantage that works alongside technology and talent" (Florida 2012, 232–233). He notes that talent (i.e., human capital) is a central force in economic progress. This central force is not static such as the amount of oil or coal reserves in an area but is dynamic, able to increase or decrease over time. People are mobile and talented, ambitious, innovative individuals are often able to move freely from one place to another. To enhance their earning capacity as well as enhance their individual freedom, and personal security, people can migrate from a place where their potential is viewed as limited to higher potential places. Charles Tiebout (1956) long ago viewed migration as an indicator of how well jurisdictions served the interests of residents. His analysis is as relevant today as in the past. Scholars such as Richard Florida expand upon Tiebout's analysis arguing that the general environment of place includes more than taxes and the quality of services delivered from those taxes. The environment includes an array of interrelated forces such as social tolerance and political stability. How successful places attract and hold talent must therefore be considered when looking at economic development.

A broad sweep of history suggests that attitudes toward ethnic and racial minorities have in the past played a role in economic development. For example, the admittance of Jews and other religious minorities into the Netherlands, the United Kingdom, and Sweden had an overall positive effect on the economies of these nations. Mokyr (1990, 12) concludes that innovation requires both diversity and tolerance. This perspective aligns with Richard Florida's views as well as others who see a clear link between cultural diversity and economic development. Jane Jacobs (1961) in her classic work *The Life and Death of Great American Cities* celebrated diversity of urban neighborhoods such as New York City's Greenwich Village. For Jacobs, creative places are places where people of all races, classes, ideas, and educational backgrounds jostle against each other thereby stimulating creative sparks. Creative energy is the antithesis of the staid, conservative, conformist, mindsets that prevailed in corporate America in the 1950s.

In theory, tolerance attracts diverse sets of individuals who fear being ostracized by others who are more conventional and dread being pressured to change their way of life. Richard Florida recounts why "rock star" college graduates from Pittsburgh (where Florida worked at Carnegie Mellon for two decades) were leaving the city and moving to places such as Austin, Texas. Florida concluded that place still matters, not just the geography of the place but its "soul" or character. He questioned why the brilliant student with spiked hair would leave Pittsburgh with its major sports franchises, museums, spectacular parks, beautiful architecture, and great neighborhoods for a place like Austin with no sports teams, museums, or cultural amenities comparable to Pittsburgh. The answer is found in Austin's multitude of young people, variety of things to do, music scene, ethnic diversity, and great outdoor recreation. The bottom line is the brilliant young man felt he could have a life in Austin as opposed to just a job; people would tolerate him, he could fit in (Florida 2012, 185). This desire to fit in is not a new phenomenon. Throughout time, people who did not feel welcome or feared for their live, moved if they could. Prominent European scientists such as Albert Einstein (Germany) and Enrico Fermi (Italy) sought the friendlier place of the United States. Greater tolerance in the United States played a role in both Einstein's and Fermi's decisions to apply for permanent U.S. residency. Einstein with his Jewish heritage and Fermi with his Jewish wife both were fearful of the government policies. In turn, both Einstein and Fermi contributed significantly to the intellectual atmosphere and future innovations of their adopted place.

The ability of people to do their own thing, to start their own company, to work hard and expand their venture has traditionally been a hallmark of U.S. society. Former chairman of the U.S. Federal Reserve Board Alan Greenspan along with Adrian Wooldridge (2018, 541) stated that the United States has rightly regarded itself as a land of entrepreneurs, where it is easier than elsewhere to found companies and then, with luck and determination turn nascent companies into giants. Greenspan and Wooldridge note that Andrew Carnegie was a penniless immigrant from Scotland and John D. Rockefeller was the son of a snake-oil salesman concluding that "for all the changes from the railway age to the information age, America still excels compared to the rest of the world in producing entrepreneurs. It sucks in talent from all over the world" (Greenspan and Wooldridge 2018, 608).

Tolerance and Immigrant Contributions to Development

Openness to people from around the world is a hallmark of the United States. Such openness has reaped economic rewards. Numerous studies indicate that immigrants contribute greatly to the overall U.S. economy, and in particular to the creation of high-tech enterprises. A significant number of the most highly valued tech companies were cofounded by first- or second-generation immigrants. Founders of Apple and Google include Steve Jobs, a second-generation Syrian immigrant, and Sergey Brin, a Russian immigrant. In 2019, 44.6 percent, or 223 companies, in the Fortune 500 were founded by immigrants or their children while 25 percent of all companies in the United States were founded by immigrants. The "new American" firms on the Fortune 500 list made important contributions to both the U.S. and the global economy. In fiscal year 2018, the 223 new American companies on the 2019 Fortune 500 list brought in $6.1 trillion in revenue (New American Economy 2019).

The immigrant companies were also strong drivers of jobs. On average, each "new American" (i.e., first or second-generation American) Fortune 500 companies employed 60,629 workers, 10.7 percent more than the average number of workers at other Fortune 500 firms. Together, the first- or second-generation American firms employed over 13.5 million people. In addition, the Fortune 500 job creation represents only one example of how immigrants and their children contribute to the overall U.S. economy. First- or second-generation American firms also provide jobs at medium and small businesses that are vital to the U.S. economy. These firms employ millions of employees at neighborhood stores, restaurants, professional services, and other local businesses. Nearly 3.2 million immigrants ran their own medium and small businesses in 2019 (New American Economy 2019).

Data from 2017 indicates that immigrants are more likely to be entrepreneurs than their U.S.-born counterparts. Research shows that large proportions of net job growth in the United States is attributed to new firms and start-ups. In 2017, immigrants in the United States comprised about 13 percent of the total population, a relatively low proportion compared to their relatively high representation among Fortune 500 firms (Koch 2017). This is indicative of the significant contributions of immigrants that some attribute to a strong work ethic combined with high skill levels. While many immigrants (such as Einstein and Fermi) were highly skilled, others were not. Data reveals a bifurcated distribution of skills among immigrants with large numbers of immigrants lacking a high school degree and many with graduate level (PhD and masters) or professional degrees. This distribution indicates that many immigrants compete with U.S. citizens at the low end suppressing wages among U.S. non-high school graduates. At the high end, immigrants add value in terms of productivity and economic development.

Utilizing data from 2007 and 2012, Kerr and Kerr (2018) found that first-generation immigrants created about 25 percent of new firms in the United States, with the share of new firm creation exceeding 40 percent in states such as California and New York. Immigrant businesses were more likely to have a higher rate of patents than other firms. These businesses were highly diverse ranging from the small "mom and pop" stores in low-tech settings to high-tech start-ups in the most innovative clusters of the country. The receptivity of places to differences types of people and different lifestyles appear to have some relevance. For example, many would agree that perceptions of the environment of places such as San Francisco and Greenwich Village differ dramatically from perceptions of places such as Boise, Idaho; Birmingham, Alabama; or Philadelphia, Mississippi.

Not unexpectedly, the distribution of immigrant-founded firms is not evenly distributed throughout the nation but differs significantly across regions and local places. At the state level, immigrant business formation range from less than 5 percent in states such as Idaho and North Dakota to more than 40 percent in gateway states such as California (Kerr and Kerr 2018, 3, 5). Differences in immigrant firm formation also exist between nations with the U.S. rate of immigrant business formation (25%) exceeding that of countries such as the United Kingdom (17%), Canada (20%), and Australia (12%). It is reasonable to infer that characteristics such as tolerance, perceptions of place, and existence of similar ethnic communities all play a role in attracting immigrants. In the nations of the United States, United Kingdom, Canada, and Australia immigrant business formation exceeded that of native-born residents. Richard Florida (2018, 8) noted that it is often stated in our age of modern communications that "geography is dead," however, he states, "nothings could be further from the truth. Place has become the central organizing unit of our time."

The United States is said to be an "immigration magnet," yet U.S. immigration policies do not favor skills or wealth over family unification. Only to some extent, the United States opens its gates to wealth. In 2019, the United States offered EB-5 visas to immigrants capable of investing a million dollars into a U.S.-based business. The United States does not throw open its gates by making visas widely available to the most highly educated. The United States lacks a program that aids foreign students graduating from prestigious U.S. universities. Large number of immigrants enter the United States through family-based visas that favor migrants from nations (such as Mexico) where strong enclaves of immigrants exist. According to the Center for Immigration Studies (2017), over the last thirty-five years, the numbers of new immigrants (through chain migration) joining family members who arrived earlier has greatly exceeded other types of immigration. Out of 33 million immigrants admitted to the United States between 1981 and 2016, about 20 million or

61 percent derived from chain migration. The largest categories of chain migrants were spouses and parents of naturalized U.S. citizens. Because admissions in these family-based categories are unlimited by law, Mexico had the highest rate of chain migration.

High-tech firms often claim that the United States needs to be more open in granting H-1B visas that help firms remain innovative, productive, and competitive. Various studies documents how high-skilled immigrants, particularly in STEM fields, boost the economy by increasing innovation and productivity. Leaders in the field of computer technology lobby for greater access to highly skilled workers. In 2008, Bill Gates testified before Congress in support of granting more H-1B visas. According to Gates, this would help compensate for what Gates viewed as a deficit of Americans with computer science degrees. A bill was introduced to Congress in 2015 to raise the cap and liberalize rules around H-1B visas. The bill was not enacted into law despite the support of major corporations in the field of high technology. In general, tech leaders emphasize the contributions high-skilled immigrants make to the economy. Advocates of expanding the H-1B program argue that the H-1B visa program allows companies to hire foreign workers for specialized jobs that are difficult to fill.

Supporters of expanding the H-1B program contend that it has benefited the tech industry enormously, as well as other sectors of the economy including health care, science, and finance. They claim that H-1B workers are needed to fill gaps in their workforces. Demand for foreign workers to enter through the H-1B program is high. In 2017, the U.S. Citizen and Immigration Services (USCIS) conducted its annual lottery for selecting H-1B visas; it received 199,000 petitions for the available 85,000 slots. Some argue that restricting the number of highly skilled workers that are permitted to enter the United States harms U.S. competitiveness in the global war for talent. Gordon Hanson of the University of California-San Diego stated that immigrant workers have helped the United States maintain its leadership in innovation and technical research, stating that "immigration is an important part of why the U.S. is able to maintain its elite status" (Torres 2017, webpage).

Others also warn that limiting the number of H-1B can have dire consequences. They note that in areas where the United States is not dominant, a diminished ability to import brains may be highly injurious. They warn that companies in nations such as Israel, Japan, or China can acquire leadership in new areas such as battery technology and that companies in nations such as Canadian, German, and Israeli could become dominant in autonomous vehicle technology. Global corporations such as Samsung, Sony and HTC, as well as Finland's Nokia, could gain dominance in virtual and augmented reality while German and Scandinavian firms might get an edge in storage technology for solar and wind plants. Bershidsky (2017) cautions that the race for the "holy grail" in these areas is wide open and companies are running full tilt to win. He stated that the United States may lose technological advantages in certain fields if it turns away as few have 100 specific engineers to be picked up by other nations. Consequences would be dire and end U.S. leadership hopes in future multibillion-dollar markets. Bershidsky (2017) cautions that it is too early for the United States to rest on its laurels since countries that keep their best tech brains or make a special effort to lure them from elsewhere will be the new kings.

The United States remains a desirable destination for the so-called opportunity-based migrations. Kerr and Kerr (2018, 7) note that the United States has long been a favored destination for prospective entrepreneurs due to its open and competitive markets. Kerr and Kerr state, "for many entrepreneurial immigrants, it [U.S.] is the dream destination." Immigration, however, remains a highly contentious issue in the United States and elsewhere. A Pew Research Center survey conducted in 2020 indicated that about three-quarters of U.S. adults say they favor granting permanent legal status to immigrants who came illegally to the United States when they were children (i.e., DACA residents). Americans also express strong support for finding a way for all undocumented immigrants (not just those brought to the country as children) to legally stay in the United States. A majority of Hispanic immigrants (94%), U.S.-born Hispanics (82%), Blacks (81%), Asians (76%), and white adults (70%) supported allowing undocumented immigrants to stay in the United States (Krogstad 2020). Despite this popular support, politicians such as Donald Trump appear to have benefited from anti-immigrant postures.

Ethnic diversity and immigrant populations were crucial factors in attracting or fostering high-tech entrepreneurship at the metropolitan level. Research indicates that in Silicon Valley, 24 percent of all high-technology firms in 1998 were run by Chinese or Indian immigrants (Saxenian 1999). The Chinese or Indian immigrant share of high-tech firms was 43.9 percent in 2012. Other research noted that nationwide, 25.3 percent of the engineering and technology companies established between 1995 and 2005 had at least one immigrant founder (Kerr and Kerr 2018, 3).

Immigrants historically have located in a few gateway cities. Figure 6.1 identifies concentrations of immigrants in specific metropolitan statistical areas (MSAs). Eighty percent of immigrant high-tech entrepreneurs were concentrated in the largest twenty-five metropolitan areas. This figure is significantly higher than the 57 percent of their U.S.-born counterparts who also concentrated in these areas (Liu et al. 2014). Three MSAs (Los Angeles, New York, San Francisco) contained more than a third (34.5 percent) of immigrant high-tech entrepreneurs. Data from the U.S. Census, American Community Survey 2007–2011.

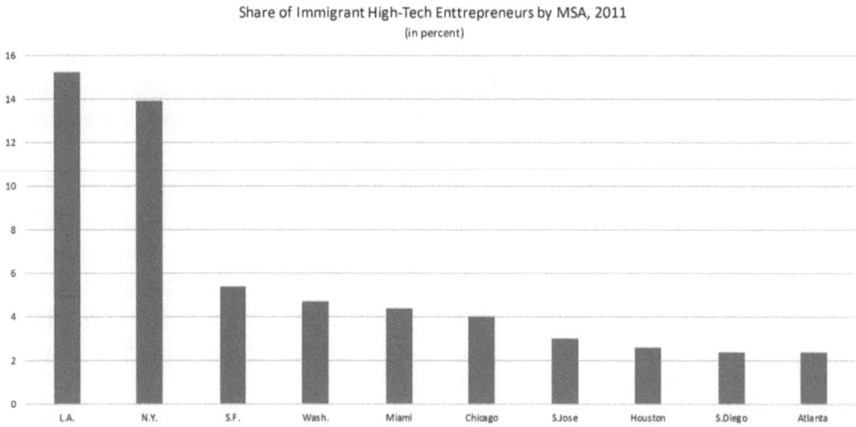

Figure 6.1 Share of Immigrant High-Tech Entrepreneurs by MSA, 2011 (in percentage). *Source*: Created by author using data from Liu et al. (2014).

Since immigrant high-tech entrepreneurship is so heavily concentrated, an important question to ask is why this is so and whether the factor of tolerance plays an important role. Does tolerance and openness have anything to do with attracting highly motivated and highly skilled immigrants (human capital) to specific places? Does the presence of higher skill levels of human capital affect development? Each of these are important questions in assessing the importance of the social climate of a place.

Some debate exists about the role of openness and tolerance in attracting human capital, however, what appears undeniable is that over the centuries the United States and specific states within the United States have attracted large numbers of immigrants. Those immigrants have contributed to the economic development of states and the nation as a whole through starting new businesses. Empirical studies support the view that immigrants have contributed to economic development by creating massively profitable enterprises. One study notes that immigrants have started more than half (55%) of America's start-up companies valued at $1 billion or more. Immigrants were also found to be increasingly important in cutting-edge companies. Immigrants have started 33 percent of U.S. venture-backed companies that became publicly traded between 2006 and 2012. In addition, nearly one-quarter of the billion-dollar start-up companies had a founder who first came to America as an international student (Anderson 2018, 1–2).

In terms of employment, leading immigrant founded billion-dollar companies include the transportation company Uber (Garrett Camp/Canada) and the aerospace company SpaceX (Elon Musk/South Africa). These companies and others with immigrant founders have produced many jobs, added tax revenue to jurisdictions, and supplied a variety of goods and services to U.S. consumers. The Uber company transformed travel by making it easier to get from place to place while the goal of SpaceX company is to provide travel to outer space. Immigrant entrepreneurs in billion-dollar start-ups come from a variety of nations. In 2016, Canada and Israel (nine each), India (eight), the United Kingdom (seven), China (six), Germany (four), France, Ireland, and Russia (three each) represented the leading countries of origin for immigrant founders of billion-dollar companies. The state of California attracted the majority of the headquarters for immigrant-founded companies. Table 6.1 describes some of the Fortune 500 companies started by immigrants.

As indicated in table 6.1, immigrant-founded companies continue to contribute greatly to the American economy. Immigrant founders of Fortune 500 companies migrated from both poor and wealthier nations including Myanmar, Columbia, Greece, Turkey, Hungary, South Africa, Poland, Taiwan, France, Germany, England, and Canada. Numerous companies were founded in the 1990s and 2000s suggesting that immigrant success is not a relic of the past but an ongoing phenomenon.

Table 6.1 Immigrant Founded Fortune 500 Companies, Founders, Nationality, and Year of Founding

Founder	*Company*	*Nationality*	*Year of Founding*
Andrew and Peggy Chen	Panda Express (restaurants)	Myanmar	1973
James Kraft	Kraft (food)	Canada	1903
Alberto Perez	Zumba Fitness (fitness)	Columbia	2001
Nigel Morris	Capital One (banking)	England	1994
Pierre Omidyar	eBay (e-commerce)	France	1995
Charles Pfizer	Pfizer (pharmaceuticals)	Germany	1849
Arianna Huffington	Huffington Post (media)	Greece	2005
Andrew Grove	Intel (technology)	Hungary	1968
Maxwell Kohl	Kohl's (retail)	Poland	1988
Sergey Brin	Google (technology)	Russia	1998
Alexander Graham Bell	Bell Telephone and AT&T (communications)	Scotland	1880 and 1875
Elon Musk	SpaceX and Tesla (aerospace and autos)	South Africa	1998
Jerry Yang	Yahoo (technology)	Taiwan	1994
Hamdi Ulukaya	Chobai (yogurt)	Turkey	2005

Source: Table made by author using data from Leadem (2017).

Empirical Studies of Tolerance and Economic Development

A variety of statistical studies explored the linkage between tolerance and economic development. Richard Florida's (2012, 246) Composite Diversity Index (CDI) provides one measure of tolerance by combining scores on the presence of gays (Gay Index), the concentration of immigrants (Melting Pot Index), and the concentration of artists, writers, designers, musicians, and actors (Bohemian Index). Florida found the CDI to be highly correlated with an index of technological development (High Tech Index). He describes linkages between diversity and high-tech cities such as San Francisco, Boston, Seattle, Los Angeles, and Washington, DC. Florida also created a Tolerance Index by including a measure of racial diversity (Integration Index) and removing the Bohemian Index. Florida's Tolerance Index was closely associated with many positive regional outcomes such as patents, technology centers, a creative class of workers, housing values, and happiness. Tolerance was negatively associated with Florida's definition of the working class (454). Cities ranking high on both tolerance and technology included cities such as Seattle, Boston, San Francisco, Austin, Denver, and Orlando.

Florida suggests that places that are welcoming to immigrants, artists, gays, bohemians, socioeconomic integration and racial integration growth are prosperous, vibrant, and dynamic (Florida 2012, 233). Tolerance, as defined by the urbanist Richard Florida, was associated with innovation, high-tech industry, higher incomes, higher levels of happiness, and general well-being. In essence, Florida suggested that the "environment of place" explains positive economic outcomes such as geographical concentrations of high-tech development. Other research confirmed Florida's assertion that immigrant entrepreneurship is related to a place's concentration of foreign-born residents, ethnic diversity, technology industries, and innovation base (Liu et al. 2014, 11).

The importance of diversity or tolerance has also been measured with regard to Canadian city-regions. Gertler et al. (2002) found linkages discussed by Richard Florida were even stronger in Canada than in the United States. The Gertler et al. (2002) Canadian study concluded that creativity, diversity, talent, and technology-intensive activity drove the economic growth of the nation's city-regions (24). Proportion of foreign-born populations as well as employment in artistic and creative occupations were found to be statistically related to a city-region's high-technology industrial output. Not all research, however, is supportive of the relationships identified in the Florida and Canadian studies. Berggren and Elinder (2010) investigated the relationship between tolerance (as measured by attitudes toward different types of neighbors) and economic growth in fifty-four countries. They found a negative relationship between tolerances toward homosexuals and growth. With regard to growth and tolerance toward people of a different race, the relationship was positive, however, weak.

Some authors posit that tolerance can have negative effects on development (Berggren and Elinder 2010) for at least three reasons. First, talented, productive, and innovate people may dislike other people and other lifestyles. The environment of tolerance may induce people to leave organizations or reduce the productivity of talented people. Second, discomfort toward those with alternative lifestyles can lead more conventional people to self-select away from the most productive jobs available to them. Third, growth at least partly depends on the productivity levels of those toward whom tolerance is extended.

The degree of openness and toleration represent just one aspect of the broader American gestalt, the holistic American environment comprising the norms, values, assumptions, and institutions that make up the entirety of the nation. The "culture" of place remains important. The contours of the American culture have been widely discussed yet agreement is lacking in regard to what it is, what values dominate, what are the culture's main characteristics. Does the distinguishing characteristics (i.e., culture) of a place contribute to wealth creation and economic development? If the broad environment and ecosystem of place are related to development, it is essential to grasp a better understanding of its dominant features. The following section describes U.S. culture and speculates about how it has contributed to economic development.

U.S. CULTURE AND ITS EFFECT ON DEVELOPMENT

In a broad sense, the social environment of a place is a product of its culture. Culture, however, has numerous definition and interpretations. The *Merriam-Webster* dictionary defines culture as the set of shared attitudes, values, goals, and practices that characterizes an institution or organization or the set of values, conventions, and social practices associated with a particular field, activity, or societal characteristic. Paradoxically, scholars hold differing views about the composition of U.S. culture. They alternatively describe the U.S. culture as pragmatic and idealistic, individualistic and egalitarian, Puritanical and licentious, democratic and elitist, spendthrift and frugal, exploitative and fair, fair and discriminatory, rigid and ever-changing. The dominant values of culture provide the setting for the social environment and in turn social environments can foster attitudes that either advance or hinder entrepreneurial development.

Like the blind man and the elephant, perspectives of concepts as global as culture have different interpretations. Some touchstones, however, exist.

A review of touchstones is useful for at least two reasons. First, one should have a general idea of what leading figures think about the construct of culture. One cannot truly assess influences of culture without a basis of agreement on its makeup. Second, culture affects outcomes. If societies agree on a desired outcome such as material prosperity, then assessments can be made regarding the extent to which it is or is not achieved. To better understand the parameters of U.S. culture, the views of various analysts are reviewed. Europeans such as Alexis de Tocqueville and Max Weber provide insight into the cultural characteristics of Americans. More modern analysts such as Daniel Elazar have also commented extensively on American culture.

Alexis de Tocqueville

In 1831, The French aristocrat Alexis de Tocqueville provides some of the most insightful analysis of U.S. political and social culture. In 1831, Tocqueville along with a friend traveled extensively through the United States in order to study the methods of local, state, and national government. In his travels, Tocqueville observed and later discussed the manners, habits, businesses, and occupations of the American people. His massive study *Democracy in America* was not written for Americans, yet it remains a work of great interest to citizens of the United States as the first comprehensive view of U.S. society, institutions, and destiny (Ingalls 2002, 9). Tocqueville's study provides insight into both the U.S. system of governing and the nature of the American people. Some of the fears that Tocqueville expressed (such as the tyranny of the majority and the subordination of the judgments of the wise to the prejudices of the ignorant) have dissipated over time yet many of those fears still exist. Ingalls (11) states that readers of Tocqueville will find encouragement in the view that the same spirit which has vanquished the perils of the past will be equally prepared for the responsibilities of the present and the future.

Tocqueville commented extensively on America's cultural characteristics. What struck Tocqueville most forcibly about America was what he perceived as equality of conditions in the United States compared to the rigid class structure of Europe. Tocqueville noted that the more he studied American society, the more he recognized that equality of conditions was the fundamental fact from which all others derived (12). Tocqueville was skeptical of the value of democracy since he believed democracy could make the nation, taken as a whole, less brilliant, less glorious, and perhaps less strong. He contended, however, that in the United States, the majority of the citizens would enjoy a greater degree of prosperity than Europeans. Tocqueville warned that the nearer people drew to each other in equality of condition, the greater their mutual hatred, and the more vehement the envy and the dread with which they resist each other's claims to power (20). Tocqueville selected America to study as an exemplar of democracy and sought to understand how democracy could be rendered more beneficial (24). In Volume Two of Tocqueville's massive work, he attempted to discern how democracy in America shaped attitudes, behavior, and sentiments. Various observations are made about the fundamental character of Americans in terms of philosophy, religion, the love of equality, addiction to practical rather than theoretical science, tendencies to join associations, restlessness, and callings.

In Tocqueville's mind, Americans paid little attention to philosophy. He contended that no country in the civilized world paid less attention to philosophy than the United States and proposed that the Americans had no philosophical school of their own. Nevertheless, he stated that without ever having taken the trouble to define the rules of a philosophical method, a philosophy common to the whole people did in fact exist. This perceived philosophy included a relative disregard for family rules, relative disregard for class opinions and relative absence of national prejudices. Tradition was accepted only as a means of information; facts were only accepted as a lesson to be used for doing better. Tocqueville proposed that the characteristic that predominates is that "each American appeals to the individual exercise of his own understanding alone. America is therefore one of the countries in the world where philosophy is least studied" (Tocqueville 2002, 489). He wrote that since Americans perceive that they can succeed in resolving difficulties without assistance, they also conclude that everything in the world may be explained, and that nothing in it transcends the limits of understanding.

In regard to religion, Tocqueville identified a separation between clergy and secular affairs where religion in America is a "distinct sphere." Beyond that distinct sphere the American religious leader basically leaves individuals to themselves and their natures (510). In America, Tocqueville states, Christianity is "clothed with fewer forms, figures, and observances"; it presents distinct, simple, and general notions. Religion in America is viewed as being consistent with productive labor. Tocqueville observed that "whilst they [clergy] never cease to point to the other world as the great object of the hopes and fears of the believer, they do not forbid him honestly to court prosperity" (511).

In regard to science, Tocqueville viewed Americans as being interested in the practical aspects of science while also paying attention to the immediate application of theory. He thought Americans displayed a clear, free, original, and inventive power of mind but noted that hardly anyone in the United States devoted time to the theoretical aspects of human knowledge. Tocqueville did not find in America a situation that existed in Europe where the aristocrats were in a state of rest because they were well-off and vast numbers of others did not strive because they did not think it was possible to improve their condition (522).

A clear distinction between American and European views of science is also articulated. While European aristocrats are thought to pursue science for the love of truth, people in democracies such as America are thought to be more inclined to pursue science for material reward. Tocqueville stated,

> The greater part of the men who constitute these nations [democracies] are extremely eager in the pursuit of actual and physical gratification. . . . They think of nothing but the means of changing their fortune, or of increasing it. To minds thus predisposed, every new method which leads by a shorter road to wealth, every machine which spares labor, every instrument which diminishes the cost of production, every discovery which facilitates pleasures or augments them, seems to be the grandest effort of the human intellect. It is chiefly from these motives that a democratic people addicts itself to scientific pursuits. (Tocqueville 2002, 525)

In contrast to the materialistic application of science in democratic societies, Tocqueville views science in European nations as being called upon to furnish gratification to the mind. Democratic societies are viewed as neglecting the loftier spheres of the intellect. Tocqueville expresses disdain of the grasping materialism he saw in American society. He emphasized the pragmatic nature of Americans and their ability to capitalize on the inventions of others. Tocqueville noted that while Americans were not at the forefront of discovery in terms of the general laws of mechanics, they applied the knowledge to introduce a highly valuable engine. The idea that Americans use technical knowledge for material gain is reinforced in the success of entrepreneurial billionaires discussed in earlier chapters. American inventors such as Thomas Edison are especially noted for using scientific discovery for practical application.

Edison's inventions such as the phonograph, the motion picture camera, and versions of the electric light bulb not only improved ordinary people's lives but also led to the creation of massive companies that created large numbers of well-paying jobs. Americans such as the Wright Brothers, Samuel Morse, and Thomas Edison created their own practical inventions yet others such as Henry Ford (who did not invent the automobile), Andrew Carnegie (who did not invent the Bessemer Process for manufacturing steel inexpensively) and Mark Zuckerberg (who did not invent the Internet) were able to very successfully apply established discoveries for profit.

According to the great French observer Alexis de Tocqueville, all democratic societies including the United States show a more ardent and enduring love of equality than of liberty. He stated that equality of conditions represented the prepondering fact which marked the democratic age. This implies rights to indulge in the same pleasures, enter the same professions, frequent the same places, live in the same manner, and seek wealth by the same means. He stated, "Ask not what singular charm the men of democratic ages find in being equal, or what special reasons they may have for clinging so tenaciously to equality rather than to the other advantages which society holds out to them: equality is the distinguishing characteristic of the age they live in" (Tocqueville 2002, 571).

The tendency of Americans to join associations is one of Tocqueville's most identifiable observations. He wrote that a cultural attribute of U.S. citizens was that Americans of all ages, all conditions, and all dispositions, constantly formed associations. These associations included not only commercial interests, but other types of associations including religious, moral, futile, open, and restricted establishments. These establishments focused on entertainment, education, religion and other activities. Associations also helped to found hospitals, prisons, and schools. Tocqueville concluded that in contrast to France where government took most action or England where individuals of rank assumed leadership, Americans formed associations (581). Tocqueville reasoned that in aristocratic societies people did not need to combine in order to act; every wealthy and powerful citizen constituted the head of a permanent and compulsory association, composed of all dependents. In contrast, in democratic societies like America, citizens were viewed as relatively independent.

Voluntary action in America was viewed as a necessity that induced people to lend assistance to each other in actions such as barn raisings where people of a community gathered to cooperatively erect the framework of a neighbor's barn, typically followed by a celebration. In Tocqueville's opinion, intellectual and moral associations of America were of fundamental importance. He stated, "If men are to remain civilized, or to become so, the art of associating together must grow and improve in the same ratio in which the equality of condition is increased" (Tocqueville 2002, 585).

Some further observations made by Tocqueville relate to restlessness of spirit and callings in the United States. Tocqueville viewed Americans as forever brooding over advantages they did not possess. He finds it strange to witness the "feverish ardor" in which Americans pursue their own welfare and to watch the dread that torments them if they do not choose the shortest path which may lead to it. He stated that in the United States a man builds a house to spend his later years, and sells it before the roof is on, plants a garden, and rents it just as the trees are bearing fruit, embraces a profession, and gives it up, settles in a place, and soon afterward leaves (Tocqueville 2002, 605). Taste for physical gratification is viewed as the chief source of this restlessness. What Tocqueville found novel in Americans was not the restlessness of single individuals but the restlessness of a whole society (Tocqueville 2002, 606).

In regard to calling, Tocqueville contended that in America labor was a necessary, natural, and honest condition of human existence. Tocqueville asserted that in America no one is degraded because of work, nor is anyone humiliated by the notion of receiving pay. He stated, "In the United States professions are more or less laborious, more or less profitable; but they are never either high or low: every honest calling is honorable" (Tocqueville 2002, 621).

Max Weber

In his influential work *The Protestant Ethic and the Spirit of Capitalism*, Weber (1904/1992) explains how specific worldviews can influence a system wide ecosystem or environment by guiding habits and behaviors of individuals. He argues that the religious ideas of groups such as the Calvinists played a key role in creating the spirit of capitalism. This spirit views profit as an end in itself, and in contrast to Roman Catholic theology views pursuit of profit as virtuous. Calvinist belief in predestination is linked with capitalists' hard work and individualism. Weber discussed the Calvinist idea of predestination or the belief that God determined everyone's fate before they even began their lives on earth. This provided Calvinists with a highly individualist attitude toward life and belief that individual efforts could establish proof of their preordained salvation. Calvinism taught a doctrine in which from the beginning God chose some people for salvation and others for damnation. It, therefore, became a duty to believe that one was chosen for salvation, and to dispel any doubt about that through worldly success.

One of Weber's greatest contributions to our understanding of economic development is his linkage between Protestantism and values that are essential for the success of capitalism. Weber reviewed occupations and economic successes of people of different religious beliefs. He found that in countries with mixed religions, business leaders, owners of capital, and higher grades of skilled labor overwhelmingly were Protestant. His analysis suggests that Protestants and Protestant-dominated places such as Great Britain, New England, Holland, and Northern Europe, will be more prosperous than Catholic-dominated places such as Southern Europe. Weber argued that some places are more prosperous because of the "mental and spiritual particularities acquired from the environment" (1904/1992, 39). He identified perceived differences between general natures of Catholics (quieter, less acquisitive, prefer security even with a smaller income) to Protestants who are perceived to be more inclined to risk taking that could bring about riches (1904/1992, 40).

Weber further explored the background of ideas which could account for economic differences. He finds in the writings of Martin Luther and John Calvin justifications for activity directed toward profit as an ethical obligation and calling. For Luther, the monastic life is thought to be devoid of value and a renunciation of duties to the world is thought to be a product of selfishness. In contrast, Luther viewed labor as an obligation and outward expression of brotherly love that is necessary to live in a manner that is acceptable to God. Weber stated, "this moral justification of worldly activity was one of the most important results of the Reformation, especially for Luther's part in it" (Weber 1904/1992, 81). Weber also commented upon the beliefs of the Puritans; their strong adherence to the doctrine of predestination, their rejection of magical means toward salvation, their antagonism toward sensual culture, and their inclination toward individualism. Weber states that the inclination toward individualism is identified in "national character and institutions" of people "with a Puritan past" (Weber 1904/1992, 105). Self-control is also viewed as essential to the Puritan ethic. A life of self-control should result in good works (Weber 1904/1992, 117).

Benjamin Franklin was presented by Weber as an exemplar of the Calvinist faith that was taught to him by his strict New England father. Franklin's aphorisms such as "time is money," "money begets money," and "the good paymaster is lord of another man's purse," reflect Franklin's views of capitalism. Weber claimed that all of Franklin's moral attitudes such as honesty, punctuality, industry, and frugality were colored with utilitarianism (Weber 1904/1992, 52). Earnings began to be linked to religion, however, Weber felt that earnings devoid of spontaneous enjoyment of life was "irrational" and "foreign to all peoples not under capitalist influence" (Weber 1904/199, 253).

CONTRIBUTIONS OF EUROPEAN POLITICAL ENVIRONMENT PHILOSOPHERS ON U.S. POLITICAL

Tocqueville also had interesting observations about the U.S. political environment. This environment is steeped in conflict between advocates of a stronger centralized government and advocates of greater decentralization. The American system of federalism reflects the unwillingness of founding fathers to place too much power in national authorities. Federalism constructs a system where states are somewhat autonomous with separate executives (governors), legislatures, and courts. Often boundaries are ambiguous with one level of government trying to expand its powers through arguments about state's rights derived from the Tenth Amendment to the Constitution or reference to the so-called supremacy clause (Article VI of the U.S. Constitution). This supremacy clause of the Constitution declares the constitution, laws, and treaties of the federal government to be the supreme law of the land. To better understand the context in which business operates in the United States, it is useful to appreciate historical tensions between the branches (executive, legislative, judicial) and levels (national, state, local) of government. Origins of the ideas and theories that influence the U.S. political system of federalism and separations of powers are traced to Europeans of the seventeenth and eighteenth centuries such as John Locke and Charles Montesquieu. Later commentators such as Tocqueville, Friedrich Hayek, and Milton Friedman further add to our understanding of the connection between the American political system and American business.

John Locke

It is important to realize that while Thomas Jefferson is credited with being the father of the U.S. Declaration of Independence and James Madison is credited with being the father of the U.S. Constitution, the ideas behind these founding documents did not spring out of thin air. Before Jefferson and Madison there was John Locke and Charles Montesquieu who developed ideas about natural rights and separation of powers. The contributions of Locke (1632–1704) and Montesquieu (1689–1755) cannot be slighted by anyone who wishes to understand the intellectual genesis of the U.S. political system.

Locke is widely regarded as one of the most influential of Enlightenment thinkers. In his work *Two Treatises of Government*, he defended the claim that men are by nature free and equal; not subject to a monarch. He argued that people have rights to life, liberty, and property; the foundation of these rights were thought to be independent of human-made laws of any particular society. For Locke, the idea that people are naturally free and equal supplied the justification for understanding government as a social contract whereby people conditionally transfer some of their rights to the government in order to better ensure the stable, comfortable enjoyment of their lives, liberty, and property. Locke posited that governments exist by the consent of the people; the people consent to a government in order to protect their rights and promote the public good. Governments that fail to do so can be resisted and replaced. Other important contributions of Locke to the U.S. political system include the principles of majority rule, the separation of legislative and executive powers and the separation of church and state. Locke opposed the use of coercion to bring people to what rulers believed was the true religion (Tuckness 2020).

Locke's contribution to the Declaration of Independence is evident in his views of universal moral truths. He contrasts natural laws that are God given with conventional law or those that operate only in certain places. His treatment of property is generally thought to be a major contribution, but it is also one of the aspects of his philosophy that has been most heavily criticized. One interpretation of his writings views Locke as a defender of unrestricted capitalist accumulation with the power of government severely limited. Libertarians interpret Locke's writings as viewing the purpose of government only in regard to protect people from infringements on their rights. Others view Locke's writings as supporting a more expansive justification of government in its power to promote the common good. They see him justifying extending government power for actions designed to increase population, improve the military, develop infrastructure and strengthen the economy. Locke also supported separation of powers with legislative power as supreme. According to Locke, legislative power derived from its ability to create laws and punish those who violate those laws. The executive power derives from its ability to implement the laws. Montesquieu later expanded upon Locke's views with inclusion of the judicial branch as a check on the powers of legislatures and executives. Montesquieu is in general agreement with Locke reaffirming the superiority of the legislative power (Tuckness 2020).

Locke was also concerned with limiting the power of government in order to protect liberty and reduce the threat of tyranny. He placed ultimate authority in the people that are governed, their consent, and their right to remove those in power who abuse their privileges. Locke was aware of the need for the people to have representatives with sufficient power to block attacks on their liberty and attempts to tax them without justification. Locke also affirmed that the community must retain the supreme power. He argues that the people retain the right to "remove or alter" the legislative power for a variety of reasons. Locke describes the occasions when the people take power back from the government to which they have entrusted it. These occasions include: (1) when the rule of law is ignored, (2) when the representatives of the people are prevented from assembling, (3) when popular consent is ignored, and (4) when the people are handed over to a foreign power. On these occasions, the people can take back their original authority. The threat of possible rebellion is a check on tyranny.

An additional contribution of Locke to the social and political environment of the United States relates to tolerance and religion. Locke believed in a separation of religious teachings from the actions of the state. He objected to the idea of using force as a proper way to bring people to salvation. Locke presents three reasons for barring governments from using force to advance religious beliefs. First, he argues that the care of men's souls has not been committed to government. Second, he observed that since the power of the government is only force, while true religion consists of genuine inward persuasion of the mind, force is incapable of bringing people to the true religion. Locke's third argument relates to the view that even if a magistrate could change a person's mind and everyone accepted the magistrate's religion, this would not bring more people to the "true religion" since there is no agreement among magistrates about the nature of a "true religion" (Tuckness 2020).

Charles Montesquieu

The eighteenth-century French aristocrat, Charles-Louis de Secondat, baron de La Brède et de Montesquieu and his views on separation of power greatly influenced the Constitution of the United States. Montesquieu asserted that to most effectively promote liberty, legislative, executive, and judicial powers should be separated and act independently. For Montesquieu, the legislative branch should be responsible for enacting the laws and appropriating the money necessary to operate the government. The executive branch should be responsible for administering the public policy enacted and funded by the legislative branch while the judicial branch should be responsible for interpreting the constitution and laws and applying their interpretations to controversies brought before it. This interpretation is widely accepted in the United States today.

Montesquieu contended that establishing political liberty on a sound footing required both the separation of the powers and the appropriate framing of civil and criminal laws. Montesquieu argued that separating functions of government would prevent attempts by one branch of government to infringe upon political liberty. He notes that liberty cannot be secure where there is no separation of powers, even in a republic. In regard to framing of laws in order to ensure personal security, Montesquieu supported what modern legal scholars call the rights to robust procedural due process. These rights included the right to a fair trial, the presumption of innocence, and proportionality in the severity of punishment. Montesquieu also opposed slavery and advocated for freedom of thought, speech, and assembly. He believed that strong political institutions might be able to constrain overreaching power. Montesquieu believed that capable individual could design governing documents in a professional manner (Levitsky and Ziblatt 2018, 166).

Montesquieu identified inequality as a potential threat to democracy. He was revered by the founding fathers as an authority on the subject of checks and balances. For Montesquieu, liberty did not consist in unlimited freedom but in doing what the laws permitted. Scholars, however, note that codification of forms of government in themselves are not sufficient to protect representative government. Constitutions survive or die depending upon their environment. Kemp (2010) states that the U.S. Constitution took root because the soil in which it was planted was receptive. He notes that in contrast to the U.S. Constitution, the French Constitution of 1789 lasted less than one year and was followed by the tyranny of the French Revolution and later by the military autocracy of Napoleon Buonaparte.

The U.S. version of Montesquieu's ideas encompasses the basic premise that one must always guard against concentrated power. Kemp (2010, 4) states that by institutionalizing different branches of government with different powers, the founders recognized that power "emanated from the people, [the people] sought to prevent the totality of such power from ever being united in untrustworthy hands. By guarding against tyranny, they sought to preserve the liberty which they saw as the hard won prize of the American Revolutionary War." It is, therefore, evident that the success of the U.S. system of government was dependent upon the environment of the United States and a willingness to accept the laws of the land. Both Locke and Montesquieu formulated precepts that later would be formally adopted in the United States. Over time, scholars and politicians would attempt to further mold the U.S. environment and the institutions that sprang from that environment. Those who influenced the U.S. political environment span the ideological spectrum as one would expect in a polity that is open to divergence of opinion. Conservative economic thought is expounded in the writings of Hayek and Friedman.

CONSERVATIVE INFLUENCES ON U.S. POLITICAL SYSTEM

Friedrich Hayek

Friedrich Hayek (1899–1992) was an economist and philosopher who is associated with classical liberalism that advocates civil liberties under the rule of law with an emphasis on economic freedom. Hayek is also identified with the Austrian School of Economics that values individualism and the Chicago School of Economics that emphasizes the ability to control economies through the supply of money. Hayek is particularly famous for his defense of free-market capitalism and as one of the greatest critics of socialism. Hayek's most famous work *The Road to Serfdom* was written between 1940 and 1943 and in 1945 the U.S. magazine *Readers Digest* published an abridged version that in turn enabled the book to reach a wide audience. The book was widely read among those advocating individualism and classical liberalism.

In *The Road to Serfdom*, Hayek (1944) argues that Western democracies progressively abandoned economic freedom. He notes that without economic freedom, personal and political freedom have never existed and that societies have mistakenly tried to ensure continuing prosperity by centralized planning. According to Hayek, centralized planning will inevitably lead to totalitarianism by replacing the anonymous mechanism of the market with the planned direction of all social forces to chosen goals. Hayek echoed the views of fellow Austrian economist Ludwig von Mises who argued that socialist central planning was unworkable and possessed negative consequences. Mises also contended that a social quagmire would result from introducing piecemeal regulations into the market economy.

Hayek claims that socialism presents a means of assuring equality yet does so through servitude while democracy seeks equality in liberty. Hayek thought that planning was an inferior method of regulating an economy compared to the competition of free markets. Free markets, according to Hayek, would allow for people to freely adjust their behavior without coercive influences of the state. Hayek contended that centralized planning is inherently undemocratic because it requires the will of a small minority imposing itself upon the majority. It allows for the power of a small number of technical experts to act in pursuit of centralized goals and does not give adequate attention to the value of individual freedom. Hayek surmised that where there is centralized planning, the individual becomes a means to achieve abstract goals such as social welfare or the good of the community. He concludes that socialism is hypocritical because its professed humanitarian goals can only be put into practice by brutal methods. The centralized system is thought to be possible through the use of propaganda that in turn brings people to embrace the collective goals of the state as their own.

Hayek believed that the only way to build a decent world in the future was to improve general levels of wealth via free markets. He saw international organization as constituting a threat to individual freedom; he concluded that a policy of freedom for the individual was the only truly progressive policy. Hayek forcefully argued that collectivism, whether it is in Germany, the former Soviet Union, Britain or the United States functions to reduce personal liberty. He concluded that the tragedy of the rise of the Nazis in Germany was that people of goodwill, by their socialist policies, prepared the way for forces which stand for everything they detested. He urged those who support a liberal social order to attack the intellectual foundations of collectivism. Hayek believed that an understanding of what led many intellectuals toward socialism was vital. He did not believe that supporters of socialism were out for selfish interests nor have evil intentions. On the contrary, he maintained that supporters of socialism were motivated by honest convictions and good intentions.

In Hayek's mind, socialism, the collectivist state, and planned economies represent the ultimate form of hubris. He proposed that those who formulate plans in the collectivist state arrogantly ignore traditions that embody the wisdom of generations, disregard customs, and cannot change people's habits with administrative rules that they can alter at whim. For Hayek, such presumption represented a road to serfdom. Hayek attempted to demonstrate that fascism and what the Germans called National Socialism (represented in the Nazi Party) were the inevitable results of the increasing growth of state control and state power. Hayek extols the value of freedom and the right to own property, stating,

> Our generation has forgotten that the system of private property is the most important guarantee of freedom. It is only because the control of the means of production is divided among many people acting independently that we as individuals can decide what to do with ourselves. When all the means of production are vested in a single hand, whether it be nominally that of "society" as a whole or that of a dictator, whoever exercises this control has complete power over us. . . . When economic power is centralized as an instrument of political power it creates a degree of dependence scarcely distinguishable from slavery. It has been well said that, in a country where the sole employer is the state, opposition means death by slow starvation. (Hayek 2005, 41)

Hayek argues that even badly paid unskilled workers in free societies are allowed to shape their own lives while employers in Nazi Germany or managers in Soviet Russia cannot change jobs or their places of residence at will. If the unskilled worker in free societies wants to spend his or her leisure in a particular way, he or she faces no absolute impediments. There are no dangers to bodily security and there are no dangers to one's freedom by brute force. Hayek also defends individualism, noting that in contrast to socialism and all other forms of totalitarianism, individualism is based on the respect of Christianity for the individual and the belief that it is desirable that people should be free to develop his or her own individual gifts and benefits.

Hayek (2005, 68) laments that the youth of his day had grown up in a world in which, in school and press, the spirit of commercial enterprise was represented as disreputable and the making of profit was viewed as immoral. He notes that influencers of public opinion depict large employers as exploiters but commanding people in the name of a collective society is viewed as honorable. Hayek supports the successful use of competition and contends competition does not preclude some types of government interference such as limiting working hours, requiring sanitary arrangements, and providing social services. Some of his clearest assertions relate to the value of free-market competition. Hayek observes that under competition, the price system automatically records all the relevant information and adjusts to them. Entrepreneurs can watch the movement of prices and act in efforts to maximize profit. Comparing central direction to automatic adjustments through the price system, Hayek (2005, 62) finds the method of central direction incredibly clumsy, primitive, and limited in scope.

Discussing the capacity to build a better world, Hayek states, "We must clear away the obstacles with which human folly has recently encumbered our path and release the creative energy of individuals. We must create conditions favorable to progress rather than 'planning progress' " (Hayek 2005, 70). Hayek refers to statements of Benjamin Franklin and their applicability to both individuals and nations. In *The Intellectuals and Socialism*, Hayek further discusses threats to freedom speculating that free societies may carry forces of its own destruction since once freedom has been achieved it is taken for granted and ceases to be valued. He writes that in countries like the United States the ideal of freedom has less real appeal for the young than it has in countries where the people have learned what its loss means. He asks whether freedom is valued only when it is lost and whether the world "must everywhere go through a dark phase of socialist totalitarianism before the forces of freedom can gather strength anew?" He hopes it is not necessary but surmises that "so long as the people who over longer periods determine public opinion continue to be attracted by the ideals of socialism, the trend will continue." To avoid such a development, Hayek (2004, 128) proposes offering programs that appeals to the imagination. He pronounces that "we must make the building of a free society once more an intellectual adventure, a deed of courage."

Hayek identifies a clear link between economic security and liberty. He states that independence of mind or strength of character is rarely found among those who cannot be confident that they will make their way by their own effort. He believed wealthy societies could still provide a safety net for food, shelter, and clothing that was sufficient to preserve health and general freedom. However, he contended that planning designed to protect individuals or groups against diminutions of their incomes had an insidious effect on liberty. Fellow University of Chicago faculty member Milton Friedman continued in Hayek's tradition in exalting freedom, competition, and the economic superiority of market systems.

Milton Friedman

Like Hayek, Milton Friedman received a Nobel Prize in economics for his contributions to his field. His book *Capitalism and Freedom* (1962) extolled the virtues of a free-market economic system with minimal intervention. The book brought Friedman national and international attention outside academia while arguing that government should only involve itself when absolutely necessary for the survival of its people and the country. The book describes both the failures of government intervention and the advantages of free-market competition. Similar to the 1776 thoughts of Adam Smith, Friedman proposes that free markets benefit both nations and individuals. Friedman then developed a ten-part television series that was broadcast by the Public

Broadcasting Service (PBS). An outcome of the television series was the bestselling book *Free to Choose* (Friedman and Friedman 1980) that eventually was translated into fourteen languages and topped the bestseller list for five weeks.

In their book, Milton and Rose Friedman present highly readable examples that describe the superiority of market economies when compared to controlled economies. The Friedmans note that after traveling to underdeveloped countries, they were impressed by the contrast between the ideas held by the intellectuals of those countries and many intellectuals in the West. Intellectuals took for granted that free enterprise capitalism represented a tool for exploiting the masses. Central economic planning was seen as the wave of the future that would set their countries on the road to rapid economic progress. The Friedmans (1980, 54) noted that the facts themselves were very different. They state that wherever there are large element of individual freedom, some measure of material progress for ordinary citizens evolves as well as hope of further progress. Hope in the future occurs under free-market systems.

A cogent example of the effect of differing economic system is given by comparisons of previously mentioned East and West Germany. They note that both East and West were originally part of one whole with "the same blood, the same civilization, the same level of technical skill and knowledge." They ask which nation has prospered and "which had to erect a wall to pen in its citizens." Which maintained "armed guards, assisted by fierce dogs, minefields, and similar devices of devilish ingenuity" in efforts to prevent desperate citizens "willing to risk their lives to leave their communist paradise for the capitalist hell on the other side of the wall?" They remark that "on one side of that wall the brightly lit streets and stores are filled with cheerful, bustling people" who "can buy freely newspapers and magazines expressing every variety of opinion." In contrast, on the other side of the wall, "the streets appear empty; the city, gray and pallid; the store windows, dull; the buildings, grimy. Wartime destruction has not yet been repaired after more than three decades" (Friedman and Friedman 1980, 55).

The "miracle" of West Germany becoming one of the strongest economies on the continent of Europe is attributed to its embrace of free-market economics. Other examples of market economy success are found in comparisons of Israel and Egypt. Despite an announced socialist philosophy, Israel had a vigorous market sector and its citizens enjoyed both more political freedom and a far higher standard of living than the citizens of Egypt, which had a much more extensive centralization of political power and which had imposed much more rigid controls on economic activity. Places such as Malaysia, Singapore, Korea, Taiwan, Hong Kong, and Japan that relied on private markets were viewed as thriving while others that embraced more centralized planning lagged behind (57). Evidence can be found that the political environment of the United States that protected property rights, limited government, and free markets contributed at least in part to America's entrepreneurial and economic success. Negative consequences of unlimited free markets, however, were also identified by those who sought to ameliorate unequal outcomes. Progressive politicians were able to limit excesses and some would argue that adjustments made by politicians such as Theodore and Franklin D. Roosevelt helped to save capitalism from more radical influences. We now briefly describe positions of the critics of unfettered capitalism that have argued for a more interventionist state.

PROGRESSIVE INFLUENCE ON THE U.S. POLITICAL SYSTEM

Progressive Movement and Franklin Roosevelt

Early roots of progressive thinking in the United States are linked to the writings of American sociologist Lester Ward (1841–1913). For most of his life, Ward worked for the federal government in the area of botany. He later shifted the focus of his work to sociology, and in 1906 at the age of 65, he was appointed professor of sociology at Brown University. Ward vigorously opposed doctrines of laissez-faire and Darwinian survival of the fittest. He argued that business had already made a travesty of the doctrine of laissez-faire and that genuine competition was the last thing that turn of the twentieth-century captains of industry desired. Ward proposed that these powerful individuals strove to replace competition with monopolies that rewarded privilege, established capital, legal acumen, and ruthlessness. He contended that the term "liberty" had been perverted to assure immunity from government interference. Ward wrote that individual freedom can only come through social regulation and the state interposing itself between the strong and the weak, the privileged and the unprivileged, the cunning and the simple. According to Ward, such interposition could be done through wise legislation (Commager 1950, 211).

Ward, however, was critical of legislation of his time since he believed such legislation to be limited in scope, reflecting the will of special interests rather than the needs of society as a whole, and more concerned with preventing crimes than releasing energies for constructive work. He pronounced that government needed to adopt positive programs that would stimulate rather than suppress and concern itself with crimes against society rather than crimes against individuals. His early embrace of a more proactive government was adopted by popular political figures such as William Jennings Bryan, Theodore Roosevelt, and Woodrow Wilson, as well as latter-day political leaders such as Franklin Roosevelt. Commager (1950, 217) stated that while Ward is largely forgotten and champions of laissez-faire and Social Darwinism such as Herbert Spencer (1820–1903) are extolled, government was moving along the lines of the former. By the early 1900s, Ward's philosophy was enacted into progressive legislation. Such legislation was viewed as necessary due to the massive inequities of the times (217). It became accepted that only the state had sufficient power to act effectively against the power of massive corporations.

William Jennings Bryan became the first major political figure to articulate the large-scale discontent that was sweeping the nation in the late nineteenth and early twentieth centuries. Bryan understood the economic problems of the nation and formulated a broad program to stir the passions of his followers. Named "The Great Commoner," Bryan was rejected by U.S. voters three times (1896, 1900, and 1908) as he ran for president under the banner of the Democratic Party. For two decades he led the fight against laissez-faire economics. While repudiated by voters, the causes he championed were vindicated by others such as Theodore Roosevelt, who many Americans considered the leader of the Progressive movement. Roosevelt advanced the "three Cs": conservation of natural resources, control of corporations, and consumer protection. Under his presidency, Congress passed legislation to curb the monopolistic power of railroads. Roosevelt directed his attorney general to bring a lawsuit on antitrust grounds against the leading meat-packers of the country that monopolized half or more of beef sales, and pushed Congress to pass legislation regarding food and drug safety.

Woodrow Wilson further advanced the ideals of progressive government. In his first Inaugural Address, Wilson stated that "society must see to it that it does not crush or weaken or damage its own constituent part; the first duty of law is to keep sound the society it serves" (quoted in Commager 1950, 219). Wilson accepted a broad interpretation of the U.S. Constitution and its powers to promote the general welfare. Specific accomplishments of the Wilson administration include establishing the Federal Reserve System that provided legal authority to issue Federal Reserve Notes, expanding antitrust powers through the Clayton Act of 1914, establishing the Federal Trade Commission to regulate business practices, and inaugurating programs to benefit farmers.

Commager (1950, 355) notes that Franklin Roosevelt extended earlier reforms in his advancement of a politics of hope, rather than a politics of regret and fear. Franklin D. Roosevelt is characterized as endlessly resourceful, always ready to experiment within permissible bounds, and respectful of precedent only when that respect is deserving (Commager 1950, 356). As a pragmatic realist, he recognized the dangers that the United States faced during his tenure. During a "Fireside Chat" of April 14, 1938, Roosevelt observed that democracy does not disappear because people dislike democracy, but because people "had grown tired of unemployment and insecurity, of seeing their children hungry while they sat helpless in the face of government confusion and government weakness through lack of leadership in government" (Commager 1950, 342). He noted that in desperation people chose to sacrifice liberty in the hope of getting something to eat. Despite the hard economic times, Roosevelt preached that American democratic institutions can be preserved and made to work.

Roosevelt's philosophy of faith over fear was affirmed with four impressive victories in the presidential races of 1932, 1936, 1940, and 1944. He successfully confronted the major crises of depression and war. Commager states that if American political thought and conduct are to be judged by the history of the Roosevelt administration, "the verdict must of necessity be positive" (Commager 1950, 357). Critics, however, denounced Roosevelt as a dictator, as a socialist, and defiant of the precepts of the founding fathers. Roosevelt's views, however, were considerably more moderate than others who adopted more socialistic postures. A number of such individuals exerted influence in U.S. politics.

Socialist Influences

Socialist ideas have a relatively long history in the United States. Dissatisfied with the American Federation of Labor (AFL), Daniel De Leon split with the AFL to found the Socialist Labor Party (SLP) in 1877. In 1897, union leader Eugene V. Debs founded the Social Democratic Party of America (SDPA). The two parties merged in 1901 to form the American Socialist Party under the leadership of Eugene V. Debs. The party supported public ownership of utilities, transportation, and communications, public ownership of monopolies, and workers' compensation insurance. Other policies were advanced such as reducing hours of work, providing higher wages, providing equal political and civil rights for all men and women, proportional representation, the referendum, initiative and recall; and universal education. Debs advanced the idea that worker interests were ignored by both major political parties and that both parties represented the interests of capitalists.

In 1910, a representative from a district in Milwaukee was elected as the first socialist member of the U.S. House of Representatives. In 1912, numerous mayors and aldermen were also elected. The pinnacle of the party's success occurred in 1912 when Debs attracted about 6 percent of the vote in the presidential race. His campaigns brought into the national dialogue issues such as child labor, civil rights, and universal suffrage. In addition to civil rights demands, the Socialist Party fought for improved labor conditions, better housing, and expanded welfare legislation. The Socialist Party attracted many of the era's leading intellectuals and hundreds of thousands of workers with its support for labor causes. Although the Socialist Party never displaced the major parties, many of its causes were adoption by the mainstream political parties (Socialist Party of America 2020).

A contemporary offspring of the Socialist Party of America (SPA) is the Democratic Socialists of America (DSA). This organization does not run their own candidates but has at times endorsed Democratic presidential candidates, including Walter Mondale, Jesse Jackson, John Kerry, Barack Obama, and Bernie Sanders. In November 2018, two DSA members, Alexandria Ocasio-Cortez and Rashida Tlaib, were elected to the House of Representatives while in 2020, two other DSA members (Cori Bush and Jamaal Bowman) were elected while running as Democratic Party candidates. American politicians such as Bernie Sanders are associated with the views of democratic socialism, advocating for an expansion of government as a force for good in people's lives. Supporters of democratic socialist generally support unions, tuition-free public universities, universal healthcare, federal jobs programs, taxes that close loopholes for the wealthy, and using taxes on the rich and corporations to pay for social welfare programs.

There is some indication that socialist ideas gained popularity after the 2008 financial crisis. The Occupy Wall Street movement made the democratic socialist tenet of closing the wage gap between the 1 percent and 99 percent part of the national conversation. A University of Chicago survey of eighteen- to thirty-four-year-olds, taken in 2018, found that 61 percent of millennial Democrats express favorable views toward socialism while a 2018 Gallup poll reported that more Democrats hold positive views of socialism than of capitalism, at 57 percent versus 47 percent respectively (Waxman 2018).

The official DSA website claims that many false ideas about socialism have developed in the United States. The website asserts that democratic socialists do not want to create an all-powerful government bureaucracy. At the same time, they do not want big corporate bureaucracies to control society. Democratic socialists reject the belief that the whole economy should be centrally planned yet also believe that democratic planning can shape major social investments like mass transit, housing, and energy. Their website claims that employers should make work more desirable by raising wages, offering benefits, and improving the work environment. A combination of social, economic, and moral incentives are advocated to motivate people. The DSA website pronounces that "although capitalism will be with us for a long time, reforms we win now—raising the minimum wage, securing a national health plan, and demanding passage of right-to-strike legislation—can bring us closer to socialism."

The ideology of socialism, however, continues to be attacked by critics, many of whom have firsthand experience with socialistic and communistic regimes. Former chess champion and former resident of the Soviet Union Gary Kasparov (2017) proposed that Americans talking about socialism in the twenty-first century was a luxury paid for by the successes of U.S. capitalism in the twentieth century. He asserts "that while inequality is a huge problem, the best way to increase everyone's share of pie is to make the pie bigger, not to dismantle the bakery." Kasparov recognized that while many of the traditional economic measures denote that America was doing fine, polls also indicated that many Americans were angry and fearful about the future. Kasparov claimed that with slower growth, stagnant wages, and the steady shift of wealth from labor to capital many people were willing to turn to the government for help and embrace socialism. Kasparov concluded that socialism was not the answer and "a society that relies too heavily on redistributing wealth eventually runs out of wealth to redistribute. The historical record is clear. It's capitalism that brought billions of people out of poverty in the 20th century. It's socialism that enslaved them and impoverished them" (Kasparov 2017, webpage).

It should be evident that influences from the social and political environment play a large role in determining what is acceptable and unacceptable, what is rewarded and distained for a given place and time. As discussed by Tocqueville and others, the social and political environment of the United States evolved over time, but was heavily influenced by the values of the original settlers. While the United States is by no means homogeneous, some agreement exists in regard to fundamental tenets and creeds of the United States. These tenets provided an environment that allowed for growth, development, individualism, capital accumulation, and entrepreneurship. Personal freedom allows individuals choice in what endeavors to pursue or not pursue.

FUTURE OF U.S. SOCIAL AND POLITICAL ENVIRONMENT

The environment has influenced people and allowed many to prosper, however, environments are not immutable, unchanging gifts from God, but environments change over time. History indicates that jurisdictions at one time or another have been open or closed, free or repressive, stagnant or resourceful, loving or hateful, strong or weak. Different environments have led to either spurts of creativity or periods of stagnation. The role of individuals fostered one type of environment or another yet individuals were also affected by their general surroundings. Their ambitions were either suppressed or encouraged. Some people passively accepted their environments and tried to survive within the existing framework; others succeeded in altering their environment in either a positive or negative direction.

The direction of the future U.S. social and political environment is unclear. On the one hand, people point to the U.S. Statue of Liberty as an enduring marker of U.S. openness to others. Signs of tolerance include greater acceptance of alternative lifestyles, gay marriage, and gay adoption of children. Acceptance of looser forms of dress and different custom also suggest greater tolerance. On the other hand, opposition to immigrations remains one of the "hot button" issues that motivates voters. Politicians such as Bernie Sanders generate huge followings yet the overall political environment for entrepreneurs and their companies remain friendly. For example, in 1996, Congress approved Section 230 of the Communications Decency Act that placed limits on companies' legal exposure for the words, photos, and videos posted by users of their websites.

Only after attacks by Democratic and Republican leaders have tech industry leaders such as Facebook's Mark Zuckerberg and Twitter's Jack Dorsey admitted that the law could be updated or expanded. Facebook has been criticized by liberals for allowing misinformation to spread and by conservatives who claim that the company takes too much right-leaning content down. Facebook and others in Silicon Valley have often pushed back vigorously against any talk of changing Section 230 of the Decency Act. Proposed changes in the law by tech giants have been interpreted as a rhetorical strategy to forestall real reform (McCabe 2020).

Throughout U.S. history, the government has propped up troubling companies and economies in trouble. The first major intervention occurred during the Panic of 1792, when Treasury Secretary Alexander Hamilton authorized purchases to prevent the collapse of the securities market. In 2008, Congress passed the Emergency Economic Stabilization Act that created the Troubled Asset Relief Program (TARP). This program authorized the U.S. Department of the Treasury to buy up to $700 billion in toxic assets from companies, which could then replenish their balance sheets with safer assets.

The Treasury Department was also authorized to buy up to $250 billion in bank shares. Companies such as Bank of America, Citigroup, and the insurance giant AIG were deemed "too big to fail" and were supported by government funds. More recently, in 2020, the Coronavirus Aid, Relief, and Economic Security (CARES) Act provided more than $2 trillion in assistance. Part of the Act included the Paycheck Protection Program, which funneled more than $500 billion to companies through the Small Business Administration to keep workers on the payrolls (Davis 2021). Although the political environment in the United States appears to be favorable toward business, recent events suggests that changes may be in store. By late 2020, a flurry of lawsuits alleging anti-competitive behavior had been launched against companies such as Google, Amazon, and Facebook. Nearly forty states launched antitrust lawsuits against Google. The U.S. government also initiated an antitrust lawsuit against Facebook (Gray 2020).

One can see from the animal kingdom that some species are more adaptable to conditions and some successfully alter their conditions to benefit themselves. The example of the beaver is instructive. The resourceful beaver is the mascot of great engineering universities such as the Massachusetts Institute of Technology (MIT), the California Institute of Technology (CalTech), and others such as my alma mater City College of New York and Oregon State University. It is interesting to note that ecologists call beavers "ecosystem engineers" because they physically alter habitats by cutting down trees, building dams, digging canals, and building lodges. Using engineering instincts, they significantly alter the ecology of place. Dam building slows the flow of water and triggers a host of changes in the plants and animals that live in the area. Aquatic plants colonize the new pond; turtles, fish, and other water creatures take up residence. Drowned trees become homes for insects and birds; larger animals follow, looking for food and shelter. Over the course of many years, a wetland forms. Beavers directly benefit from their environmental alterations. A beaver on land has been described as a slow-moving snack for wolves, bears, and cougars. By contrast, beavers are incredibly powerful and agile swimmers. So building dams increases the safety of their habitat (Dennehy 2018).

One must be knowledgeable of one's environment in order to sustain or change it for the better. It is proposed by many that the U.S. environment or ecosystem has been relatively successful in terms of supporting entrepreneurs and generating wealth creation. Measures such as gross national product, per capita income, population growth, tax base, business creation and others suggest that the U.S. environment has been conducive to development. Problems such as wealth and income distribution nevertheless still remain. According to Franklin D. Roosevelt, hope over fear has often triumphed in the face of adversity. Sustaining the environment that fostered U.S. prior successes demands constant attention. The United States and other leaders need to think like beavers and should be ready to change their environments as conditions demand.

Part III

DECLINE OF U.S. ENTREPRENEURIAL DYNAMISM?

Chapter 7

Challenges to U.S. Entrepreneurship

ENTREPRENEURSHIP, INSTITUTIONAL SETTING, AND ECONOMIC DEVELOPMENT

The basic thesis of this book is that entrepreneurship and economic development are inextricably tied to an overall "ecosystem" identified in a place's legal, educational, social, and political environment. The role of individuals is significant yet one must also recognize that individual action takes place within a broad environment that can deter or foster development. Nobel laureate Douglas North's (1990) discussion of institutions helps to explain how the broad environment and "rules of the game" in that environment affect growth and decline. North contends that societal rules structure incentives and supplies cues to people as they make their choices. Perceived opportunities and blockages affect choices regarding economic development and other activities.

North claimed that rules of the game can derive from official documents (such as the U.S. Constitution) or evolve over time as in common law. The organizations that are created and how they evolve are influenced by this broad societal framework. A clear benefit of stable rules of interaction is that of reducing uncertainty. Informal rules provide stability yet are subject to incremental change. Formal rules are more likely to be subject to quick change as informal rules are embedded in relatively stable customs, traditions, and codes of conduct (6).

North asserts that we cannot feel, touch, or measure norms and rules of the game (termed institutions) since they are constructs of the human mind. Nevertheless, he asserts that institutions represent "the underlying determinant of the long-run performance of economies" (North 1990, 107). According to North, some constraints (such as the inability of societies to enforcement of contracts) represent important sources of both historical stagnation and contemporary underdevelopment (54). North stated that in developed countries because of effective judicial systems "one has confidence that the merits of a case rather than private payoffs will influence outcomes. In contrast, enforcement in Third World economies is uncertain" (North 1990, 59). He sees significant differences between the institutional framework of countries such as the United States, England, France, Germany, and Japan and Third World countries. The institutional framework in turn is identified as "the critical key to the relative success of economies" (North 1990, 69).

Numerous examples are given regarding how institutional rules (such as the norm of enforcing contracts) affect economic development in various societies. North contrasts historical evolutions of England with that of Spain. He observes that both faced the need to raise revenue to survive in the face of rising costs. In England, financial pressures "led to the evolution of a polity and economy that solved the fiscal crisis and went on to dominate the Western world." In Spain, "in spite of initially more favorable conditions, it led to unresolved fiscal crises, bankruptcies, confiscation of assets, and insecure property rights and to three centuries of relative stagnation" (North 1990, 113).

In England, Parliament and the legislative branch of government eventually gained the right to make laws, enquire into abuses, and share in the guidance of national policy. In Spain, the monarchy gained control over the aristocracy and church policy; its centralized monarchy controlled the state bureaucracy. The monarchy subsequently shaped norms, values, and individual expectations (North 1990, 114). Decentralization of power in England made a critical difference. The Parliament in England provided the beginning of representative government and a reduction in "rent seeking" (seeking to gain wealth through political or social connections without contributing to productivity) behavior. Parliament's ascension also helped ensure property rights and led to a more effective, impartial judicial system. In contrast, Spain established a centralized bureaucracy that attempted to manage details of economic life with the objective of furthering the interest of the monarchy. Eventually, poor management of Spain's finance led to fiscal demands that outstripped revenue, higher taxes, insecure property rights, and bankruptcy (North 1990, 114).

North (1990, 33) places special emphasis on the role of property rights. He notes that one only has to compare property rights in Beirut in the 1980s with those of a modern small U.S. community. In the former, property can be seized by violence, in the latter the legal structure defines and enforces rights. Historical precedence matters. Path dependency (the idea that present decisions are dependent on prior decisions) plays a key role in economic growth and entrepreneurship. The role of history in shaping English institutions is relevant. Some argue that from the thirteenth century, English society differed from others (Macfarlane 1978). In contrast to traditional peasant societies, English society is seen as being more fluid, and individualistic with an array of formal rules that protected property, inheritance, and the legal status of women. English differences then migrated to the United States. Douglas North (1990, 103) asserts that the U.S. Constitution embodies the ongoing heritage of Britain. This heritage and the ideals supporting them fostered economic growth and development. The historical background laid the groundwork for development of private lending, property rights, removal of mercantilist restrictions, and expanded opportunities. Both growing markets and patent laws encouraged innovation (North 1990, 114).

As discussed in earlier chapters, a relatively high concentration of the wealthiest and most successful entrepreneurs exists in the United States. Precisely why this is the case are difficult to discern. This book highlights the importance of culture/tolerance, returns from education, political structure, and legal protections as contributing factors that encourage development. No doubt, other factors play a part, however, it is reasonable to infer that individual initiative is influenced by perceptions of the returns from effort. Environment, norms, and rules shape perceptions of opportunity. It is logical and economically rational that negative cues from the environment deter risk taking, effort, and investment. If rewards that derive from labor are perceived as likely to be confiscated and subject to arbitrary seizure, rational economic actors (in the absence of severe coercion) will reduce effort. Entrepreneurship therefore is dependent upon perception of opportunities for reward as well as the ability to retain those rewards.

TOLERANCE, POLITICS, LAWS, EDUCATION, AND ECONOMIC DEVELOPMENT

Tolerance

Tolerance is one component of the overall "culture of place." It is dependent upon its historical past as well as contemporary developments. Tolerant attitudes foster economic growth by attracting highly productive people who are searching to live in a more conducive environment. Richard Florida (2012) in *The Rise of the Creative Class* indicates that a lack of tolerance can drive away talented individuals. Tolerance, however, should not be viewed as a dichotomy, but as a continuum ranging from love of others to hatred of others with a middle ground of cool indifference. At various times in history, visceral hatred has produced tragic consequences. The examples of (1) Balkan genocide, (2) the World War II holocaust, and (3) the Armenian genocide of 1915–1916 provide examples of how the intolerance can corrode social norms and lead to reprehensible action. Throughout history these are not the only unconscionable acts of intolerance but represent fairly recent examples. In addition, hatred can diminish productivity by shifting priorities away from commerce and productive activities toward identifying and killing perceived enemies.

The Armenian genocide refers to the massacre of Christian Armenians who lived in the Muslim Ottoman Empire. The official date of the beginning of the Armenian genocide is often cited as April 25, 1915, yet the Armenian genocide was preceded by earlier displays of hatred toward Armenians. Some history is instructive in order to more fully understand the background of the Armenian massacres. The history of the Armenian people who dwelt in the Caucasus region of Eurasia dates back 3,000 years. At one period of time, the kingdom of Armenia was an independent entity. At the beginning of the fourth century AD, Armenia became the first nation in the world to make Christianity its official religion. During the fifteenth century, Armenia was absorbed into the Islamic Ottoman Empire and as "infidels," Armenians were subjected to harsh treatment. In spite of these obstacles, the Armenian community thrived under Ottoman rule. The Armenian people tended to be better educated and wealthier than their Turkish neighbors, who grew to resent their success. In an effort to solve "the Armenian question," the Turkish Sultan approved the sacking of Armenian cities by Turkish military officials and others. Massacres of hundreds of thousands of Armenian citizens occurred between 1894 and 1896.

In 1914, the Ottoman Empire entered World War I on the side of Germany and the Austro-Hungarian Empire. Religious authorities of the Ottoman Empire subsequently declared a holy war against all Christians except their allies. Military leaders of the Ottoman Empire argued that the Armenians could not be trusted, that they were traitors and would be eager to fight for the enemy. The Turkish government subsequently arrested and executed Armenian intellectuals. Ordinary Armenians were sent on death marches through the Mesopotamian desert without food or water. Armenian marchers were stripped naked and forced to walk until they died; people who stopped to rest were shot. Government squads kidnapped children, converted them to Islam and gave them to Turkish families. Government squads raped Armenian women and forced them to join Turkish harems or serve as slaves. Muslim families seized Armenian property and moved into the homes of deported Armenians. Reports vary, however, most sources agree that about 2 million Armenians lived in the Ottoman Empire prior to the time of the genocide. After the war, in 1922, estimates of the Armenian population approximated 388,000 (History.com editors 2019).

The Bosnian genocide of 1990 also has long historical roots. Paris (1961, 4) notes that between 1941 and 1945, in the name of racial purity and religion, 750,000 Serbs, 50,000 Jews, and 26,000 Gypsies were killed by agents of the Ustashi Croatian government. The Ustashi regime was supported by the Axis powers (Germany, Italy, and Japan) as well as by the Croatian Catholic hierarchy. Eastern Orthodox Christian Serbs living in Croatia barely escaped complete extermination. Victims were for the most part Serbs who belonged to the Serbian Orthodox Church. Between 1941 and 1945, the Ustashi government forced Christian Serbs to dig their own graves, tied their hands tied behind their backs, and buried them alive. Others were killed with knives and thrown into deep crevices, many were tortured. Paris (1961, 5) stated, "it is difficult for the world to believe that a whole people could be doomed to extermination by a government and a religious hierarchy of the twentieth century, just because it happened to belong to another ethnical and racial group and which had inherited the Christianity of Byzantium rather than that of Rome."

The Croatian genocide of World War II represented the greatest massacre of World War II, in proportion to a nation's population. The persecution of the Eastern Orthodox Serbs did not occur in a vacuum. Followers of the Eastern Orthodox religion were persecuted for centuries by the Roman Catholic monarchs of Hungary. By the nineteenth century, hatred for the Eastern Orthodox Serbs (previously confined to the Roman Catholic priesthood) spread to the general Croatian population. By the 1990s, the seeds were laid for the atrocities of the 1992–1995 Bosnian War. During this time, Eastern Orthodox Bosnian Serbs with the backing of the Yugoslav army perpetrated genocide against Bosnian Muslims and Croatians. This resulted in the deaths of approximately 100,000 people (80% of them Bosnian Muslims). Serbians attacked Bosnian Muslim (Bosniak) dominated towns and forcibly expelled civilians. In what became known as the Srebrenica Massacre, Bosniak women were raped while the men and boys were killed. Estimates of Bosniaks killed by Serb forces at Srebrenica range from around 7,000 to more than 8,000 (Hisory.com editors 2020a).

The intolerance and hatred that fueled Adolf Hitler's rise to power is well documented. Hitler swayed public opinion by using pseudo-scientific arguments to assert the superiority of the German race and the inferiority of other races. The pseudo-scientific arguments of racial superiority presumably justified a natural right for Germans to rule over Europe, if not over the entire world. According to the Nazi racial ideology, a person's characteristics, attitudes, abilities, and behavior were determined by his or her racial makeup. Hitler believed that all of human history could be explained in terms of a racial struggle. Inherited characteristics related not only to outward appearance but also were believed to have shaped ways of thinking, creative abilities, intelligence, taste, physical strength, and military prowess.

Hitler classified Jews as the priority enemy, but targeted other groups for annihilation including Gypsies, people with disabilities, Poles, Soviet prisoners of war, and Afro-Germans. The Nazis also targeted political dissidents, Jehovah's Witnesses, homosexuals, and security risks either because they opposed the Nazi regime or some aspect of their behavior did not fit Nazi perceptions of social norms. The Nazis sought to eliminate racial threats through a purging of German society. They contended that superior races had not just the right but the obligation to subdue and even exterminate inferior ones. This ideology, however, appears to simply provide philosophical cover for deep-seated hatred and intolerance of the "other." The Nazis believed that groups such as the Slavs must work for their overlords; they believed the Jews could never be assimilated and therefore must be killed (Paris 1961, 3).

The genocide of the Armenians by the Turks in 1915, the holocaust of World War II, or the genocide in Bosnia did not produce great economic prosperity by the perpetrators of the genocides. Turkey and Bosnia languished economically; after World War II, Germany lay in ruins. Killings in the name of racial or religious purity did not produce widespread prosperity; killings were the outward expression of hatred and intolerance of others. This intolerance coincided with military aggression, scapegoating, military overextension, and eventual destruction.

This discussion may seem tangential to entrepreneurship, yet is instrumental in highlighting the insidious impact of hatred on the norms and rules of society. It reaffirms the idea that social environment cannot be separated from development. In contrast to the extreme hatred exhibited over time in various societies, the atmosphere of relative tolerance in the United States encouraged development. The in-migration of generations of people coming to the United States in search of a better life added significantly to U.S. prosperity and growth. Extreme hatred may have produced short-term satisfaction from real or perceived grievances, but in reality, it did not lead to long-term economic prosperity. The German Third Reich lasted considerable less time than the promised 1,000 years, the Ottoman Empire crumbled, and the countries of the Balkans lived up to their reputation for division into small mutually hostile groups. The term "balkanization" reflects the history of division in this part of Southeastern Europe.

Politics

Alexis de Tocqueville provides keen insight into American life and political structure. Many of the observations he wrote about in 1835 are remarkably still relevant today. Although highly critical of some aspects of the U.S. political structure, Tocqueville also identified numerous strengths. His comments about popular sovereignty, decentralization, and checks and balances are particularly pertinent. Tocqueville notes that the government of consent of the governed is a particularly important aspect of U.S.

democracy but warns readers about the dangers of tyranny of the majority. According to Tocqueville, after the Revolutionary War the upper classes in the United States acquiesce to expanded sovereignty in order to gain the goodwill of the people. Legislation expanded the right to vote. The ethos of expanded participation in government is most clearly observed in New England townships where local liberties were deeply rooted. In the New England townships, administrative duties were designated to leaders who were elected on a yearly basis. These leaders or "selectmen" generally acted on already established principles agreed upon by the majority. To enact changes in precedent, selectmen needed to summon all voters by calling a town meeting.

Tocqueville claimed New Englanders were attached to their township not only by birth but by contributions and participation. He states, residents of New England were attached to the township "because it is independent and free." Cooperation in township affairs enhances allegiance to the collective interest. The well-being of the township secures the affection of residents and the welfare of the township is a primary aim of exertions (Tocqueville 2002, 86). The ideas of affiliation and participation in governing therefore has strong roots in the United States and remains of source of governing legitimacy. Tocqueville concluded that the only means for a nation to have true freedom is through local institutions. It is evident from Tocqueville that both decentralization of power to the lowest levels of governance and stout adherence to the principle of rule by the consent of the people date to the earliest period of the U.S. colonies.

Another concern of the U.S. political system is its ability to attain and conserve liberty. Division of power helps to prevent despotism and foster individual freedom. Tocqueville concluded that in the United States no one person had extreme power. In a small New England townships, there were nineteen officials, each with limited sphere of authority. Tocqueville observed that in the United States, executives were subject to the courts and legislatures. Standing for election by the people, executives needed to foster goodwill of constituents. All of these checks helped to assure individual rights and protect against concentrated power.

According to Tocqueville, while Americans disagree on almost everything, they were unanimous in their love of freedom. The courts acted as a safeguard for freedom and a check on the potential tyranny of the majority. The role of the judicial branch was to limit the powers of other branches; it was viewed as being less political than the other branches of government with judges appointed to very long terms. Tocqueville admired the decentralized American system and its ability to protect individual freedom. He applauded the distribution of authority and showed disdain for centralization which tended to maintain the status quo (109).

Protection of freedom remains a dominant concern of Tocqueville. He contrasts the subservient nature of the people in many of the states or Europe with the greater activism of people under the decentralized structure of U.S. governance. Tocqueville admits that villages and counties of the United States might more usefully be governed by a remote authority and perhaps the country would be more secure. However, he ultimately prefers the political advantages of the decentralized United States to that of more centralized systems, stating, "It profits me but little, after all, that a vigilant authority should protect the tranquility of my pleasures and constantly avert all dangers from my path" if the state is in absolute control over life and liberty (Tocqueville 2002, 111).

Laws

Legal protections are essential for freedom and prosperity. The ability to acquire and retain property (physical assets or intellectual property rights) motivates many to start businesses and strive to achieve the American Dream. Entrepreneurs start and grow companies to fulfill individual dreams. In contrast to autocratic societies where rulers can arbitrarily confiscate property, in the United States and other democracies, rule of law offers valuable protections. Various studies support the view that the United States strongly supports rule of law. The idea of "rule of law rather than men" has long historical roots in the United States dating back at least to the time of the Revolutionary War. The founding fathers railed against the arbitrary authority of the king of England and endeavored to create a society where rules could be neutrally enforced regardless of social standing or wealth. The first ten amendments to the U.S. Constitution strove to ensure fundamental rights and protect individual liberties.

Rule of law is significantly more apparent in the United States than in authoritarian nations. The United States also compares relatively well (although not the highest performers) with European nations in terms of securing property rights. The World Bank provides an Annual Report to assess security of property rights, government effectiveness, and regulatory quality. The assessment of rule of law captured perceptions of the extent to which people had confidence in and abided by the rules of society, in particular the quality of contract enforcement, property rights, the police, and the courts. Security of property rights captured the degree to which individuals could fortify rights to their property. Government effectiveness assessed the quality of public services and the degree of their independence from political pressures. Regulatory quality captured assessments of governments' ability to formulate and implement sound policies. The United States ranked relatively high on measures (although not the highest) when compared to twenty-eight

European nations in terms of rule of law (8th), security of property rights (9th), government effectiveness (9th), and regulatory quality (9th). Countries perceived to have the strongest legal protections included the Nordic, Anglo-Saxon, and Benelux countries. Scores of Eastern European nations such as Greece, Italy, Spain, and Portugal were relatively low (Elert et al. 2019, 26).

Economic actors often compensated for weaknesses in the rule of law and property rights protection by participating in underground, nontaxed activity. In countries such as Bulgaria and Romania where the rule of law and property rights protection were assessed to be weak, the off-the books underground economy was thought to be powerful. In Bulgaria and Romania, the shadow economy was estimated to be approximately 30 percent of the nation's official gross domestic product. In Northern European countries, the proportions of the shadow economy were assessed at less than half of the estimated 30 percent in Bulgaria and Romania. Shadow economy activity is less efficient in that it creates unfair competition for firms that adhere to rules and regulations (Elert et al. 2019). Innovation is affected by legal protections, however, other factors also shape innovation. According to the Institute for Management Development (IMD), an independent academic institution with Swiss roots, in 2018, ranked the United States first among the top twenty nations in a measure of innovation (3).

Implicit in the concept of property rights is the idea that protection against arbitrary authority establishes a framework for individual and collective prosperity. At the operational level, the tension between government prerogatives and individual rights is observed in the controversy surrounding eminent domain and "takings." The extent to which government takeover of private property ("takings") inhibits or fosters economic development is not fully known. Some studies decry the erosion of individual freedom in "takings" while others contend that government's responsibility to ensure economic development, at times, call for acquiring private property.

The logic behind granting government the power to confiscate private property for its own use without the owner's consent (eminent domain) is that the government will occasionally need large tracts of land for public projects such as highways, schools, parks, and hospitals. The Fifth Amendment's "takings clause" grants the U.S. federal government authority to use eminent domain provided the taking is for "public use" and the property owner receives "just compensation." The conditions of public use and just compensation attempt to ameliorate abuse by placing constraints on the government's eminent domain power. Various studies indicate that insecure property rights drive productive economic activity underground. Secure property rights diminish uncertainty. The uncertainty related to "takings" is less severe in the United States than in other countries, however, fears regarding the ability of the state to weaken property rights remain (Boettne et al. 2010, 336).

The "public use" requirement in eminent domain is intended to limit government power to transfer property from one private owner to another. The "just compensation" condition requires the government to pay the market rate for confiscated property. This condition aims to prevent the government from arbitrarily seizing private property. In the past, the courts have supported the government's right to use eminent domain in order to create jobs. For example, in 1954, the U.S. Supreme Court supported the city of Detroit's right to use eminent domain to displace several thousand private residents for the construction of a General Motors factory. In the more recent *Kelo v. City of New London* case, the Supreme Court ruled that benefits from economic gain could justify the taking of private property.

The *Kelo* ruling sparked a backlash against eminent domain powers and led to calls to strengthen private property protections. Opposition to the *Kelo* ruling came from groups such as American Association of Retired Persons (AARP), the National Association for the Advancement of Colored People (NAACP), the Libertarian Party, the American Conservative Union, and the Institute for Justice. Much of the public viewed the *Kelo* decision as a violation of property rights, the consequence of which would benefit large corporations at the expense of individual homeowners and local communities. Owners of family farms also disapproved of the ruling. In 2006, President George W. Bush issued an Executive Order instructing the federal government to restrict the use of eminent domain for general public goals rather than for the purpose of advancing the interest of private parties. Following the *Kelo* decision, a large number of states amended their eminent domain laws to strengthen private property protections. Attitudes about "takings" varied by jurisdiction. In state and local governments that were accustomed to high taxation, regulation of labor, regulation of products, and other policies, legislatures were less inclined to restrict takings power. In contrast, jurisdictions that were characterized by more economic freedom placed greater limitations on takings (Lopez et al. 2009).

Protection of intellectual property represents another legal concern. According to the official website of the U.S. State Department, intellectual property is the lifeblood of the U.S. economy. A branch of the U.S. State Department, the Office of Intellectual Property Enforcement (IPE) advocates for the effective protection of intellectual property rights (IPR) by working with U.S. ambassadors and diplomats to ensure that the interests of American rights holders are protected. The Office of IPE views intellectual property protection as vital for economic development since such property rights represent a large proportion of the U.S. gross national product. The IPE emphasizes that a strong system of IPR assures inventors, industrial designers, and creative artists that their ideas will be protected. The agency notes that development and enforcement of IPR makes it possible for the United States to continue to be one of the most innovative countries in the world. The IPE proclaimed that innovation is a hallmark of the United States and it has contributed enormously to new developments of immense importance. The IPE website states, "American scientists, engineers, and entrepreneurs invented the microchip, created the Internet, invented the smartphone, started the biotechnology revolution, sent astronauts to the Moon, and saved millions of lives through innovative medicines. America's creative artists—authors, musicians, film directors and gamers—have captivated the imagination of people all over the world" (U.S. State Department n.d. webpage).

Education

Education has previously been discussed in chapter 5 as a historical strength of the United States. While warning signs exist in terms of the overall quality of the U.S. educational system, U.S. universities remain a source of strength. Many of America's most successful entrepreneurs either attended or graduated from one of its top-rated universities. While some argue that entrepreneurship taps innate qualities that cannot be taught, others look at entrepreneurship as a skill (such as mathematics) that is transmitted through good pedagogy at good universities. Educational quality is somewhat subjective; however, the quality of educational institutions is regularly assessed in popular magazines and other outlets. One such outlet assesses masters of business administration programs in entrepreneurship by combined overall rankings with data such as graduates starting their own businesses, employer perceptions, and research output. In 2019, four of the world's highest-ranking programs in entrepreneurship and the highest-ranked program were located in the United States. This represents a higher proportion of top-ranked schools than any other country. The top-ten programs include in descending order: Stanford (U.S.), Imperial College (U.K.), IE (Spain), Oxford (U.K.), ESADE (Spain), IESE (Spain), Harvard (U.S.), UC-Berkeley (U.S.), University of Pennsylvania (U.S.), and University of Cambridge (U.K.) (Kiersz 2019).

Growth of entrepreneurship programs in U.S. universities represents another indicator of the perceived importance it holds. Entrepreneurship education has become increasingly popular at U.S. universities. In the early 1980s, approximately 300 universities offered entrepreneurship courses; by the 1990s, over 1,000 universities offered courses in entrepreneurship. In 2005, the number of universities offering entrepreneurship courses had reached 1,600 (Kuratko 2005). Several organizations including the National Foundation for Teaching Entrepreneurship, the Kauffman Foundation, and the Consortium for Entrepreneurship Education established curriculum for effective entrepreneurship education programs.

In general, student in entrepreneurship programs are encouraged to learn through experience. Entrepreneurship courses attempt to inspire students to look at problems differently; courses often challenge the status quo and nurture creativity by looking at the world in a different light. Entrepreneurship education programs try to instill self-confidence and boost the self-esteem. Students in entrepreneurship classes are encouraged to stand behind their ideas, to learn how to accept failure and to stay motivated when presented with obstacles. Students often come from various background (Bridges 2008).

U.S. EXCEPTIONALISM AND ENTREPRENEURIALISM?

Entrepreneurialism is not unique to the United States, however, it appears to represent a comparative advantage of the nation. The role of the national environment or the ecology for development cannot be ignored. The question of why entrepreneurship and innovation is relatively strong in the United States is a fundamental question to be explored in future research. One must ask, is the United States unique in certain characteristics? Is the United States not unique in its political and legal organization, but better able to achieve goals because of its history and path dependence? Is the United States "exceptional" in a way that promotes economic growth? Is there something in the water or is there a secret sauce that led to U.S. economic advancement? The term "U.S. exceptionalism" has historically referred to as the belief that the United States differs qualitatively from other nations on many dimensions. Differences are assigned to national beliefs, historical evolution, or distinctive political and religious institutions. Commonly cited in discussion of American exceptionalism is the idea that the United States and its people hold a special place in the world by offering opportunity for individuals and hope for humanity. This idea is supported by a balance of public and private interests and constitutional ideals that focus on personal and economic freedom. Some have used the concept of American exceptionalism to claim moral superiority for America or Americans, however, opponents of the concept content that it is little more than ethnocentrism and propaganda. Critics argue that the United States is similar to other countries that have claimed an exceptional nature or destiny; they argue that all great powers of the past (such as the Egyptians, Greeks, Chinese, and Romans to name a few) have asserted superiority over "barbarian" others.

Historical support for the concept of American exceptionalism is often traced to the Protestantism of Puritan settlers of New England. The metaphor of a "city upon a hill" described by early Puritan leader, John Winthrop, expressed the view that the Puritan community of New England should serve as a model for the rest of the world. This metaphor is often used by proponents of exceptionalism. The Puritans' deep moralistic values were inculcated into the national identity of the United States and retain influence. The settlers of New England viewed themselves as participants in creating a kingdom of God on earth. These beliefs combine with attitudes toward democracy, immigration, liberty, individualism, and mobility shape the argument for U.S. exceptionalism (New World Encyclopedia contributors 2016).

The U.S. belief in a form of government in which a state is ruled by representatives of citizens (i.e., Republicanism) was forged in the view that sovereignty belonged to the people, not to a hereditary ruling class. Thomas Paine's 1776 pamphlet *Common Sense* expressed the opinion that America was not just an extension of Europe but a new land, a country of nearly unlimited potential and opportunity that had outgrown the British mother country. Proponents of American exceptionalism highlight the nation's founding on a set of republican ideals, rather than on a common heritage, ethnicity, or ruling elite. Another factor supportive of U.S. exceptionalism refers to immigration and the fact that America has been unusually attractive to immigrants from all parts of the world. Advocates of American exceptionalism contend that the United States possesses an unusually high degree of social and economic mobility. The term "American Dream" conceptualizes the perceived abundance of opportunities in the American system. During the Cold War, the value of liberty in the United States was often contrasted with tyranny and oppression of Communism and the Soviet Union.

Following Frederick Jackson Turner's "Frontier Thesis," proponents of American exceptionalism also claimed that the "American spirit" was created at the frontier where rugged conditions gave birth to the country's national vitality. Under this perspective, American society is best understood when viewed from the lens of a response to new conditions; not as a continuation of European ideas. For most of its history, the United States has been associated with mobility. Known as the land of opportunity, the United States promoted itself on providing people with the opportunity to escape from the contexts of their class and family background. Advocates of U.S. exceptionalism argue that in the United States children could easily choose careers which were not based upon their parents' vocations; geographical location was not static, and citizens were free to move without barrier. In regard to status, as in most countries, family standing and riches were often a means to remain in a higher social circle. However, the United States is viewed as unusual in the perceptions that anyone who worked hard could aspire to higher social standing. Birth circumstances were not taken as a social barrier to the upper echelons or to high political standing. These views stood in contrast to prevailing attitudes in other countries where many higher offices were socially determined, and usually difficult to enter without being born into the suitable social group (New World Encyclopedia contributors 2016).

Seymour Martin Lipset (1996, 17–19) helped to refine the construct of American exceptionalism. According to Lipset, "Americanism" and "American exceptionalism" is based on liberty, equality before the law, individual responsibility, republicanism, and laissez-faire economics. America is seen as having a unique mission to transform the world. In a Public Broadcasting System interview, Lipset contended that Europe has always been more stratified than the United States because of their history of feudalism with greater respect for the privileged classes. In contrast, the United States was called a "settler society," formed by immigrants. The frontier served as an outlet for people who were perceived to be troublemakers, people who wanted to change society, and people who were frustrated because of their economic condition. Instead of making revolution these people were able to migrate to the frontier to start over again. This was not as readily possible in other societies. Lipset saw the frontier as a place that helped reduce revolutionary pressure for change and as a safety value. Lipset noted that there are various positives associated with U.S. exceptionalism but also negatives such as the high crime rate, high rate of violence; relatively low rate of voting, and high incarceration rate (Seymour Martin Lipset Interview, n.d. website).

Another perspective of U.S. exceptionalism focuses on the relative weakness of socialist ideas compared to Europe. Socialist candidates have run for office at various times in the United States, however, in the past have not met with great success. The relative success of Senator Bernie Sanders in mobilizing voters suggests that contemporary economic condition may be ripe for candidates that call for more government activism. However, Sanders failed twice in his bids for the Democratic Party nomination. Voter support and a lack of ultimate success at the national level indicates that people hold both positive and negative perceptions of socialism.

An area of U.S. strength is education; the roots of this strength is traced to religion. Lipset observed that because Protestant sectarianism demands that people read the Bible and interpret it for themselves, there was a high emphasis on education in the United States. The early emphasis on literacy in order to read the Bible pressured schools and colleges to train teachers as well as preachers. In earlier times, more Americans went to high school than any other country. Lipset also noted that U.S. exceptionalism seemed to have declined because Europe was becoming more like the United States in terms of education and standards of living. He believed differences still existed in terms of pride in nation (U.S. higher), approval of state intervention (U.S. lower), and ideology with the U.S. ideology based to a larger degree on the concepts of social equality and equality of opportunity.

POLITICAL AND ECONOMIC VALUE OF ENTREPRENEURSHIP

Entrepreneurship adds political stability and economic strength to jurisdictions (Elert et al. 2019, 3). A lack of opportunity coupled with few new business creations are signs of economic stagnation that in turn can foster xenophobia and radical populism. Economic growth in contrast reduces such threats as people become absorbed in achieving success of their businesses (Friedman 2005). In a stagnant economy, people no longer see opportunities for improvement and can turn to strong leaders who blame outsiders for poor economic conditions and promise improvement. In an open, vibrant entrepreneurial environment, the simplistic recipes of strong leaders lose much of their appeal. Political and social reforms foster inclusive growth and therefore reduce the threat of instability (Elert et al. 2019, 1). In theory, the political benefits of entrepreneurialism are clear. Entrepreneurialism leads to fuller employment, more wealth creation, and greater satisfaction with the economic system in general. People become fully focused on improving their economic lot in life and believe that their efforts will bear fruit. Stability results as a product of both satisfaction with one's economic prospects and a lack of incentive to commit to political causes. Economic despair and blocked opportunity traditionally has been a harbinger for political instability.

The success of the United States in terms of entrepreneurial ventures remains the envy of others. Elert et al. (2019, 1) found that while the aggregate self-employment rate (often small businesses) was considerably lower in the United States than in Western Europe and East Asia, the number of U.S. billionaire entrepreneurs per capita was three times greater. Other measures of entrepreneurship such as total venture capital (VC) and investment as a share of gross domestic product were also indicative of a positive entrepreneurial environment. The number of large firms founded by entrepreneurs since 1990 was more than three times greater in the United States than in Western Europe. The number of unicorns (privately held start-up companies valued at over $1 billion) was almost seven times greater in the United States. These differences are attributed to success in "Schumpeterian entrepreneurship" defined as entrepreneurship that introduces new products and technologies. The "ecosystem" for Schumpeterian, high-impact entrepreneurship was perceived to be significantly greater in the United States than in other developed nations (6).

The overall value of entrepreneurship to a nation's economy should be self-evident. Entrepreneurs have the ability to change the way we live; their innovations improve standards of living, and in addition to creating individual wealth, entrepreneurs also create jobs thereby expanding a nation's tax base. Entrepreneurs can produce a cascading effect, with new businesses stimulating the creation of related enterprises that arise in order to support the new ventures. This cascading effect furthers economic development. Entrepreneurs create new and improved products, services, or technologies that enable new markets to be developed and new wealth to be created. All of this adds to national income. By offering unique goods and services, entrepreneurs reduce dependence on obsolete systems and technologies. This can result in an improved quality of life, improved morale for citizens, and greater economic freedom (Seth 2020).

In the United States, entrepreneurism is part of America's identity and self-image. Entrepreneurism is seen as a route to upward mobility and a means for average people to build wealth. Technology further enables entrepreneurs to expand into regional and global markets. Exports from entrepreneurial companies then contribute to a region's productivity and earnings thereby promoting the overall welfare of a population. New and growing businesses represent principal sources of job creation and innovation. Entrepreneurs can create economic value in a variety of manners. They can increase productivity by intensifying competition. They can enhance awareness of what is technically viable and what consumers prefer by introducing variations of existing products.

Entrepreneurs may also be inclined to work longer hours and more efficiently since their income is strongly linked to their working effort. Entrepreneurs often play vital roles in the early evolution of industries. The economic impact of entrepreneurship, however, does not seem to be the same for all places. Van Stel et al. (2005, 313) found that the impact of entrepreneurship on growth differs for countries at different stages of development. The economic effect of entrepreneurship for relatively poor countries was negative but positive for relatively rich countries. A possible explanation for the negative effect in poorer countries is that entrepreneurs in poor countries have lower human capital levels compared to entrepreneurs in developed countries. Entrepreneurs in the relatively poor nations may reflect the presence of shopkeepers in small crafts compared to more innovative entrepreneurs in new sectors (such as computer software) who reside in relatively wealthy places. Entrepreneurship in poor countries may reflect the absence of other opportunities and the emergence of entrepreneurism as a last resort for earning a subsistence living. Wealthy countries, in contrast, are better able to provide the education and consumer market for those with fresh ideas, ambition, and drive.

SUMMARY OF KEY POINTS AND TAKEAWAYS OF AUDIENCES

A few basic points need to be reemphasized. First, the United States has produced a disproportionate number of the world's richest entrepreneurs.

Individual attributes such as ability and motivation appear to play a role, however, environment also appears to be a salient factor. The U.S. environment fosters achievement that at least partially derives from: (1) a superior educational system (particularly at the top-ranked university level), (2) a culture of relative tolerance that accepts differences, (3) a legal system that protects private property, and (4) a political system that defends individual freedoms. All of these factors contribute to an overall environment that can reward innovation, effort, and risk taking.

Second, the view that Americans cannot achieve today, as they did in past generations is dispelled by the phenomenal wealth generated by contemporary entrepreneurs. Massive fortunes have been made within a single lifetime by highly motivated, well-educated, innovative entrepreneurs that were fortunate to be able to operate in an environment conducive to wealth building. A relatively large proportion of these entrepreneurs in one way or another leveraged capabilities in new technologies (such as software design) to start companies that later became enormously profitable.

Third, the creation of products such as high-speed calculators, search engines, and word processors increased productivity. The application of technology through social networking and e-commerce has enhanced people's ability to communicate with each other and revolutionized purchasing. The success of these innovations is consistent with Schumpeter's conceptualization of the new driving out the old in competition over profits. Innovations have in many ways made people's lives more interesting and more productive.

Fourth, a significant number of the world's most successful entrepreneurs seem to have come from relatively modest family circumstances. This suggests that upward mobility is not exhausted, not a relic of a bygone era, but a possibility for some with luck, pluck, motivation, and ability. The idea of intergenerational mobility (compared to rigid class structures of other societies) has long been a conceptual marker of the United States. The successes of U.S. entrepreneurs suggest (although with very limited sample size) that the prospects for fabulous wealth creation is greater in the United States than elsewhere and that the class structure in the United States is fluid.

Fifth, success is not a birthright. Many profound problems such as income inequality, inequities in student performance, lack of opportunity for many, relatively high rates of incarceration, loss of relatively good-paying jobs, drug use, family instability, global competition, discrimination and others still exist in the United States. How these and other problems are addressed will determine what the future holds in store for the U.S. economy and U.S. society as a whole.

Sixth, average citizens and leaders can shape their environment for good or bad. Education systems can rot or develop excellence; legal systems can motivate citizens by protecting private property or inhibit effort by failing to secure protections; social environments can inculcate hatred or tolerance. Finally, political systems can enslave or free the human spirit. Like the beaver, societies can create environments that are more conducive to survival.

Seventh, the United States has been remarkably successful in regard to measures such as the number of billionaire entrepreneurs per capita, total VC investment as a share of gross domestic product, the number of relatively young large firms founded by entrepreneurs and the number of privately held start-up companies valued at over $1 billion. Much of this success can be linked to institutions (rules of the game for society) and path dependency (past decisions and experiences). At the same time, past success is not a guarantee of future success. Underpinnings of past success (such as educational, legal, social, and political structure) need to be sustained.

Eighth, the role of government in fostering or inhibiting entrepreneurship will remain essential. Debate surrounding the benefits of unfettered market economies versus centralized controlled economies versus a mixed regulatory economy is ongoing. Economic growth of more controlled economies (such as China) raises renewed questions about the relative merits of unfettered market economies, mixed market economies, and centralized planned systems.

Entrepreneurial behavior has marked U.S. development in the past. Wealth creation in prior times at least partially stemmed from a mixture of Protestant values (frugality, thrift, and effort), individual freedoms, respect for education, acceptance of heterogeneity, and a legal structure that protected property and secured contracts. The endurance of such conditions is an open question. How well they are sustained in the United States will undoubtedly have a large impact on the future wealth and security of U.S. citizens. One specific takeaway from this book is the importance of a positive overall framework for economic development. Enforceable contracts, low levels of corruption, a strong scientific base, incentives for entrepreneurs to achieve, individual freedom, property rights, tolerance, and other factors contribute to establishing such an environment.

CONTRIBUTIONS OF THE BOOK, TAKEAWAYS, AND IMPLICATIONS OF ENTREPRENEURSHIP

Entrepreneurship remains a topic of great interest for a variety of audiences. At the individual level, people want to know how to assess their chances of success in starting a new business and how to increase their chances of success. At the macroeconomic level, governments want to increase the number of multibillion-dollar businesses that will enhance their tax bases. At a practical level, aspiring entrepreneurs need to have determination, encouragement, and some rational conviction that they can succeed. Narratives of people who became billionaires through entrepreneurship is not representative of an entire population, however, the narratives serve as confirmation that enormous wealth can be attained. Success stories do not assure that all persons who engage in entrepreneurship become billionaires, however, they may provide enough encouragement for people to take risk and eventually attain relative prosperity.

Different audiences should find interest in this book. Students in business, planning, public administration, and other programs may find the real-life narratives of highly successful entrepreneurs to be energizing. In contrast to dry numbers, narratives describe relatable details that can be motivating to aspiring entrepreneur. Politicians have clear incentives to promote development that can enrich constituents. Bureaucratic officials that provide incentives though industrial policies need to be aware of how to wisely utilize scarce resources. Scholars, political leaders, and others need to also look at the macroeconomic framework for development. A bias toward a relatively unfettered market system has been accepted by many in the United States. Advantages of such a system are reinforced in narratives of entrepreneurs who started with little and wound up with a great deal. This model, however, has come under scrutiny not only by those who focus on massive wealth and income inequities but also by those who look warily at the rise of centrally controlled economies such as the Chinese economy.

The concept of entrepreneurship has also been applied to the nonprofit sector. Nonprofit organizations increasingly face pressures through heightened competition for funds and a changed role of government in providing social services. These developments have caused nonprofit organizations to adopt a more innovative and entrepreneurial approach to survive. This approach offers the possibility of improved services in the social realm, and increased cost-effectiveness. Social entrepreneurship has been identified as incorporating the same tendencies of business in for-profit organizations. While the primary motivation for nonprofits is to serve a social purpose, elements of success for both nonprofit and for-profit entrepreneurs (such as innovativeness, a proactive posture and risk taking) are similar. Therefore, narratives of success can encourage aspiring entrepreneurs in both sectors.

Entrepreneurship is said to represent a comparative advantage of the United States. Entrepreneurs in the United States have been able to leverage advantages of a favorable environment in terms of political stability, educational excellence, a sound legal system, and a relatively tolerant setting in order to start and grow enterprises. Individual traits play a role but the relevance of environment must be recognized. Future research should further explore the link between environmental factors and entrepreneurial success. Such studies can assess needs to sustain or alter existing environments.

Bibliography

Adam Smith Institute. n.d. "The Wealth of Nations." https://www.adamsmith.org/the-wealth-of-nations.

Ahlers, Annie L., and Gunter Schubert. 2011. "Adaptive Authoritarianism' in Contemporary China: Identifying Zones of Legitimacy Building." In *Reviving Legitimacy: Lessons for and from China*, edited by Dend Zhenglai and Guo Sujian, 61–81. Lanham, MD: Lexington Books.

Alba, Richard. 2019. "Beyond the Melting Pot." *City & Community* 18 (2): 446–450.

Aldrich, Howard E. 1999. *Organizations Evolving*. London: SAGE.

Aldrich, Howard E., and Roger Waldinger. 1990. "Ethnicity and Entrepreneurship." *Annual Review of Sociology* 16 (1): 111–135.

Allen, Robert. C. 2003. *Farm to Factory: A Reinterpretation of the Soviet Industrial Revolution*. Princeton, NJ: Princeton University Press.

Amancio Ortega Gaona. n.d. "Biography."*Astrum People* website. https://astrumpeople.com/amancio-ortega-gaona-biography/.

Anderson, Robert D. 2016. "The German (Humboldtian) University Tradition." *Encyclopedia of International Higher Education Systems and Institutions*. https://link.springer.com/referenceworkentry/10.1007/978-94-017-9553-1_4-1.

Anderson, Stuart. 2018. "Immigrants and billion Dollar Companies." *National Foundation for American Policy*. NFAP Policy Brief. https://nfap.com/wp-content/uploads/2019/03/2018-BILLION-DOLLAR-STARTUPS.NFAP-Policy-Brief.2018.pdf.

Anokhin, Sergey, and William S. Schulze. 2009. "Entrepreneurship, Innovation, and Corruption." *Journal of Business Venturing* 24 (5): 465–476.

Audretsch, David B., and Zoltan J. Acs. 1994. "New-Firm Startups, Technology, and Macroeconomic Fluctuations." *Small Business Economics* 6 (6): 439–449.

Auletta, Kenneth. 2009. *Googles: The End of the World as We Know It*. New York: Penguin Press.

Avnimelech, Gil, Yaron Zelekha, and Eyal Sarabi. 2011. "The Effect of Corruption on Entrepreneurship." Paper presented at Druid Society, Copenhagen Denmark,

June 15–17, 2011. https://conference.druid.dk/acc_papers/1944qlhkqrqpnsq5gmk f4yvuy4m2.pdf.

BankBoston. 1997. *MIT: The Impact of Innovation.* http://saveourheritage.com/ Library_Docs/Bank%20Boston%20Impact%20of%20Innovation.pdf.

Baron, Robert A. 2000. "Psychological Perspectives on Entrepreneurship: Cognitive and Social Factors in Entrepreneurs' Success." *Current Directions in Psychological Science* 9 (1): 15–18.

Barro, Robert J. 1996. "Democracy and Growth." *Journal of Economic Growth* 1 (1): 1–27.

Bartik, Timothy J. 1991. *Who Benefits from State and Local Development Policies?* Kalamazoo, Michigan: W.E. Upjohn Institute for Employment Research.

Baskerville, Rachel F. 2003. "Hofstede Never Studied Culture." *Accounting Organizations and Society* 28 (1): 1–14.

Bates, Timothy. 1995. "Self-Employment Entry Across Industrial Groups." *Journal of Business Venturing* 10 (2): 143–156.

Baumol, William. 1990. "Entrepreneurship: Productive, Unproductive and Destructive." *Journal of Political Economy* 98 (5): 893–921.

Bell, Daniel. 1996. "The Protestant Ethic." *World Policy Journal* 13 (3): 35–39.

Bennett, Tim. 2015. "A View on U.S. Industrial Policy." *Trans-Atlantic Business Council.* http://www.transatlanticbusiness.org/wpcontent/uploads/2015/05/ VDMA-article-re-industrial-policy.pdf.

Berggren, Niclas, and Mikael Elinder. 2010. "Is Tolerance Good or Bad for Growth?" *Research Institute of Industrial Economics.* Working Paper No. 846. http://www .ifn.se/wfiles/wp/wp846.pdf#:~:text=Tolerance%20can%20have%20both%20 positive%20and%20negative%20effects,the%20generation%20and%20spread %20of%20ideas%20and%20values.

Bershidsky, Leonid. 2017. "H1B Visa Squeeze Threatens US Tech Leadership." *Mint.* https://www.livemint.com/Opinion/fQaktf5sbzuh6f2u6o8IoM/Donald-Trumps-H1B-squeeze-threatens-US-tech-leadership.html.

Blackwell, Ken. 2014. "Milton Friedman's Property Rights Legacy." *Forbes*, July 31, 2014. https://www.propertyrightsalliance.org/news/2019-international-property-rights-index-press-release-draft/.

Blanchflower, David G., and Andrew J. Oswalt. 1998. "What Makes an Entrepreneur?" *Journal of Labor Economics* 16 (1): 26–60.

Boettne, Peter J., Christopher J. Coyne, and Peter T. Leeson. 2010. "Takings." *The Georgetown Journal of Law & Public Policy* 8: 327–338.

Boissaneault, Lorraine. 2017. "How the 19th-Century Know Nothing Party Reshaped American Politics." *Smithsonian Magazine.* https://www.smithsonianmag.com/ history/immigrants-conspiracies-and-secret-society-launched-american-nativism-1 80961915/.

Bollingtoft, Anne, and John Ulhoi. 2005. "The Networked Business Incubator—Leveraging Entrepreneurial Agency?" *Journal of Business Venturing* 20 (2): 265–290.

Bondarenko, P. 2019. "Enron Scandal." *Encyclopedia Britannica.* https://www. britannica.com/event/Enron-scandal.

Bonnett, Celia, and Adrian Furnham. 1991. "Who Wants to be an Entrepreneur? A Study of Adolescents Interested in a Young Enterprise Scheme." *Journal of Economic Psychology* 12 (3): 465–478.

Borjas, George. 1986. "The Self-Employment Experience of Immigrants." *The Journal of Human Resources* 21 (4): 485–506.

Bostaph, Samuel. 2013. "Driving the Market Process: 'Alertness' Versus Innovation and 'Creative Destruction.'" *Quarterly Journal of Austrian Economic* 16 (4): 421–458.

Bradshaw, Ted K., and Edward J. Blakely. 1999. "What are 'Third-Wave' State Economic Development Efforts? From Incentives to Industrial Policy." *Economic Development Quarterly* 13 (3): 229–244.

Brandt, Richard. 2011. *The Google Guys*. New York: Penguin.

Braswell, Shawn. 2015. "Carlos Slim's Worldwide Portfolio." *OZY*. https://www.ozy.com/news-and-politics/carlos-slims-worldwide-portfolio/62341/.

Bridges, Carla. 2008. "Entrepreneurship Education and Economic Development: Preparing the Workforce for the Twenty-First Century Economy." Masters Thesis, Clemson University.

Briffault, Richard. 2010. "The Most Popular Tool: Tax Increment Financing and the Political Economy of Local Government." *The University of Chicago Law Review* 77 (1): 65–95.

Brockhaus, Robert H. 1982. "The Psychology of the Entrepreneur." In *Encyclopedia of Entrepreneurship*, edited by Calvin A. Kent, Donald L. Sexton, and Karl H. Vesper, 39–56. Englewood Cliffs, NJ: Prentice Hall.

Brooks, Oliver J. 1986. "Economic Development through Entrepreneurship: Incubators and the Incubation Process." *Economic Development Review* 4 (2): 24–29.

Brown, Christopher, and Mark Thornton. 2013. "How Entrepreneurship Theory Created Economics." *Quarterly Journal of Austrian Economics* 16 (4): 401–420.

Buchanan, James, and Gordon Tullock. 1962. *The Calculus of Consent: Logical Foundations of Constitutional Democracy*. Ann Arbor, MI: University of Michigan Press.

Bureau of Labor Statistics. 2020. *Career Outlook*. https://www.bls.gov/careeroutlook/subject/education_level.htm.

Bush, Vannevar. 1945. *Science the Endless Frontier*. https://www.nsf.gov/od/lpa/nsf50/vbush1945.htm.

Business Vibes. 2015. *6 Reasons Why a Relocation is Good Business*. https://www.business2community.com/business-intelligence/6-reasons-relocation-good-business-01407703.

Camera, L. 2019. "U.S. Students Show No Improvement in Math, Reading, Science on International Exam." *U.S. News & World Report*, December 3, 2019. https://www.usnews.com/news/education-news/articles/2019-12-03/us-students-show-no-improvement-in-math-reading-science-on-international-exam.

Carter, T. (2021). The True Failure Rate of Small Businesses. *Entrepreneur*. https://www.entrepreneur.com/article/361350.

Cassidy, John. 2013. "Steve Ballmer and the Art of Managing a Monopoly." *The New Yorker*, August 26, 2013. https://www.newyorker.com/news/john-cassidy/steve-ballmer-and-the-art-of-managing-a-monopoly.

Casson, Mark. 1995. *Entrepreneurship and Business Culture*. Aldersot, UK: Edward Algar.

CB Insights. 2019. *The top 20 Reasons Startups Fail*. https://www.insight.com/reports/.

Center for Immigration Studies. 2017, September 27. "Immigration Multipliers Trends in Chain Migration." September 27, 2017. https://cis.org/sites/default/files/2018-01/vaughan-chain-migration_0.pdf.

Chappelow, Jim. 2019. "Centrally Planned Economy." *Investopedia*. https://www.investopedia.com/terms/c/centrally-planned-economy.asp.

Chen, James. 2008. "Amancio Ortega." *Investopedia*. https://www.investopedia.com/terms/a/amancio-ortega.asp.

Cheng, Allen T. 2017. "Alibaba vs. The World." *Institutional Investor*, July 25, 2017. https://www.institutionalinvestor.com/article/b1505pjf8xsy75/alibaba-vs-the-world.

Cherry, Kendra. 2019. "The Big Five Personality Traits." *Very Well Mind*. https://www.verywellmind.com/the-big-five-personality-dimensions-2795422.

Ciccone, Antonio, and Elias Papaioannou. 2006. "Red Tape and Delayed Entry," CEPR Discussion Paper No. 5996. https://papers.ssrn.com/sol3/papers.cfm?abstract_id=976061.

Clarke, Susan E., and Gary Gaile. 1992. "The Next Wave: Post-federal Local Economic
Development Strategies." *Economic Development Quarterly* 6(2): 187–198.

Clarke, Susan E., and Gary Gaile. 1997. "Local Politics in a Global Era: Thinking Locally, Acting Globally." *The Annals of the American Academy of Political and Social Science* 551 (1): 28–43.

Colonial America. 1999. *Oregon State University School of Education*. http://oregonstate.edu/instruct/ed416/ae1.html.

Commager, Henry S. 1950. *The American Mind*. New Haven: Yale University Press.

Conroy, Tessa, and Steven C. Deller. n.d. *Regional Growth and Development Strategies: Business Relocation*. Madison, WI: University of Wisconsin-Extension.

Council of Development Finance Agencies. n.d. "Revolving Loan Funds & Development Finance." *Council of Development Finance Agencies*. https://www.cdfa.net/cdfa/cdfaweb.nsf/pages/revolving-loan-funds.html.

Cremin, Lawrence A. 1957. *The Republic and the School: Horace Mann on the Education of Free Men*. New York: Teachers College Press.

Cremin, Lawrence A. 1962. *The Transformation of the School: Progressivism in American Education, 1876–1957*. New York: Knopf.

Cremin, Lawrence A. 2020. "Horace Mann." *Encyclopedia Britannica*. https://www.britannica.com/biography/Horace-Mann.

Cross, Elizabeth. 2018. "The Game of Life Versus Real Life: How the Data Compare." *Bureau of Labor Statistics*. https://www.bls.gov/careeroutlook/2018/article/game-of-life-vs-real-life.htm.

Davis, M. 2020. "US Government Financial Bailouts." *Investopedia*, January 24. https://www.investopedia.com/articles/.

Deller, Steven, and Matt Kures. n.d. "Columbia County Economic Patterns, Trends & Regional Niches." *University of Wisconsin-Madison Extension*. http://www.co.columbia.wi.us/columbiacounty.

Dennehy, Ben. 2018. "Let the Rodent Do the Work: Reflections of a Beaver Believer." *Yale School of the Environment*. https://environment.yale.edu/news/article/let-the-rodent-do-the-work-reflections-of-a-beaver-believer/.

Department of Justice. 2006, May 25. *Federal Jury Convicts Former Enron Chief Executives*

Ken Lay, Jeff Skilling on Fraud, Conspiracy and Related Charges. https://www.justice.gov/archive/opa/pr/2006/May/06_crm_328.html.

Detroit County Day School. 2020. https://web.archive.org/web/20070408053318/http://www.dcds.edu/page.cfm?p=356.

Dickes, Lori. 2011. "The Theory and Practice of Third Wave Regional Economic Development Strategies." PhD Dissertation, Clemson University.

Djankov, Simeon, Rafael La Porta, Florencio Lopez-DeSilanes, and Andei Shleifer. 2002. *Quarterly Journal of Economics* CXVII (1): 1–37.

Dolbeare, Kenneth, and Patricia Medcalf. 1971. *American Ideologies*. Chicago: Markham.

Driouchi, Ahmed, and Alae Gamar. 2015. "Entrepreneurship and its Link to Corruption: Assessment with the Most Recent World and Country-Group Data." *Munich Personal RePEc Archive*. https://mpra.ub.uni-muenchen.de/62271/1/MPRA_paper_62271.pdf.

Drucker, Peter F. 1985. *Innovation and Entrepreneurship*. New York: Harper & Row Publishers.

Dye, Richard F., and David F. Merriman. 2006. "Tax Increment Financing: A tool for Local Government." *Land Lines* 18 (1): 2–7. https://www.nassauinstitute.org/economic-ideas-the-french-physiocrats-and-the-case-for-laissez-faire/.

Ebeling, Richard M. 2017. "Economic Ideas: The French Physiocrats and the Case for Laissez-faire." *The Nassau Institute*. https://www.nassauinstitute.org/economic-ideas-the-french-physiocrats-and-the-case-for-laissez-faire/.

Editors of the Encyclopedia Britannica. 2020. "Michael Bloomberg." *Encyclopedia Britannica*. https://www.britannica.com/biography/Michael-Bloomberg.

Educational Reform: The Example of Horace Mann. n.d. *Lumen*. https://courses.lumenlearning.com/teachereducationx92x1/chapter/educational-reforms/.

Eilperin, J. 2012. "Why the Clean Tech Boom Went Bust." *Wired*. https://www.wired.com/2012/01/ff_solyndra/.

Eisinger, Peter K. 1989. *The Rise of the Entrepreneurial State: State and Local Economic Development Policy in the United States*. Madison, WI: The University of Wisconsin Press.

Elazar, Daniel. 1984. *American Federalism: A View from the States* (3rd ed.). New York: Harper & Row.

Elert, Niklas, Magnus Henrekson, and Mark Sanders. 2019. *The Entrepreneurial Society: A Reform Strategy for the European Union*. Berlin, Germany: Springer Open.

Evans, David, and Linda Leighton. 1989. "Some Empirical Aspects of Entrepreneurship." *American Economic Review* 79 (3): 519–535.

Evans, Peter. 2017. "Behind Trump's Rhetoric of Economic Nationalism." *Global Dialogue: Magazine of the International Sociological Association* 7 (4). http://globaldialogue.isa-sociology.org/behind-trumps-rhetoric-of-economic-nationalism/.

Ewing Marion Kauffman Foundation. 2021. *Indicators of Entrepreneurship.* https://indicators.kauffman.org/indicator/rate-of-new-entrepreneurs.

Festus, Nikpoyen, Glory Bassey, and Francis Uyang. 2014. "Entrepreneurship, Corruption and the Challenge of Development in Nigeria." *European Journal of Business and Social Sciences* 3: 104–112.

Finkelsein, Barbara. 1990. "Perfecting Childhood: Horace Mann and the Origins of Public Education in the United States." *Biography* 13 (1): 6–20.

Florida, Richard. 2002. "The Economic Geography of Talent." *Annals of the Association of American Geographers* 92 (4): 743–755.

Florida, Richard. 2012. *The Rise of the Creative Class, Revisited Edition.* New York: Basic Books.

Forbes. 2020. "World's Billionaire List." *Forbes.* https://www.forbes.com/billionaires/.

Forbes. 2021. *Best States for Business, 2019 Rankings.* https://www.forbes.com.

Fosler, R. Scott. 1992. "State Economic Policy: The Emerging Paradigm." *Economic Development Quarterly* 6 (1): 3–13.

Frankel, Mathew. 2017. "8 Warren Buffett Deals That Won Big." *The Motley Fool*, November 13, 2007. https://www.fool.com/investing/2017/11/13/8-warren-buffett-deals-that-won-big.aspx.

Frey, Renato S. 1984. "Does n-Achievement Cause Economic Development? A Cross-Lagged Panel Analysis of the McClelland Thesis." *The Journal of Social Psychology* 122 (1): 67–70.

Friedman, Benjamin. 2005. *The Moral Consequences of Economic Growth.* New York: Alfred A. Knopf.

Friedman, Milton. 1962. *Capitalism and Freedom.* Chicago: University of Chicago Press.

Friedman, Milton. 1970. "The Social Responsibility of Business is to Increase its Profits." *New York Times Magazine*, September 13, 1970.

Friedman, Milton, and Rose Friedman. 1980. *Free to Choose.* New York: Harcourt, Brace, Jovanovich.

Frølund, Lars, Fiona Murray, and Max Riedel. 2018. "Developing Successful Strategic Partnerships with Universities." *MIT Sloan Management Review.* https://sloanreview.mit.edu/article/developing-successful-strategic-partnerships-with-universities/.

Fukuyama, Francis. 1995. *Trust: The Social Virtues and the Creation of Prosperity.* New York: Free Press.

Fukuyama, Francis. 2014. *Political Order and Political Decay: From the Industrial Revolution to the Globalization of Democracy.* New York: Farrar, Straus and Giroux.

Galiani, Sebatian, and Itai Sened, eds. 2014. *Institutions, Economic Growth, and Property Rights: The Legacy of Douglass North*. New York: Cambridge University Press.

Gertler, Meric S., Richard Florida, Gary Gates, and Tara Vinodrai. 2002. *Competing on Creativity: Placing Ontario's Cities in North American Context*. A report prepared for the Ontario Ministry of Enterprise, Opportunity and Innovation and the Institute for Competitiveness and Prosperity. http://www.urban.org/sites/default/files/publication/60786/410889-Competing-on-Creativity.PDF.

Glaeser, Edward L. 1998. "Are Cities Dying?" *Journal of Economic Perspectives* 12 (2): 139–160.

Glaeser, Edward L., Jed Kolko, and Albert Saiz. 2001. "Consumer City." *Journal of Economic Geography* 1 (1): 27–50.

Glaeser, Edward L., Jose A. Sheinkman, and Andrei Shleifer. 1995. "Economic Growth in a Cross-Section of Cities." *Journal of Monetary Economics* 36 (1):117–143.

Glaeser, Edward L., Rafael La Porta, Florencio Lopez-de-Silanes, and Andrei Shleifer. 2004. "Do Institutions Cause Growth?" *Journal of Economic Growth* 9 (2): 271–303.

Glazer, Nathan, and Daniel Moynihan. 1963. *Beyond the Melting Pot: The Negroes, Puerto Ricans, Jews, Italians, and Irish of New York City*. Cambridge, MA: MIT Press.

Gottlieb, Paul D. 1995. "Residential Amenities, Firm Location and Economic Development." *Urban Studies* 32 (9): 1413–1436.

Granovetter, Mark. 1973. "The Strength of Weak Ties." *American Journal of Sociology* 78 (6): 1360–1380.

Granovetter, Mark. 1985. "Economic Action and Social Structure: The Problem of Embeddedness." *American Journal of Sociology* 91 (3): 481–510.

Gray, P. 2020. "What the Antitrust Lawsuits Against Big Tech Companies Could Mean for Tech Leaders." *TechRepublic*. https://www.techrepublic.com/article/.

Green, Gary P. 2001. "Amenities and Community Economic Development: Strategies for Sustainability." *Journal of Regional Analysis & Policy* 31 (2): 61–75.

Greenspan, Alan, and Adrian Wooldridge. 2018. *Capitalism in America: A History*. New York: Random House Large Print.

Gregersonm, Erik, and Mark Hall. 2020. "Larry Ellison." *Encyclopedia Britannica*. https://www.britannica.com/biography/Larry-Ellison.

Greve, Arent, and Janet W. Salaff. 2003. "Social Networks and Entrepreneurship." *Entrepreneurship Theory and Practice* 28 (1): 1–22.

Hackett, Sean M., and David Dilts. 2004. "A Systematic Review of Business Incubation Research." *Journal of Technology Transfer* 29 (1): 55–82.

Hanson, Phillip. 2003. *The Rise and Fall of the Soviet Economy*. New York: Routledge.

Hayek, Friedrich. 1944. *The Road to Serfdom*. Chicago: University of Chicago Press.

Hayek, Friedrich. 2005. *The Road to Serfdom with the Intellectuals and Socialism*. London: The Institute of Economic Affairs.

He, L. 2020. "China Launches Antitrust Investigation into Alibaba." *CNN Business*. https://edition.cnn.com/2020/12/24/tech/alibaba-china-antitrust-investigation/index.html.

Hébert, Robert, and Albert Link. 2006. "The Entrepreneur as Innovator." *Journal of Technology Transfer* 31: 589–597.

Held, James R. 1996. "Clusters as an Economic Development Tool: Beyond the Pitfalls." *Economic Development Quarterly* 10 (3): 249–261.

Henderson, Harry. 2012. *Larry Page and Sergey Brin: Information at Your Fingertips*. New York: Chelsea House.

Hirschman, Charles. 1982. "Immigrants and Minorities: Old Questions for New Directions in Research." *International Migration Review* 16 (2): 474–490.

History.com Editors. 2019. "Armenian Genocide." *History*. https://www.history.com/topics/world-war-i/armenian-genocide.

History.com Editors. 2020a. "Bosnian Genocide." *History*. https://www.history.com/topics/1990s/bosnian-genocide.

History.com Editors. 2020b. "Jim Crow Laws." *History*. https://www.history.com/topics/early-20th-century-us/jim-crow-laws.

Holtz-Eakin, Douglas, David Joulfaian, and Harvey Rosen. 1994. "Entrepreneurial Decisions and Liquidity Constraints." *The RAND Journal of Economics* 25 (2): 334–347.

Hopkins, Erin A. 2017. "John Dewey and Progressive Education." *The Journal of Educational Thought* 50 (1): 59–68.

Howes, Candace, and Ann R. Markusen. 1993. "Trade Industry and Economic Development." In *Trading Industries, Trading Regions: International Trade, American Industry, and Regional Economic Development*, edited by Hetzi Nopenen, Juli Graham, and Ann R. Markusen, 1–44. New York: Guilford Press.

Hsueh, Roselyn. 2011. *China's Regulatory State: A New Strategy for Globalization*. Ithaca, NY: Cornell University Press.

Hull, D. 2011. "The Man Behind Solyndra's Rise and Fall." *East Bay Times*. https://www.eastbaytimes.com/2011/11/27/the-man-behind-solyndras-rise-and-fall/.

Hunter, Holland. 1973. "The Overambitious First Soviet Five-Year Plan." *Slavic Review* 32 (2): 237–257.

Huntington, Samuel. 2004. *Who Are We? The Challenges of America's National Identity*. New York: Simon & Schuster.

Hyman, Wilton. 1998. "Empowerment Zones, Enterprise Communities, Black Business, and Unemployment." *Journal of Urban and Contemporary Law* 53: 143–170.

Ingalls, John J. 2002. "Special Introduction." In *Democracy in America, Volumes One and Two*, 9–12. Translated by Henry Reeves. Hazleton, PA: Pennsylvania State University, Electronic Classics Series. http://seas3.elte.hu/coursematerial/LojkoMiklos/Alexis-de-Tocqueville-Democracy-in-America.pdf.

International Property Rights Index 2019. 2019, October 16. *Property Rights Alliance*. https://www.propertyrightsalliance.org/news/2019-international-property-rights-index-press-release-draft/.

Ireland, R. Duane, Jeffrey G. Colvin, and Donald F. Kuratko. 2009. "Conceptualizing Corporate Entrepreneurship Strategy." *Entrepreneurship Theory Practice* 33 (1): 19–46.

Jacobs, Harvey. 2009. "U.S. Private Property Rights in International Perspective." In *Property Rights and Land Policies*, edited by Gregory K. Ingram and Yu-Hung Hong, 52–69. Cambridge, MA: Lincoln Institute of Land Policy.

Jacobs, Jane. 1961. *The Life and Death of Great American Cities*. New York: Random House.

Jao, Nicole. 2018. "Alibaba Market Value Hits the $500 Billion Valuation Mark." *Technode*, January 25, 2018. https://technode.com/2018/01/25/alibaba-500-million-market-cap/.

Jarillo, Carlos J. 1989. "Entrepreneurship and Growth: The Strategic Use of External Resources." *Journal of Business Venturing* 4 (2): 133–147.

Jepson, Edward J., and Anna Haines. 2003. "Under Sustainability: Rebuilding the Local Economic Development Tool Box." *Economic Development Journal* (Summer): 45–53.

Jeynes, William H. 2007. *American Educational History: School, Society, and the Common Good*. Thousand Oaks: Sage Publications.

Johnson, Kenneth M., and Calvin L. Beale. 1994. "The Recent Revival of Widespread Population Growth in Nonmetropolitan Areas of the United States." *Rural Sociology* 59 (4): 655–667.

Johnson, Landy C. 2018. "Balance Agriculture with Industry Program (BAWI)." *Mississippi Encyclopedia*. https://mississippiencyclopedia.org/entries/balance-agriculture-with-industry-program/.

Kasparov, Gary. 2017. "Garry Kasparov: Hey, Bernie, Don't Lecture Me About Socialism. I Lived Through It." *The Daily Beast*, April 13, 2017. https://www.thedailybeast.com/garry-kasparov-hey-bernie-dont-lecture-me-about-socialism-i-lived-through-it.

Kemp, Christopher J. 2010. *Madison, Montesquieu and the Separation of Powers*. Institute of Local Government Studies Conference, University of Birmingham. https://www.researchgate.net/publication/270286063_Madison_Montesquieu_and_the_Separation_of_Powers.

Kennedy, Jan. 2018. "A Corporate Entrepreneurship Definition and Four Other Things You Should Know About It." *Academy for Corporate Entrepreneurship*. https://www.afce.co/corporate-entrepreneurship-definition/.

Kennedy, Scott. 2015. "Made in China 2025." *CSIS*. https://www.csis.org/analysis/made-china-2025.

Kerr, Sari P., and William R. Kerr. 2018. "Immigration Entrepreneurship in America: Evidence from the Survey of Business Owners, 2007 & 2012." Working Paper 24494, NBER Working Paper Series. https://www.nber.org/system/files/working_papers/w24494/w24494.pdf.

Kerr, Sari P., William R. Kerr, and Tina Xu. 2017. "Personality Traits of Entrepreneurs: A Review of Recent Literature." Working Paper 18-04. Harvard

Business School. https://www.hbs.edu/faculty/Publication%20Files/18-047_b0074a64-5428-479b-8c83-16f2a0e97eb6.pdf.

Kiersz, Andy. 2019. "The 25 Best MBA Programs in the World for Ambitious Entrepreneurs." *Business Insider*, March 27, 2019. https://www.businessinsider.com/best-mba-programs-entrepreneurship-2019-3.

Kirzner, Israel. 1973. *Competition and Entrepreneurship*. Chicago: University of Chicago Press.

Klapper, Leora, Luc Laeven, and Raghuran Rajan. 2006. "Entry Regulation as a Barrier to Entrepreneurship." *Journal of Financial Economics* 82 (3): 591–629.

Kleinfield, N. R. (1985). "ABC Is Being Sold for $3.5 Billion; 1st Network Sale." *The New York Times*, March 19, 1985. www.nytimes.com/1985/03/19/business/abc-is-being-sold-for-3.5-billion-1st-network-sale.html.

Knight, Edgar W. 1922. *Public Education in the South*. Boston, MA: Ginn and Company.

Knight, Frank. 1921. *Risk, Uncertainty and Profit*. Boston, MA: Houghton Mifflin Company.

Knopf, Linda. 2016. "Profiles of Entrepreneurs: Discriminant and Cluster Analyses of the Romans 12 Motivational Gifts and Locus of Control as Predictors of Entrepreneurs and a Canonical Analysis of the Romans 12 Motivational Gifts and IEO." PhD Dissertation, Regent University.

Koch, Sarah. 2017. "Immigrants, We Create Jobs." *The Case Foundation*. https://casefoundation.org/blog/immigrants-we-create-jobs/.

Kotkin, Stephen. 2001. *Armageddon Averted: The Soviet Collapse, 1970–2000*. Oxford, UK: Oxford University Press.

Koven, Steven G. 1999. *Public Budgeting in the United States: The Cultural and Ideological Setting*. Washington, D.C.: Georgetown University Press.

Koven, Steven G., and Andrea C. Koven. 2018. *Growth, Decline, and Regeneration in Large Cities: A Case Study Approach*. New York: Routledge.

Koven, Steven G., and Frank Götzke. 2010. *American Immigration Policy: Confronting the Nation's Challenges*. New York: Springer.

Koven, Steven G., and Thomas S. Lyons. 2003. E*conomic Development: Strategies for State and Local Practice*. Washington, D.C.: International City/County Management Association.

Koven, Steven G., and Thomas S. Lyons. 2010. *Economic Development: Strategies for State and Local Practice* (2nd ed.). Washington, D.C.: International City/County Management Association.

Kraujalis, Vytautas. 2012. "China's First Five-Year Plan: Achievement at the Expense of a Generation." *gbtimes*. https://gbtimes.com/chinas-first-five-year-plan-achievement-at-the-expense-of-a-generation.

Krogstad, Jens M. 2020. "Americans Broadly Support Legal Status for Immigrants Brought to the U.S. Illegally as Children." *Pew Research Center*. https://www.pewresearch.org/fact-tank/2020/06/17/americans-broadly-support-legal-status-for-immigrants-brought-to-the-u-s-illegally-as-children/.

Krueger, Anne O., Alexander Nove, John Hackett, and Hla Myint. n.d. "Economic Planning." *Encyclopedia Britannica*. https://www.britannica.com/topic/economic-planning.

Kuratko, Donald F.2005. "The Emergence of Entrepreneurship Education: Development, Trends, and Challenges." *Entrepreneurship Theory and Practice* 29 (5): 577–597.

Kuratko, Donald F. 2009. "The Entrepreneurial Imperative of the 21st Century." *Business Horizons* 52 (5): 421–428.

Kuratko, Donald F., Jeffrey S. Hornsby, and James Hayton. 2015. "Corporate Entrepreneurship: the Innovative Challenge for a New Global Economic Reality." *Small Business Economics* 45 (2): 245–253.

Kuratko, Donald, and William LaFollette. 1987. "Small Business Incubators for Local Economic Development." *Economic Development Review* 5 (2): 49–55.

Kwabena, Nkansah, and Kwabena Simpeh. 2011. "Entrepreneurship Theories and Empirical Research: A Summary Review of the Literature." *European Journal of Business and Management* 3 (6): 1–8.

Laffer, Arthur. 2004. "The Laffer Curve: Past, Present, and Future." *The Heritage Foundation.* https://www.heritage.org/taxes/report/the-laffer-curve-past-present-and-future.

Lambert, Thomas E., and Paul Coomes. 2001. "An Evaluation of the Effectiveness of the Louisville Enterprise Zone Program." *Economic Development Quarterly* 15 (2): 168–180.

Larry Ellison. 2019. *Biography.* https://www.biography.com/business-figure/larry-ellison.

Leadem, Rose. 2017. "The Immigrant Entrepreneur Behind Major American Companies (Infographic)." *Entrepreneur.* https://www.entrepreneur.com/article/288687.

Leibovich, Mark. 2000. *Alter Egos.* www.washingtonpost.com/archive/politics/2000/12/31/alter-egos/91b267b0-858c-4d4e-a4bd-48f22e015f70/?utm_term=.8f687ecc7e7c.

Leigh, Nancy G., and Edward J. Blakely. 2016. *Planning Local Economic Development* (6th ed.). Thousand Oaks, CA: Sage Publications.

LeSage, Edward Jr., and Lorna Stefanick. 2004. Paper Presented at the Canadian Political Science Association meetings. http://www.china-up.com:8080/international/case/case/1434.pdf.

Lester, Connie. 2004. "Economic Development in the 1930s: Balance Agriculture with Industry." *Mississippi History Now.* http://www.mshistorynow.mdah.ms.gov/articles/224/economic-development-in-the-1930s-balance-agriculture-with-industry.

Levitsky, Steven, and Daniel Ziblatt. 2018. *How Democracies Die.* New York: Crown.

Levy, Steven. 2011. *In the Plex: How Google Thinks, Works, and Shapes Our Lives.* New York: Simon & Schuster.

Levy-Carciente, Sara. 2019. *International Property Rights Index: Full Report.* https://atr-ipri2017.s3.amazonaws.com/uploads/IPRI_2019_FullReport.pdf.

Lichtenstein, Greg A., and Thomas S. Lyons. 1996. *Incubating New Enterprises: A guide to Successful Practice.* Washington, D.C.: The Aspen Institute.

Light, Ivan, and Carolyn Rosenstein. 1995. *Race, Ethnicity, and Entrepreneurship in Urban America.* New York: AldineDeGruyter.

Lindh, Thomas, and Henry Ohlsson. 1996. "Self-Employment and Windfall Gains: Evidence from the Swedish Lottery." *Economics Journal* 106 (439): 1515–1526.

Lipset, Seymour M. 1996. *American Exceptionalism: A Double-Edged Sword*. New York: W.W. Norton.

Liu, Cathy Y., Gary Painter, and Qingfang Wang. 2014. *Lessons for U.S. Metro Areas: Characteristics and Clustering of High-Tech Immigrant Entrepreneurs*. Kansas City, Missouri: Ewing Marian Kaufman Foundation.

Lopez, Edward J., R. Todd Jewell, and Noel D. Campbell. 2009. "Pass a Law, Any Law, Fast! State Legislative Responses to the Kelo Backlash." *Review of Law & Economics* 5(1): 5–5.

Lowenstein, Roger. 2008. *Buffett: The Making of an American Capitalist*. New York: Random House.

Lucas, Robert E., Jr. 1988. "On the Mechanics of Economic Development." *Journal of Monetary Economics* 22 (1): 3–42.

Lyons, Thomas S., Theodore R. Alter, David Audretsch, and Darline Augustine. 2012. "Entrepreneurship and Community: The Next Frontier of Entrepreneurship Inquiry." *Entrepreneurship Research Journal* 2 (1): 1–26.

Malecki, Edward. J. 1997. *Technology and Economic Development: The Dynamics of Local, Regional and National Competitiveness* (2nd ed.). Edinburgh Gate, UK: Addison, Wesley, Longman.

Manes, Stephen. 1994. *Gates: How Microsoft's Mogul Reinvented an Industry-and Made Himself the Richest Man in America*. New York: Touchstone.

Markusen, Ann R. 1995. "Growing Pains: Thoughts on Theory, Method, and Politics for a Regional Science of the Future." *International Regional Science Review* 17 (3): 319–326.

Marples, David. R. 2009. "Ethnic Issues in the Famine of 1932–1933 in Ukraine." *Europe-Asia Studies* 61 (3): 505–518.

Marshall, Alfred. 1920. *The Principles of Economics*. Basingstoke, UK: Palgrave Macmillan.

Martin, George H. 1894. *The Evolution of the Massachusetts Public School System*. New York: Appleton.

Maxwell, Frederick A. 2002. *Bad Boy Ballmer: The Man Who Rules Microsoft*. New York: William Morrow.

McCabe, D. 2020. "Tech Companies Shift Their Posture on a Legal Shield, Wary of Being Left Behind." *New York Times*, December 15, 2020. https://www.nytimes.com/2020/12/15/.

McClelland, David C. 1961.*The Achieving Society*. Princeton, NJ: Van Nostrand.

McClosky, Herbert, and John Zaller. 1984. *The American Ethos: Public Attitudes Toward Capitalism and Democracy*. Cambridge, MA: Harvard University Press.

McFarlane, Alan. 1978. *The Origins of English Individualism: The Family, Property and Social Transition*. Oxford, UK: Blackwell.

Merriam, David. 2018. *Improving Tax Increment Financing (TIF) for Economic Development*. Cambridge, MA: Lincoln Institute of Land Policy.

Meyer, Bruce D. "Why Are There So Few Black Entrepreneurs?" National Bureau of Economic Research Working Paper No. 3537. Cambridge, MA. https://www.nber.org/papers/w3537.

Michael Bloomberg Biography. n.d. *IMDb*. https://www.imdb.com/name/nm0089255/bio.

Miller, Danny. 1983. "The Correlates of Entrepreneurship in Three Types of Firms." *Management Science* 29 (7): 770–791.

Min, Pyong G. 1986/1987. "Filipino and Korean Immigrants in Small Business: A Comparative Analysis." *Ameraria Journal* 13 (1): 53–71.

Mohamed, Theron. 2020. "Warren Buffett's Berkshire Hathaway Raked in More Than $3 Billion from its Goldman Sachs Bailout." *Market Insider*, May 18, 2020. https://markets.businessinsider.com/news/stocks/warren-buffett-berkshire-hathaway-goldman-sachs-sale-billions-return-bailout-2020-5-1029212109#.

Mokyr, Joel. 1990. *The Lever of Riches: Technological Creativity and Economic Progress*. Oxford: Oxford University Press.

Montgomery, Scott L. 1994. *Minds for the Making: The Role of Science in American Education, 1750–1990*. New York: Guilford Press.

Moody, J. 2019. "Where, How International Students Are Studying in the U.S." *U.S. News & World Report*. https://www.usnews.com/education/best-colleges/articles/.

Moretti, Enrico. 2013. *The New Geography of Jobs*. Boston: Mariner Books.

Morris, Michael H., Donald F. Kuratko, and Jeffrey Covin. 2011. *Corporate Entrepreneurship and Innovation* (3rd ed.). USA: Cengage/Southwestern.

Morrison, Wayne M. 2004. *China's Economic Rise: History, Trends, Challenges and Implications for the United States*. Washington, D.C.: Congressional Research Service.

Murphy, Patrick J., Jianwen Liao, and Harold P. Welsch. 2006. "A Conceptual History of Entrepreneurial Thought." *Journal of Management History* 12 (1): 9–24.

Murray, Henry. A. 1938. *Explorations in Personality*. New York: Oxford University Press.

Myrdal, Gunnar. 1944. *An American Dilemma: The Negro Problem and Modern Democracy*. New York: Harper & Brothers.

Nebehay, Stephanie. 2020. "In a First, China Knocks U.S. from Top Spot in Global Patent Race." *Reuters*. https://www.reuters.com/article/us-usa-china-patents/.

New American Economy. 2019. "New American Fortune 500 in 2019: Top American Companies and Their Immigrant Roots." July 22, 2019. https://data.newamericaneconomy.org/en/fortune500-2019/.

New World Encyclopedia Contributors. 2016. "American Exceptionalism." *New World Encyclopedia*. https://www.newworldencyclopedia.org/p/index.php?title=American_exceptionalism&oldid=994552.

Newby, Les. 1999. "Sustainable Local Economic Development: A New Agenda for Action?" *Local Environment* 4 (1): 67–72.

North, Douglas C. 1990. *Institutions, Institutional Change, and Economic Performance*. Cambridge, UK: Cambridge University Press.

North, Douglas C. 1991. "Institutions." *Journal of Economic Perspectives* 5 (1): 97–112.

North, Douglas C., John J. Wallis, and Barry R. Weingast. 2009. "Violence and the Rise of Open-Access Orders." *Journal of Democracy* 20 (1): 55–68.

Nystöm, Kristin. 2010. "Business Regulation and Red Tape in the Entrepreneurial Economy." CESIS Electronic Working Paper Series, Paper Number 225. https://static.sys.kth.se/itm/wp/cesis/cesiswp225.pdf.

O'Connell, Jonathan. 2017. "As Companies Relocate to Big Cities, Suburban Towns Are Left Scrambling." *Washington Post*, July 16, 2017. https://www.washingtonpost.com/business/economy/as-companies-relocate-to-big-cities-suburban-towns-are-left-scrambling/.

Olberding, Julie. "The Formation, Structure, and Processes, and Performance of Regional Partnerships for Economic Development in U.S. Metropolitan Areas." PhD Dissertation, University of Kentucky.

O'Neil, Thomas. 2005. "Evolving a Successful University-Based Incubator: Lessons Learned from the UCF Technology Incubator." *Engineering Management Journal* 17 (3): 11–25.

Origins of Prussian Education System. 2004–2020. *K12 Academics*. https://www.k12academics.com/Education%20Worldwide/Education%20in%20Germany/History/Prussian%20Education%20System/origin.

Palley, Thomas I. 2011. "The Rise and Fall of Export-led Growth." Levy Economic Institute, Working Paper No. 675. http://www.levyinstitute.org.

Paris, Edmond. 1961. *Genocide in Satellite Croatia, 1941–1945: A Record of Racial and Religious Persecutions and Massacres*. Chicago: The American Institute for Balkan Affairs.

Pastor, Manuel, Jr., Peter Dreier, P., and J. Eugene Grigsby III. 2000. *How Cities and Suburbs Grow Together*. Minneapolis: University of Minnesota Press.

Peters, Allan H., and Peter S. Fisher. 2002. *State Enterprise Zone Programs: Have They Worked?* Kalamazoo, Michigan: W.E. Upjohn Institute.

Petro, Greg. 2012. "The Future of Fashion Retailing: The Zara Approach." *Forbes*, October 25, 2012. https://www.forbes.com/sites/gregpetro/2012/10/25/the-future-of-fashion-retailing-the-zara-approach-part-2-of-3/#25ded2bb7aa4.

Pillon, Annie. 2019. "25 Diverse Startup Incubators." *Small Business Trends*. https://smallbiztrends.com/2013/11/list-of-startup-incubators.html.

Pillsbury, Michael. 2016. *The Hundred Year Marathon: China's Secret Strategy to Replace America as the Global Superpower*. New York: St. Martin's Press.

PISA 2018 WorldWide Ranking. 2018. *FactsMap*. https://factsmaps.com/pisa-2018-worldwide-ranking-average-score-of-mathematics-science-reading/.

Poprawe, Marie. 2014. "A Panel Data Analysis of the Effect of Corruption on Tourism." *Applied Economics* 47 (23): 2399–2412.

Porter, Michael E. 1985. *Competitive Advantage: Creating and Sustaining Superior Performance*. New York: Free Press.

Porter, Michael E. 1990. *The Competitive Advantage of Nations*. London: Macmillan Press.

Porter, Michael E. 1995. "The Competitive Advantage of the Inner City." *Harvard Business Review* 73 (3): 56–71.

Porter, Michael E. 1998a. "Clusters and the New Economics of Competition." *Harvard Business Review* 76 (6): 77–90.

Porter, Michael E. 1998b. "Creating Tomorrow's Advantages." In *Rethinking the Future*, edited by Rowan Gibson, 48–61. London: Nicholas Brealey Publishing.

Porter, Michael E. 1998c. "The Adam Smith Address: Location, Clusters, and the 'New' Microeconomics of Competition." *Business Economics* 33 (1): 7–13.

Porter, Michael, E. 2000. "Location, Competition, and Economic Development: Local Clusters in a Global Economy." *Economic Development Quarterly* 14 (1): 15–34.

Prestowitz, Clyde. 2012. "America's Industrial Policy." *Foreign Policy*, March 6, 2012. https://foreignpolicy.com/2012/03/06/americas-industrial-policy/.

Rauch, Andreas, and Michael Frese. 2000. "Psychological Approaches to Entrepreneurial Success: A General Model and an Overview of Finding." In *International Review of Industrial and Organisational Psychology*, edited by Cary. L. Cooper and Ivan Robertson, 101–143. New York: John Wiley & Sons.

Rauch, James E. 1993. "Productivity Gains from Geographic Concentrations of Human Capital: Evidence from Cities." *Journal of Urban Economics* 34 (3): 380–400.

Reich, Robert. 1983. *The Work of Nations*. New York: A. A. Knopf.

Report of the World Commission on Environment and Development: Our Common Future. 1987. http://www.un-documents.net/ocf-02.htm#I.

Reynolds, Paul D. 1991. "Sociology and Entrepreneurship: Concepts and Contributions." *Entrepreneurship Theory and Practice* 16 (2): 47–70.

Riasanovsky, Nicholas V. 2011. *A History of Russia*. New York: Oxford University Press.

Riggins, Nash. 2019. "What is a Business Incubator?" *Small Business Trends*. https://smallbiztrends.com/2017/06/what-is-a-business-incubator.html.

Ross, Sean. 2019. "Is the United States a Market Economy or a Mixed Economy?" *Investopedia*. https://www.investopedia.com/ask/answers/031815/united-states-considered-market-economy-or-mixed-economy.asp.

Rotter, Julian B. 1966. "Generalized Expectancies for Interval Versus External Control of Reinforcement." *Psychological Monographs* 80: 1–28.

Sach, Jeffrey D. n.d. *Stages of Economic Development*. https://www.earth.columbia.edu/sitefiles/file/about/director/documents/china_speech061904.pdf.

Savitch, H. V., and Ronald K. Vogel. 2000. "Metropolitan Consolidation Versus Metropolitan Governance in Louisville." *State and Local Government Review* 32 (3): 198–212.

Saxenian, Annalee. 1994. *Regional Advantage: Culture and Competition in Silicon Valley and*

Route 128. Cambridge, MA: Harvard University Press.

Schmidt, Eric, and Jonathan Rosenberg. 2014. *Google: How Google Works*. New York: Grand Central Publishing.

Schroeder, Alice. 2009. *The Snowball: Warren Buffett and the Business of Life*. New York: Bantam Books.

Schumpeter, Joseph A. 1934. *The Theory of Economic Development*. Cambridge, MA: Harvard University Press.

Schumpeter, Joseph A. 1976. *Capitalism, Socialism and Democracy* (3rd ed.). London: George Allen and Unwin.

Scott, Virginia. 2008. *Google*. Westport, CT: Greenwood Press.

Segal, T. 2021. "Enron Scandal: The Fall of a Wall Street Darling." *Investopedia*. https://www.investopedia.com/updates/enron-scandal-summary.

Sergey Brin Biography. 2020. *Astrum People*. https://astrumpeople.com/sergey-brin-biography.

Seth, Shobhit. 2020. "Why Entrepreneurship Is Important to the Economy." *Investopedia*. https://www.investopedia.com/articles/personal-finance/101414/why-entrepreneurs-are-important-economy.asp.

Seymour Martin Lipset Interview. n.d. *PBS. The First Measured Century (host B. Wattenberg)*. http://www.pbs.org/fmc/interviews/lipset.htm.

Shane, Scott. 1993. "Cultural Influences on National Rates of Innovation." *Journal of Business Venturing* 8 (3): 59–73.

Shane, Scott. 1996. "Hybrid Organizational Arrangements and Their Implications for Firm Growth and Survival: A Study of New Franchisers." *Academy of Management Journal* 19 (7): 697–707.

Shane, Scott. 2003. *A General Theory of Entrepreneurship: The Individual-Opportunity Nexus*. Cheltenham, England: Edward Elgar Publishing.

Shane, Scott, and Sankaran Venkataraman. 2000. "The Promise of Entrepreneurship as a Field of Research." *Academy of Management Review* 25 (1): 217–226.

Shaver, Kelly G., and Linda R. Scott. 1991. "Person, Process, Choice: The Psychology of New Venture Creation." *Entrepreneurship Theory and Practice* 16 (2): 23–46.

Slednik, Karol. 2003. "Schumpeter's View on Innovation and Entrepreneurship." *SSRN Electronic Journal*. https://www.researchgate.net/publication/256060978_Schumpeter's_View_on_Innovation_and_Entrepreneurship/link.

Smith, Michal. 1989. *Behind the Glitter: The Impact of Tourism on Rural Women in the Southeast*. Lexington, KY: Southeast Women's Employment Coalition.

Soares, Louis. n.d. "Community College and Industry Partnerships." *Center for American Progress*. https://www2.ed.gov/PDFDocs/college-completion/02-community-college-and-industry-partnerships.pdf.

Sobel Russell. 2008. "Testing Baumol: Institutional Quality and the Productivity of Entrepreneurship." *Journal of Business Venturing* 23: 641–655.

Socialist Party of America. 2020. *Encyclopedia.com*. www.encyclopedia.com/history/encyclopedias-almanacs-transcripts-and-maps/socialist-party-america.

Stenberg Peter. 1993. "Rural Business Incubators and Economic Development." In *Issues for the 1990's: Rural Economy. Economic Research Service*, 139–140. Washington, D.C.: U.S. Department of Agriculture, Agriculture Information Bulletin No. 664-50.

Stevens, Ashley. 2004. "The Enactment of Bayh-Dole." *Journal of Technology Transfer* 29 (1): 93–99.

Stevenson, Howard H., and J. Carlos Jarillo. 1990. "A Paradigm of Entrepreneurship: Entrepreneurial Management." *Strategic Management Journal* 11 (5): 17–27.

Stewart, Emily. 2019. "How Mike Bloomberg Made His Billions: A Computer System You've Probably Never Seen." *Vox*, December 11, 2019. https://www.vox.com/

2020-presidential-election/2019/12/11/21005008/michael-bloomberg-terminal-net-worth-2020.

Swanstrom, Todd. 1995. "Philosopher in the City: The New Regionalism Debate." *Journal of Urban Affairs* 17 (3): 309–324.

Tax Foundation. 2021. *State Income Tax Rates and Brackets for 2020*. https://taxfoundation.org/state-business-corporate -income-tax-rates-brackets-2020/.

Tax Policy Center. 2020. *Briefing Book*. https://www.taxpolicycenter.org/briefing-book/how-do-us-taxes-compare-internationally.

Tepperman, Jonathan. 2018. "China's Great Leap Backward." *FP*. https://foreignpolicy.com/2018/10/15/chinas-great-leap-backward-xi-jinping/.

TheFamousPeople.com Editors. n.d. "Steve Ballmer Biography." *TheFamousPeople.com*. https://www.thefamouspeople.com/profiles/steve-ballmer-6404.php.

The World University Rankings. 2020a. https://www.timeshighereducation.com/world-university-rankings/2020/world-ranking#!/page/0/length/25/sort_by/rank/sort_order/asc/cols/stats.

The World University Rankings, 2020b. https://www.timeshighereducation.com/world-university-rankings/2020/subject-ranking/computer-science.

Thornton, Patricia H. 1999. "The Sociology of Entrepreneurship." *Annual Review of Sociology* 25 (1): 19–46.

Tiebout, Charles. 1956. "A Pure Theory of Local Expenditures." *Journal of Political Economy* 64 (5): 416–424.

Tocqueville, Alexis de. 1956. *Democracy in America* (Mentor ed.). New York: New American Library.

Tocqueville, Alexis de. 2002. *Democracy in America* (Vol. 1, 2). Translated by Henry Reeves. Hazleton, PA: Pennsylvania State University, Electronic Classics Series. http://seas3.elte.hu/coursematerial/.

Torre, Nicole. 2017. "The H-1B Visa Debate, Explained." *Harvard Business Review*. https://hbr.org/2017/05/the-h-1b-visa-debate-explained.

Torrey, Zachary. 2018. "China Prepares for Big Pharma." *The Diplomat*, March 14, 2018. https://thediplomat.com/2018/03/china-prepares-for-big-pharma/.

Tran, Sang K. 2017. "GOOGLE: A Reflection of Culture, Leader, and Management." *International Journal of Corporate Social Responsibility* 2 (10). https://doi.org/10.1186/s40991-017-0021-0.

Transparency International. 2020. *Corruption Perceptions Index 2019*. https://images.transparencycdn.org/images/2019_CPI_Report_EN_200331_141425.pdf.

Tuckness, Alex. 2020. "Locke's Political Philosophy." *The Stanford Encyclopedia of Philosophy*, Spring 2020. https://plato.stanford.edu/archives/spr2020/entries/locke-political/.

U.S. Census Bureau. 2019. *Nativity in the United States American Community Survey 1-Year Estimates, Table B0512*. https://censusreporter.org.

U.S. Census Bureau. 2021. *State Population Total and Components of Change: 2010–2019*. http://proximityone.com/states2019.

U.S. Small Business Administration. 2020. *2020 Small Business Profiles for the States and Territories*. https://advocacy.sba.gov/2020/05/20/2020-small-business-profiles-for-the-states-and-territories/.

U.S. State Department. n.d. *Intellectual Property Enforcement*. https://www.state.gov/intellectual-property-enforcement/.

Van Stel, André, Martin Carree, and Roy Thurik. 2005. "The Effect of Entrepreneurial Activity on National Economic Growth." *Small Business Economics* 24: 311–321.

Vargas, Jose A. 2010. "The Face of Facebook." *The New Yorker*, September 13, 2010. https://www.newyorker.com/magazine/2010/09/20/the-face-of-facebook.

Vernon, Raymond. 1966. "International Investment and International Trade in the Product Cycle." *Quarterly Journal of Economics* 80 (2): 190–207.

Vise, David A., and Mark Malseed. 2005. *The Google Story*. New York: Bantam Dell.

Walia, Ashni, and Priya Chetty. 2020. "The Economic Theories of Entrepreneurship." *Project Guru*. https://www.projectguru.in/the-economic-theories-of-entrepreneurship/.

Wang, S. (2021). "Jack Ma Was Almost Bigger Than China. That's What Got Him Into Trouble." *CNN Business*. https://www.msn.com/en-us/news/world/.

Warren Buffett. 2020. *Biography*. https://www.biography.com/business-figure/warren-buffett.

Watson, Garrett, and Nicole Kaeding. 2019. "Tax Policy and Entrepreneurship: A Framework for Analysis." *Tax Foundation*. https://files.taxfoundation.org/20190403131203/Tax-Policy-and-Entrepreneurship-A-Framework-for-Analysis1.pdf.

Waxman, Olivia B. 2018. "Socialism Was Once America's Political Taboo. Now, Democratic Socialism is a Viable Platform. Here's What to Know." *Time*, October 24, 2018. https://time.com/5422714/what-is-democratic-socialism/.

Wayne, L. 2002. "Enron's Collapse; Before Debacle, Enron Insiders Cashed In $1.1 Billion in Shares." *New York Times*, January 13, 2002. https://www.nytimes.com/2002/01/13/.

Weber, Max. 1904/1992. *The Protestant Ethic and the Spirit of Capitalism*. New York: Routledge.

Wheeler, Stephen M. 2002. "The New Regionalism Key Characteristics of an Emerging Movement." *Journal of the American Planning Association* 68 (3): 267–278.

Wilder, Margaret G., and Barry Rubin. 1996. "Rhetoric Versus Reality: A Review of Studies on State Enterprise Zone Programs." *Journal of the American Planning Association* 62 (4): 473–491.

Williams, Champaign. 2017. "These Companies Are Relocating Headquarters in Search of Young, Qualified Talent." *Biznow*, February 9, 2017. https://www.bisnow.com/national/news/office/8-companies-that-have-relocated-expanded-offices-in-pursuit-of-young-talent-70823.

Williams, Morgan K. 2017. "John Dewey in the 21st Century." *Journal of Inquiry & Action in Education* 9 (1): 91–102.

Wingfield, Nick, and Nellie Bowles. 2018. "Jeff Bezos, Mr. Amazon, Steps Out." *New York Times*, January 12, 2018. https://www.nytimes.com/2018/01/12/technology/jeff-bezos-amazon.html.

Winship, A. E. 1937. "Horace Mann." *The Journal of Education* 120 (3): 68–70.

WorldAtlas. 2021. *U.S. Literacy Rates by State*. https://www.worldatlas.com/articles/us-literayratebystate/html/.

World Bank Group. 2020. *Doing Business Rankings: Comparing Business Regulation in 190 Economies*. https://openknowledge.worldbank.org/bitstream/handle/10986/32436/9781464814402.pdf.

Yuan, L. (2020). "Why China Turned Against Jack Ma." *NYT News Service*. https://timesofindia.indiatimes.com/business/international-business/.

Zainal, Zaidah. 2007. "Case Study as a Research Method." *Jurnal Kemanusiaan*. https://www.researchgate.net/publication/41822817_Case_study_as_a_research_method.

Zehner, William, Dariusz Trzmielak, Edyta Gwarda-Gruszczyńska, and Jacquelyn A. Zehner. 2014. "Business Incubation in the USA." In *International Cases on Innovation, Knowledge and Technology Transfer*, edited by Dariusz M. Trzmielak and David Gibson, 145–162. Lotz, Poland: University of Lotz.

Zhou, Min. 2004. "Revisiting Ethnic Entrepreneurship: Convergencies, Controversies, and Conceptual Advancements." *International Migration Review* 38 (3): 1040–1074.

Zucker, Lynne G., and Michael R. Darby. 2001. "Capturing Technological Opportunity via Japan's Star Scientists: Evidence from Japanese Firms' Biotech Patents and Products." *Journal of Technology Transfer* 26 (1–2): 37–58.

Index

About the Author

Steven G. Koven teaches in the Department of Urban and Public Affairs at the University of Louisville. His areas of specialization include Economic Development and Ethics. Koven received a PhD in political science in 1982 and an MBA degree in 1975. He has written extensively across various disciplines. With degrees in both business and political science, he is able to provide insight into the world of business creation and assess the geopolitical implications of such creation. In addition to questions of ethics, his current research is committed to investigating entrepreneurship and how it affects the place of the United States in the global economy.

www.ingramcontent.com/pod-product-compliance
Ingram Content Group UK Ltd.
Pitfield, Milton Keynes, MK11 3LW, UK
UKHW041842031026
15587UKWH00002B/943

9 781793 649843